University of
Hertfordshire

Learning and Information Services
Watford Campus Learning Resources Centre
Aldenham Watford Herts WD2 8AT

This book must be returned or renewed on or before the last date
and time stamped below. Renewal by telephone is not allowed
for short loan items. A substantial fine will be charged on an
hourly basis for the late return of items.

SHORT LOAN

21.11.01		

Questioning
the Master

Questioning
the Master

Gender and Sexuality
in Henry James's Writings

Edited by
Peggy McCormack

DELAWARE

Newark: University of Delaware Press
London: Associated University Presses

Associated University Presses
440 Forsgate Drive
Cranbury, NJ 08512

Associated University Presses
16 Barter Street
London WC1A 2AH, England

Associated University Presses
P.O. Box 338, Port Credit
Mississauga, Ontario
Canada L5G 4L8

The paper used in this publication meets the requirements of the American National Standard for Permanence of Paper for Printed Library Materials Z39.48-1984.

Library of Congress Cataloging-in-Publication Data

Questioning the master : gender and sexuality in Henry James's writings / edited by Peggy McCormack.
    p.   cm.
  Includes bibliographical references and index
  ISBN 0-87413-712-8 (alk. paper)
  1. James, Henry, 1843–1916—Criticism and interpretation.   2. Sex in literature.   3. Psychological fiction, American—History and criticism.   4. Sex (Psychology) in literature.   5. Gender identity in literature.   6. Sex role in literature.   7. Desire in literature. I. McCormack, Peggy.
PS2127.S48Q47   2000
813'.4—dc21
                                                          99-33518
                                                          CIP

PRINTED IN THE UNITED STATES OF AMERICA

For my father and his devoted wife,
James and Catherine McCormack,
And in loving memory of my stepson,
Paul Taylor McNamara

Contents

Acknowledgments

Introduction   11
   PEGGY MCCORMACK

The Janus Faces of James: Gender, Transnationality,
and James's Cinematic Adaptations   37
   PRISCILLA L. WALTON

Strange Meetings: Henry James and *The Siege of London*   54
   ANNY BROOKSBANK JONES

The Functions of Women in the Art Tales of Henry James   68
   BRUCE HENRICKSEN

Working at Gender: *In the Cage*   86
   JOHN CARLOS ROWE

"To Feel is Such a Career": Gender and Vocation in
The Tragic Muse   104
   MICHAEL L.J. WILSON

"His little heart, dispossessed": Ritual Sexorcism in
The Turn of the Screw   133
   ERIC HARALSON

Jamesian Sadomasochism: The Invisible (Third) Hand of
Manhood in *The Golden Bowl*   149
   LELAND S. PERSON

James and the Representation of Women: Some Lessons
of the Master(')s   176
   SARAH B. DAUGHERTY

Anerotic Excursions: Memory, Celibacy, and Desire in
The American Scene   196
   MARY ESTEVE

Contributors   217
Works Cited   220
Index   229

Acknowledgments

THERE ARE MANY PEOPLE WHO HELPED MAKE THIS BOOK A REALITY. First, I would like to thank the contributors to this collection for their enthusiasm and patience as we have seen it into publication. I very much appreciate the excellent assistance I have received from the University of Delaware Press editorial staff. And I am deeply indebted to my friend and Loyola colleague, Dana Bartelt, for the creation of the book's cover design. In addition, I would like to thank Mary McCay, my friend and department chairperson, for her generous and loyal support of this project. This manuscript is better edited thanks to Kristen Provenza and Steven Benko, who will produce great works in the not so distant future, as well as the excellent work of Cynthia Toups and Susan Schiber.

I would also like to acknowledge several people who, while I was far from Loyola and its support network, facilitated my revisions of the manuscript: my good friend of now more than twenty years, Dr. Barry Munitz, CEO and president of the Getty Trust, as well as University of California at Riverside administrators Dr. Raymond Orbach, chancellor; Dr. Carlos Velez-Ibanez, dean of Humanities, Arts, and Social Sciences; and Dr. John Ganim, chair of the English Department. Also among those southern Californians who assisted me with the preparation of this manuscript, Julie Newcome was a miracle worker who, genially and professionally, came through for me when I really needed eleventh-hour help.

In particular, I want to thank my friend and Loyola colleague, Katherine Adams, who always encouraged me and generously availed me of her superior knowledge of the discipline of writing. Last and most significantly, I want to thank my wonderful husband, Stephen Pinell, who believed in and saw this project through with me from its inception to its publication.

Introduction

PEGGY McCORMACK

THE ESSAYS IN THIS COLLECTION WERE COMMISSIONED FOR THE BOOK and thus appear in print here for the first time. This book is, to my knowledge, the only collection of essays examining representations of gender and sexuality in James's writing that does not have an a priori premise about how James lived and how his life may be read into his works. Our essays read the texts, not his life, and apply a variety of perspectives to his writings. The women and men who contributed to this volume have given it a diversity in terms of the articles' subjects, critical perspectives and judgments. In content, the book considers works (and films made from these texts) from James's early, middle, and major phases, his literary criticism, journal writing, and travel writing. For this breadth and for the excellence of the essays, I am indebted to the contributors, and I am pleased to have been a part of this collection of essays focused upon James's portrayals of gender and sexuality.

In December 1996, in *Slate,* an electronic magazine, Sheldon M. Novick and Leon Edel—with several fillips from Fred Kaplan—argued about the reliability of Novick's conclusions regarding James's sex life in Novick's recent biography of James.[1] That three James scholars debated the difficulties involved with Novick's inferences about James's sexuality and its expression in his writings through the venue of an on-line magazine was in itself intriguing to me. An argument among three James scholars published in a general news on-line magazine so that any of *Slate*'s 150,000 readers (*Slate*'s estimate of its readership) could read the discussion struck me as felicitous. No doubt that was in large part due to my work as editor of this volume, but I also think that this on-line debate as well as the vigorous debate about these issues occurring daily on the Henry James List Serv may well indicate that another marker has occurred in the history of James criticism. While there are as many versions of the history of James scholarship as there are James scholars, my own sense of it is that, from the earliest biographies until rela-

11

tively recently, James's sexuality was not discussed or was understood to operate subliminally according to a Freudian model of "repressed homosexuality," an admittedly nebulous psychoanalytic construct. However, in the last ten years, critics from cultural studies, deconstructive, feminist, gender, and queer theory perspectives have reconsidered James's sexuality and gender identification and his writing's sexual imagery as well as his depiction of gender relationships. The essays published here for the first time represent some of the best of these revisions of sexual representation in James's writings. The nine essays in this book focus upon sexual language in James's writings and examine the significance of gender representation in his works rather than focus upon James's sexuality itself, a relief to many critics and a disappointment to others, perhaps.[2] I believe that these articles have much to offer readers in terms of thoughtful examination of the language of gender and sexuality in James's writing. I have learned much from my work on this volume, and I hope other readers will also appreciate the wide-ranging, undogmatic approaches of these essays. Regarding the order of the nine essays, the first four, by Professors Priscilla L. Walton, Anny Brooksbank Jones, Bruce Henricksen, and John Carlos Rowe, focus more closely on female characters in James's fiction. The next three, by Professors Michael L. J. Wilson, Eric Haralson, and Leland S. Person, emphasize male or male and female roles in James's fiction. The last two, by Professors Sarah B. Daugherty and Mary Esteve, examine gender relations and sexual imagery in James's nonfiction: his literary criticism and travel writing.

The first essay, by Priscilla Walton, is an intriguing study of films made from James's fiction entitled "The Janus Faces of James: Gender, Transnationality, and James's Cinematic Adaptations." It considers the ways in which films adapted from James's fiction in general and these films' women characters in particular serve the political ideologies of their filmmakers, critics who respond to these works, and the historical and cultural contexts in which these groups operate. Walton contextualizes her examination theoretically by connecting the fluidity of national identity articulated by Homi K. Bhabha's explanation of film as a product of national and transnational "cultural and social climate[s]" with Anne McClintock's insights into the gendered aspects of imperialism (Walton 37). From Bhabha and Brian McFarlane, Walton applies the insight that "[t]he 'locality' of national culture is neither unified nor unitary in relation to itself. . . . The boundary [of cultural identity] is Janus-faced and . . . must always be a process of hybridity, incorporating new 'people' in relation to the body politic, generating other sites of meaning. . . . What emerges as an effect of such 'incomplete signification' is a turning of" what we once thought of as fixed "boundaries and limits into the *in between* spaces through which the meanings of cultural and political authority are negotiated" (Walton 39). Thus, Walton's essay gives us new reasons to rethink James's "in-between" status as neither American nor British: first, McFarlane's recognition that films made from literary texts "must be critiqued textually as well as analyzed and placed contextually"; and second, Bhabha's awareness that films, like all cultural productions, reflect a culture's fluidity or "Janus face" (Walton 39).

Walton structures her essay by first examining an American film production, the 1949 version of *Washington Square* retitled *The Heiress*. She then contrasts this earlier U.S. production with British-American coproductions made of *The Bostonians* and *The Europeans*. Her analyses of these films form a prequel to the essay's major focus, the recent film productions of *The Portrait of a Lady, The Wings of the Dove,* and *Washington Square.*

Walton begins with *The Heiress* not only because it is the earliest of the films she considers but also for two other significant elements: the political significance of its 1949 production and its completely American character. *The Heiress* demonstrates the profound cultural pressure that postwar America exerted upon women to leave the workforce and become full-time mothers. As Catherine Sloper, Olivia de Havilland becomes an un-Melanie, the opposite of her passive, compliant character in *Gone With the Wind.* Walton shows Catherine's revenge upon her mercenary suitor, Morris Townsend, to be the perverse consequences of her mother's death and the malign influence of Catherine's inane guardian, Aunt Lavinia, a combination of events that represents the negative results that 1949's post-World War II cultural milieu conveys about part-time or absent mothers. Forty-eight years later, Agnieszka Holland's remake of this film, *Washington Square* (1997), no longer reflects the same cultural pressure to keep women in the home. Interestingly, Holland's version "is much more critical of [Catherine's father's] behavior. . . . suggest[ing] that Dr. Sloper resents Catherine because her birth deprived him of his wife (as in the novel, Mrs. Sloper dies in childbirth)" (52–3). Thus, the 1997 take on this story criticizes not an absent mother and dithering mother substitute for Catherine's gullibility and subsequent cruelty but rather her overbearing father, while the novel emphasizes neither the women nor her father for Catherine's behavior.

Among the "more than twenty-nine films" made from James's stories, Walton also considers Ismail Merchant and James Ivory's 1979 production of *The Europeans,* which "dramatizes female sexuality" to reflect Merchant and Ivory's postcolonial, and therefore politically outdated (from some critics' perspectives), pro-European, anti-American sensibilities (44). Like both *The Heiress* and *The Europeans,* the 1984 Merchant-Ivory production of *The Bostonians* conveys the inappropriateness of women acting independently of male control.

Walton concludes her essay with examinations of Jane Campion's 1996 film *The Portrait of a Lady,* Iain Softley's 1997 treatment of *The Wings of the Dove,* and Holland's *Washington Square,* which she characterizes as multinational productions that are 'contradictory' products of "intense nationalistic [as well as international] fervor," such as those examined in Benjamin Barber's book *Jihad vs. McWorld: How Globalism and Tribalism are Reshaping the World* (47). Returning to McClintock's argument from *Imperial Leather,* Walton demonstrates that these films emblematize "three of the governing themes of Western imperialism . . . : the transmission of white, male power through control of colonized women; the emergence of a new global order of cultural knowledge; and the imperial command of commodity capital" (47). In Campion's film, Isabel's body and her sexual passion function as the contested colonial territories that her various imperialist suitors seek to possess. Walton notes that at the film's end, the success of Isabel's marriage and, more broadly, her life remains in question as it does in James's novel, but "Campion's depiction of James's heroine as a victim of her own sexuality in an era when female sexuality went unacknowledged and unspoken breaks" with the "pattern" she has outlined in *The Heiress, The Europeans,* and *The Bostonians* (49).

Like Campion's *Portrait,* Iain Softley's version of *The Wings of the Dove* breaks the pattern of the older James films and revisions James's novel in such a way that the film reflects its own cultural milieu as much as its literary source. While "mov[ing] along the trajectory" opened by Campion's *[Portrait],* Softley's film translates the sexual/economic war waged over a woman's

body into a more highly pitched, sensual conflict with significant battles taking place in London and Venice (49–50). Walton's reading emphasizes gender relationships, class struggle,
and cross-national themes.

Softley's shifting of the setting from the end of the nineteenth century to 1910 with a pre-World War I atmosphere enables him to translate the more muted sexual yearning of
James's novel into a more overtly sexualized depiction of Kate
Croy as a young woman torn between the conflicting demands
of Merton Densher and Aunt Maud. Helena Bonham-Carter as
Milly Theale is erotically attracted to both Maud's money and
Densher's sexuality. Softley creates Milly's money *and* beauty
as a third alternative to the story's unresolveable choice between only money or love. The film repeatedly tantalizes the
audience with the prospect of a ménage à trois as Softley creates as much sexual attraction on Kate's part to Milly as to Densher: "In this film the love triangle of James's novel takes on a
new dimension, and twists Eve Kosofsky Sedgwick's definition
of the homosocial, for here Densher is cast as the conduit
through which Milly and Kate's love can be consummated" (50).
In a scene "that surely had James rolling in his grave" (51),
Kate and Densher consummate their love in a Venetian street
while disguised (or revealed) as a Spanish matador and flamenco dancer, respectively. But following the film's homoerotic
spark, this heterosexual consummation becomes Kate's good-
bye gift to both Densher and, in handing him over to Milly, to
the heiress as well. When Densher and Kate meet again in London, she presents Milly's bequest letter to him as well as herself
sexually. Densher rejects both offers. Thus, Walton suggests
that "Densher and Kate's rejection of Milly's bequest spotlights
a refusal of the transference of capital in favor of an exchange
of desire, both lesbian and heterosexual" (51).

Walton concludes that "[m]uch like *The Portrait of a Lady, The
Wings of the Dove* clearly demonstrates the imbrications of nation, narration, and the female body. It goes further than Campion's feature in that it allows for a consummation of female
sexuality, although its consummation too is ultimately abrogated. . . . The films based upon James's writings open alternative readings of the written texts, shedding light on divergent
cultural endeavors that, to whatever ends they serve, illustrate
how nationality is often staked on and through the female body
and underscore the importance of gender in the construction of
a nation" (52).

The second essay, "Strange Meetings: Henry James and *The Siege of London*," is by Anny Jones, an English scholar in James studies at the University of Leeds. Jones's reading of James's 1883 novella *The Siege of London* expands, appropriately enough, on the theme of foreignness or alienation to which Mrs. Headway, the story's American protagonist, is subjected throughout the story by her Europeanized expatriate friends and the British society into which she so desperately wants "to get." Jones explores this theme of alienness or difference as it is entwined with another theme, that of uncanny doubling among the characters and plot events. Doubling begins with *L'Aventurière*, the Dumas *fils* play within the story, which James's two Europeanized American male protagonists, Littlemore and Waterville, are attending at the Comédie-Française as the story opens. Two pages into the novella, James has already evoked at least four levels of doubling: first, the imitative play; second, James's spoof of it; third, the understudies playing in the Jamesian spoof; and finally, the characters in James's story who echo the play's central question of whether a gentleman should "tell" about a lady's past misconduct. Specifically, Mr. Littlemore faces the dilemma of disclosing or keeping secret potentially socially ostracizing revelations about Mrs. Headway's past.

James mixes these themes of doubling and "telling" with his familiar international conflict, here in the form of Mrs. Headway's American alienness from European and English society. The "difference" that the old world society imputes to Mrs. Headway has more to do with her gender and her multiple divorces than with her being the most recently arrived American expatriate in its midst. Thus, Jones suggests that, for James, his international theme is additionally complicated when the "alien" who wishes to integrate into European society is a woman who does not conform to the seemingly ultraconservative sexual mores of Europeans and Europeanized Americans who have already climbed "into society" and pulled up the drawbridge against newer interlopers. Mrs. Headway's divorces, her consequent wealth, her beauty, and her blunt outspokenness "fix" her within a stereotype prevalent in the English society into which Mrs. Headway wishes to marry: the superficial, uncultivated, and promiscuous American woman. This stereotype, persisting into this century, from Wallace Simpson to as recent a version as Andie McDowell's American character in the 1994 comic film "Four Weddings and a Funeral," suggests that an

American woman who does not repress her sexuality has greater difficulty in breaching the old world's social divide than her male compatriots.

By combining Luce Irigaray's interpretation of "woman as Other" (Jones 60–62) with Freud's view of the uncanny, Jones provides a reading of *The Siege of London* that is complex, theoretically sophisticated, yet accessible. Jones maintains an organic unity of textual analysis and essay format by beginning her essay on "woman as Alien" with a note on how her English diction, spelling, and citation practices place her among the contributors to this collection in a role analogous to that of Mrs. Headway as "Other," a difference that she has asked me not to obscure by editing her essay into "American" format (54); thus, I have printed her essay just as she submitted it to me.

Bruce Henricksen, well versed in contemporary theory as his recent studies of Conrad demonstrate, suits the theory to the scholarly task in his essay and discovers much about James's depiction of gender relationships in his art tales through Proppian structuralist analyses. His article, "The Functions of Women in the Art Tales of Henry James," examines ten artists' stories written by James from 1873 and 1903. Like Laura Mulvey's revelatory analysis of Sophocles's Oedipus trilogy using Propp in *Visual and Other Pleasures*,[3] Henricksen relies on Propp's linguistic analysis of/from *The Morphology of the Folktale* as a basis for his examination. Henricksen's interest in the art tales stems from his notion that they "often deal with theories concerning the production and reception of art, the relationship of the artist to the world, and the nature of aesthetic experience. The tales not only speculate upon the social consequences of such theories and concerns, but upon the way that talk about the arts often works as an alibi in struggles for power and domination. The theory of art is not, for James, an autonomous and self-justifying realm, but is always, in a loose sense of the current phrase, ideologically freighted" (Henricksen 68).

Henricksen notes that the "current debate" about gender relations in James is "complex" for a variety of reasons (68–9). Since currency and complexity mark this discussion, Henricksen suggests that "rather than try to approach final judgments about James and 'the woman question,' [he will] offer a typology of the representations of women in the art tales" that describes the "functions" of women in the plots of these stories (69).

Henricksen describes four functions governing women's

roles in these stories: "(1) women as artists, (2) women as subjects of art, (3) women as prizes, and (4) women as gatekeepers. ... Each of these functions can be presented so as to encourage in the reader a positive, negative, or ambivalent evaluation" (Henricksen 84). I find that the most interesting women's roles occur when James fuses more than one function into a single woman's character and subverts a woman's function from its original purpose. Henricksen, in keeping with his Proppian model, remains neutral toward the functions that he examines. But these fusions and subversions become sites of considerable tension in James's fiction, positions from which Henricksen's readings against the grain prove most intriguing.

As a beginning point in his analysis of women's functions, Henricksen quotes Margaret Homans's observation of "the death or absence of the mother" that "sorrowfully but fortunately makes possible the construction of language and culture" (Henricksen 84). Homans, in turn, notes that Jacques Lacan offers a psychoanalytic explanation of this founding myth by dividing the child's world into the mother's immediate, prelinguistic realm and the father's symbolic realm of language, the law, and the phallus. In Lacan's metanarrative, while the phallus symbolizes sexual difference and language, the mother who is exiled from the "Law of the Father" represents the absent signified. Every child enters the symbolic order of language and begins a lifelong search for the lost mother, who can only be represented in the symbolic order by figurative language. Figurative language or metaphor involves "a series of substitutions along chains of signifiers" that can only evoke but never "fully embrac[e] the absent signified" or lost mother (69). Connecting these ideas for his analysis, Henricksen notes that this Lacanian myth explains both woman's subordinate or absent position within language and culture as well as the commentary by James's narrators in the art tales who "make women the subject of their discourses" (70). These male narrators can be understood to be commenting upon this underlying metanarrative of woman as a silent or seemingly absent foundation upon which man creates art.

In his analysis of "Greville Fane," representative of the "Woman as Artist" Henricksen proves that Fane, a woman author of the Victorian equivalent of Harlequin Romance novels, "subverts" the Lacanian, patriarchal myth because, as a woman novelist, she is producing language and thus intruding into the realm of the phallus—even if her novels are written just to please a female audience with simple tastes.

Illustrating the function of "Woman as Subject," Henricksen examines "The Madonna of the Future" in which a woman becomes the intended subject of a male painter's art and the actual subject of the male narrator's verbal art. Just as we never know Greville Fane's "own" name, so also we know this woman only as the painter's sentimentalized vision of the Madonna or the narrator's " 'plain prose' " version of her as a tawdry, middle-aged woman of no beauty and less ambition steadily " 'growing stout' "—an unrealized idealization or a " 'plain prose' . . . 'vulgarization' " (73). In both cases, woman eludes representation, except in these antithetical, patriarchal clichés.

Henricksen suggests that the function of "Woman as Prize" is "[p]erhaps the least complimentary role women can play in a male-dominated cultural establishment . . . recalling the exchanges of women Claude Lévi-Strauss describes in primitive societies," and his study of "The Lesson of the Master" perfectly illustrates his point (74–5). Just as woman is known in "Greville Fane" only as widow or pseudonymously as a male novelist (both terms identifying the woman in male-defined categories) and as woman is represented only in the pair of antithetical clichés devised by the male painter and the male narrator of "The Madonna of the Future," so also woman is circumscribed by the functions of either "prize" or its antithesis as "burden" in "The Lesson of the Master." Thus, a pattern appears to emerge when analysis focuses upon the women's functions. In this last story, Henricksen sees woman as a "prize" only in the future tense, when she is an unattained goal; after the "prize" is possessed by the artist, she becomes a "burden" as in the cases of the first Mrs. St. George, who "is conveniently killed off" (74), and of Mrs. Mark Ambient, also dispatched by death in "The Author of Beltraffio," which Henricksen examines later under the function of "Woman as Gatekeeper."

Henricksen points out that "Beltraffio" has been read as either misogynistic or as exposing society's misogyny, "depending upon just how one characterizes the irony of the [Boothean] inferred author" (78). Henricksen argues that "'Beltraffio" gives "shape and form to patriarchal desires concerning the position of women in relation to language and culture and to patriarchal paranoia concerning the results of woman escaping this position" (75). The author, Mark Ambient, and his wife are locked in a primal struggle for possession of their son. Mrs. Ambient judges her husband's writing as immoral, and thus she questions, from a Lacanian point of view, the position of the Father, the Law, and his Word. As gatekeeper, she denies her son access to his father to the extent that, when the boy falls ill, she locks herself in a room with the boy and, thanks to the male narrator, with her husband's latest manuscript. According to this "meddlesome" narrator (77), Mrs. Ambient is so horrified by her husband's latest manuscript that she lets the boy die "rather than be corrupted by the father's novels" (77). Henricksen suggests that "[s]uch a negative representation of unchecked maternal bonding—turning it into a death force—can [my emphasis] certainly be read as blatant patriarchal propaganda" (77). However, he questions the reliability of the narrator, whose entire tale is couched in homoerotic terms toward Ambient and, more particularly, Ambient's "extraordinarily beautiful" son, on whom the narrator confesses a desire to lay "a longing hand" (78). Thus, this narrator, "whose homoerotic temperament seeks the exclusion of women according to its own agenda" is "in competition for the function of cultural gatekeeper" with Mrs. Ambient (78). Henricksen concludes that the narrator's "unconscious intention is to offer a warning concerning unbridled feminine influence" (80), a Jamesian anxiety about which Daugherty has also written in her essay, "James and the Representation of Women: Some Lessons of the Master(')s."

John Carlos Rowe, in "Working at Gender: *In the Cage*," once again proves his own explicative mastery when reading James. Here, he is considering a novella published in 1898, the same year as *The Turn of the Screw*. But Rowe's examination of the social consequences regarding *In the Cage*'s changing means of production, its telegraphic communications, makes that story seem light-years away from *The Turn of the Screw*, wherein the young governess is enveloped by an earlier, pre-telegraphic, gothiclike setting that isolates Bly from the outside world.

The nameless female protagonist of *In the Cage* becomes fascinated by the romantic liaisons of Captain Everard, which are kept afloat by the telegrams she sends between him and his lady friends. Rowe notes that previous critics have seen this story as akin to other James fictions in which a naive young working woman, "primarily occupied with a system of representation and thus with symbolic relations," mistakes the "limitation[s]" of this "discursive mode" in which she labors as "artistic representation," a realm that remains "the province of the Master, for whom the 'feminine' has once more served a purpose in an aesthetic ideology operating still according to the old patriarchal authority" (Rowe 86). However, Rowe argues that this story represents a "change in view" and thus a change in the "technique of social representation occasioned in large part by James's uncertainty before new kinds of work, including the growing number of service-sector jobs employing women. Whereas James had previously represented nonartistic modes of communication as, at root, the same: lacking the figurative complexity requiring active interpretation and thus social instrumentalities, he views the telegraph as a mode of communication that marks an important difference in the usual conduct of social relations and thus conventional class distinctions" (Rowe 109).

Just as James commented in *The American Scene* on the proliferation of hotels in America as breaking down the distinction between public and private realms, so also Rowe interprets the telegraph of *In the Cage* as breaking down an older world's barriers between public and private spheres. Because of the telegraph's unique triad of sender, telegraphist, and receiver, "[t]he secret world of the ruling class is increasingly open to view" (87). While the uncle in *The Turn of the Screw* can command the governess "'never [to] trouble him . . . nor write about anything' with some expectation [that] the class divisions of his world will support this taboo," the "private world" of *In the Cage*'s aristocrats is written by these aristocrats themselves in front of the working-class telegraph clerks who then transmit the secret liaisons of their "betters" (87). Rowe convincingly argues that while *In the Cage*'s telegraphist, for reasons specific to her character, understands little of the technological power she holds over Captain Everard, James nonetheless "makes explicit" the potential held by "the working classes to understand and perhaps even seize what James had always understood as the primary mode of social production: discourse" (87). And Rowe's analysis demonstrates convincingly that language reveals a culture's political economy.

In the Cage's telegraphist is an unusual Jamesian character, a working-class female confronting a "nominal[ly] aristocratic hero . . . with her combination of independence, frankness . . . familiarity and . . . knowledge of his complicated, trivial liaisons" (88). However, while the telegraphist claims to know "the discourse of high society" (89), she makes no use of it to improve her own position. Thus, James creates a young woman who is capable of controlling discourse but does not exercise this power because of her nostalgia regarding her own class slippage; she is a " 'lady' fallen down the steep slope" of social and economic decline (90).

The reason she remains at Cocker's is her "infatuation with Captain Everard and vain hope that her continuance at the 'PO' . . . might lead to a genuine romance" (91). Thus, she vainly aspires to be restored to her former status as a "lady" in the old-fashioned way: by marrying a gentleman—her own late-Victorian romance fantasy that effectively keeps her in her place, literally and psychologically.

Her traditionalist characteristics mix paradoxically with the telegraphist's seemingly modern spirit. But Rowe demonstrates that gender is an unstable mix of our own and culture's expectations for us. Just as she is a combination of discordant qualities, so also her fiancé, the inelegantly named Mr. Mudge, is, despite previous critics' dismissal of him, also a diverse blend of gender and class qualities. While he is a "classic petit-bourgeois" who supports the class system because he believes that it benefits him economically, he also surprises us by responding supportively rather than jealously to the telegraphist's disclosure of her meeting with Everard (93–4).

Rowe thus suggests that, in both the telegraphist and her fiancé, "some of Judith Butler's sense of the postmodern constructions of gender through discourse are already present in James's text, albeit not entirely under his control. New representations of gender establish new relations of gender, and both are often enough the consequence of new working and living conditions" (95). At one level, *In the Cage* follows "the customary Jamesian narrative of feminine limitation" in which "the young woman is incapable of becoming not only Artist but Mother, especially those characters who pursue careers of their own" (96). On the other hand, "[a]t a certain level, the telegraphist assumes the phallus of a newly empowered 'mother,' especially as she assumes *maternal* functions outside the conventional and literal roles of 'mother' reserved for a young, affianced working-class girl" (98). As a consequence of her assumption of these different mothering roles, " '[m]othering' has been refigured by association with the powers of communication, and the degree to which the telegraphist dons those powers is some measure of an authority that no longer is *precisely* that of 'mother' or 'father' but of some 'authority' for transmission that exceeds their outmoded and gender-specific roles" (98).

Rowe concludes his essay with a reading of *In the Cage*'s ending, in which the telegraphist provokes Jamesian high comedy by misunderstanding Mrs. Jordan's explanation of just who and what Mr. Drake, butler first to Lord Rye and then to Lady Bradeen *and* Mrs. Jordan's fiancé, has been and will be to these three people. Like a highbrow version of Abbott and Costello's "Who's on First?" routine, the telegraphist's conversation with Mrs. Jordan operates on at least three levels: "the confusion of [Mrs. Jordan's reference to Mr. Drake as a] 'gentleman' to be either aristocrat or servant; confusion of Mr. Drake's sexual preference as either straight or gay; confusion of what amounts to a *ménage à quatre* of Drake, Lord Rye, Lady Bradeen, and Mrs. Jordan with the confused relations of the telegraphist, Captain Everard, Lady Bradeen, and Mrs. Jordan" (98–99).

Rowe declares that "James open[s] the doors to our repressed fears of homoeroticism" (100) by creating these women's unintentional "confusions of gender and class . . . produced nonetheless by the new circumstances of work, communication, and social relations" (100). Finally, we remain unclear of James's own awareness that "he shares the anxieties of Lady Bradeen, Captain Everard, and the others once in 'charge' of the symbolic discourse of culture" (101). While it is "difficult to determine from the surface of a novella with such depths" the extent of James's awareness of his own anxiety in becoming and remaining the "Master," Rowe argues that we must once again admire his "encourage[ment]," even his "provo[cation]" of our interest in "[s]ounding the depths" of his " 'coded' texts" (101–2).

Turning from the first four essays, which focused primarily upon female characters, Michael Wilson's study presents an ideal method of analysis to shift to the essays concentrating more upon male roles in James. In Wilson's fascinating essay, " 'To Feel is Such a Career': Gender and Vocation in *The Tragic Muse*," he focuses upon a comparative analysis of two artists, Nick Dormer and Miriam Rooth, to reveal valuable elements of James's sexual ideology during the middle phase of his career. The novel's male and female protagonists/artists enable Wilson to compare James's gendered understanding of the artist's public role and private self. In particular, Wilson "concentrate[s] on how the novel explores the pervasive and often invidious articulation of gender norms in late-Victorian society . . . .[He is]

especially interested here in how James deploys gender difference in his depiction of two contemporary social issues: . . . the
coercive power of social expectations, and the contentious uncertainty about the role of the artist in modern society" (Wilson
106). Overall, what Wilson discovers is that for the male artist,
James perceives a conflict, even a crisis, between social norms
and individual desires; however, for a woman artist, James sees
no conflict between the self and society but rather a situation
resolvable by appearances, suggesting that a woman artist does
not generate such a crisis because she experiences life and work
more superficially.

In the first half of the novel, which focuses upon Nick's crisis
of masculinity, Wilson notes that there are no adequate males
in the older generation to whom Nick could turn as role models,
and the women surrounding him enact the familiar demanding,
devouring role of James's middle-phase fiction. Caught between
his lack of understanding about how to be a man and the financial and psychological expectations women impose upon him,
Nick initially copes with this conflict by hiding behind a "double
nature" (112).

Wilson connects Nick's division into two selves, one socially
respectable and the other privately indulgent, to the fin de siècle Jekyll/Hyde tradition. But James moves his male artist
through this divided self into a more mature resolution, which
requires Nick to confront "his own conscience, his family, and
the disapprobation of society in order to realize his private ambitions" (114).

To the women surrounding Nick—his mother, sisters, and fi-
ancée—Nick appears to abandon his dutiful masculine role as
their caretaker. But Wilson notes that James is showing us that
Nick is learning to be himself, a man and an artist, through two
negatives, his steady renunciation of the women's demands and
the world's hollow rewards, and one positive step, his immersion in the long, painful struggle to paint as he believes he
must. While Nick's coming to terms with his process of masculine self-creation occupies the first half of the novel, his artistic
battle recedes in the second half of the novel as an essentially
undramatizable labor. Miriam's transformation into a rather
celebrated young actress occupies the forefront of the novel's
second half.

Like Nick, Miriam, in choosing the theater, pursues a vocation that requires at once "a renunciation of gender norms *and*
an emphatic reinscription of gender identity" (119). Having

noted this similarity, Wilson goes on to note more acute differences between the two artists: "The tale of Miriam's pursuit of a career on the stage is narrated in counterpoint to Nick's abandonment of politics for painting, but James's employment of the two stories forestalls any simple accounting. Nick and Miriam are never precisely each other's double nor are they each other's opposite; their situations are never entirely commensurate. James seems to suggest by this that the fine arts are as different as men and women" (106,118).

Miriam differs from every other woman in the novel by pursuing a career. Contradictorily, though, she writes herself off lightly in doing so by invoking gender as an excuse for her career: " 'Oh, I'm an inferior creature, of an inferior sex, and I have to earn my bread as I can' " (119). In addition to gender, Miriam inhabits other margins wherein she is allowed to have a public career: her "obscure social" and national origins (120). These hybrid elements coalesce in her choice of acting as a career, but they also point up James's limited treatment of this female character. While Nick experiences a "crisis of masculinity," which he resolves through his artistic dedication, Miriam suffers no conflict between "being" and "doing," as does Nick. Instead of Nick's effort to resolve the conflict between his public and private selves, Miriam works to eliminate any such differences in herself. She learns in the second half of the novel to become a fairly accomplished actress, which appears in part to involve learning to act like a lady when she is offstage. Once she has polished her persona, she becomes irresistible to Peter Sherringham, Nick's politically correct cousin. But he is fascinated in order to put her on his own life's stage in the role of his wife; he admits to feeling that such a woman is a kind of monster unless she plies her trade in private service as his wife.

Miriam, then, learns to act onstage and offstage as an effective success strategy, while Nick feels that any behavior in which he did not believe, any acting, betrays him and his art. In addition, Miriam's lack of class betrays itself in excessive emotion—indecorousness—of which the aristocratic Nick would never be guilty. More significantly, as Miriam learns her craft, she depends on many people: her mother, her teachers, and, for financial support, Peter. Nick already knows he must learn his art—not merely a craft—in solitude while depending on no one. Similar to Priscilla Walton's connection of Eugenia Munster's use of veils as disguise, Miriam's acting seems merely to represent "a female masquerade, the assumption of a culturally sanctioned femininity to conceal an originary lack" (Walton 45; Wilson 121–2).

Most telling is James's decision never to show Miriam's subjectivity; she remains the object of everyone's spectacle in contrast to James's interiorization of Nick's artistic struggle. Wilson cogently analyzes Miriam's struggle "to carve out a space for herself economically and socially. . . . Since [James] will not 'go behind' Miriam, [he] can demonstrate the intelligence animating Miriam's 'posing' only in her dialogue with the other characters" (128). Wilson describes the degree of Miriam's knowledge of her own inferiority as "perverse" and adds that "[i]n this moment, James reveals his stake in the articulation of gender and vocation all too clearly: despite his sympathy for all those aspirants whose lives are constrained by patriarchal society, the artist 'who happened to be born a woman' cannot escape either marriage or the marketplace and thus must always defer to the solitary male genius" (132).

Eric Haralson's essay, " 'His little heart, dispossessed': Ritual Sexorcism in *The Turn of the Screw*," combines historicism and cultural criticism in examining James's popular potboiler. Haralson reads the story as an allusion to the 1889 Cleveland Street homosexual brothel affair as well as an allegory of Oscar Wilde's 1895 immorality trial involving Lord Alfred Douglas. Overall, Haralson groups his interpretations under the umbrella of late-Victorian homosexual panic toward which James is cannily ambiguous: he manages to sell his story of repressed homosexuality exorcised "murderous[ly]" by the governess as the "handmaiden of patriarchy" at the same time that the tale laments her role as "a ruthless enforcer of heteronormative investment" (Haralson 139).

Haralson opens his essay by pointing out that contemporary reviewers of the story divided between those who saw "lurid," "deprav[ed]," and "sickening" corruption in the story's exposure of children to evil and "more cosmopolitan readers" who "gave into the [tale's] gothic frisson" (133). By analogy, readers repeat the governess's compulsion and then resistance to "playing this game of fill-in-the-blank, their keenness for explanatory details being continually blunted by a sense of (as she says) 'directions in which I must not . . . go' (even as she proceeds to do so)" (135). In effect, her terror and fascination in reading the children's behavior becomes our own, which makes her subsequent ruthlessness a stand-in for ours as well.

However, Haralson points out that readers today are prone to suspect James's refusal to name the evil encountered in the text as "disengenuousness or at a minimum . . . self-blinkering," which is as much as Virginia Woolf suggests in 1921 about James and his readers (135). Haralson shows that E. M. Forster moves past Woolf's implied unnamed homosexual element in author and readers toward an explicit interpretation of " 'homosex' as the disavowed subtext of *The Turn of the Screw*" (136). According to Forster, the " 'fluster' that James so effectively communicates was none other than his own, as he went on steadily 'declining to think about' what he was all the while thinking about" (136). It is here, Haralson notes, that James nimbly manages to excoriate his homosexual theme while simultaneously exploiting it: "[A]n author who could retail yet another period euphemism for homosexual love—'a union against nature,' as James's own criticism refers to it . . . without noticing or acknowledging that he was doing so" (136). Thus, the story clearly draws out for our perverse enjoyment the suspense of Peter Quint's unnamed evil menacing the children at the same time that it manifests a well-established Victorian obsession with "codifying, regulating, and punishing forms of sexuality *contra naturam*, with special attention to (homo)sexual acts that traversed boundaries of age and/or social class" (136).

While describing *The Turn of the Screw* as a Segdgwickian "allegory of sexual panic," Haralson also identifies Quint and Miss Jessel as "threats to the developing child—especially the male child as heritor of class and state power" (139). The governess, then, becomes the frightening but necessary enforcer of heterosexual and class norms. In the context of the Cleveland Street homosexual brothel affair and Wilde's trial for homosexuality, *The Turn of the Screw* (1898) becomes both a vigilant defense of the Victorian era's idealization of children's innocence and of its class boundaries: "Her 'dispossession' of Miles's little heart—that word which so nicely conjoins economic, lineal, and spiritual disfranchisements—indexes the heavy sacrifice that British society stood ready to incur to prevent 'little gentlemen' like him from straying into the 'wrong path altogether' taken by redheaded corrupters like Quint (better dead than red?)" (139).

Haralson concludes his provocative essay by musing upon the endangered status of the term "gentleman," in the late-Victorian era. Like Stevenson's *Dr. Jekyll and Mr. Hyde*, *The Turn of the Screw* speculated on the horror uncovered when this signifier slips from its social moorings. He closes with a reminder that Miles's claim to gentlemanliness is tentative to begin with since he is the son of the younger brother and—according to the English law of primogeniture—therefore without inheritance. All the more reason that, now that his father is dead and his uncle unmarried, he must continue to act as the little gentleman who would inherit his uncle's estate. According to the governess, he remains a gentleman, but Haralson points out that the price Miles pays for this pedigree is his life, and the governess has become the "ritual sexorcis[t]" of his essay's title.

Leland Person has established his authority as an explorer of the psychological and gendered complexities of America's renaissance master writers and of James in his previous books. In his essay here, he explores the psychosexual sadomasochism inherent in the relationships of *The Golden Bowl*. His article, playfully entitled "Jamesian Sadomasochism: The Invisible (Third) Hand of Manhood in *The Golden Bowl*," examines Prince Amerigo's relationships to Maggie Verver, Adam Verver, and Charlotte Stant. Person suggests that within the novel's sexual economy, "James transposes his [four major] characters, making them subjects *and* objects of [one another's] diversified desires . . . and dividing male subjectivity between Prince Amerigo and Adam Verver, making each man the codependent of the other. James unsettles male subjectivity even further, feminizing it in the process, when he delegates authority to Maggie in the second half of the novel" (Person 150–51). Amerigo's "potent manhood works for Adam" in the form of producing a male heir. But in fulfilling his designated role, Amerigo renders himself useless. As Person articulates Amerigo's impossible position, "Phallically and seminally empowered through the female subject position delegated by the patriarchal capitalist to his daughter, Amerigo becomes the invisible third hand of the Ververs' capitalist economy, laboring to remain more a complex male subject than a passive, feminized male victim" (151).

Applying Kaja Silverman's psychoanalytic exploration of female and male masochism to *The Golden Bowl*, Person notes that female masochism is a required aspect of " 'normal' female subjectivity" in which woman "eroticiz[es her genital] lack" and her culturally determined "subordination" (Person 150). However, whenever a male is placed in the feminine masochistic position as Amerigo is when he marries Maggie, his culturally-determined masculine role is threatened. First made use of and then ignored by both Ververs, Amerigo is left alone to reconstruct his sexual subjectivity through his sexual domination of Charlotte in their affair.

Person suggests that Gilles Deleuze's "masochistic tableau" of the relationship between male masochist and cold, maternal, and severe woman reflects effectively Maggie and the Prince's marriage: " 'Through the dispassionate and highly ritualized transaction that takes place between these two figures, the [male masochist] is stripped of all virility, and reborn as a 'new, sexless man,' and the [cold maternal woman] is invested with the phallus.' . . . In this 'utopian' rereading of masochism, Deleuze 'celebrates' a 'pact between the mother and the son to write the father out of his dominant position within both culture and masochism, and to install the mother in his place' " (154). Adam's calculating connoisseurship, demonstrated in his purchase, use, and reification of Amerigo and Charlotte, constitutes the grandiose sadism that requires Maggie's reconfiguration of the couples and her father and Charlotte's exile to America.

Person examines the imagery with which Adam and Amerigo take mutual pleasure in the older man's buying, surveilling, and deploying Amerigo as a surrogate lover to both of his daughter-wives. This imagery's tenor is both homoerotic and homosocial. Its frequency and the intensity of this language prompts Person to ask which of the partners [in Amerigo and Maggie's marriage] Adam actually uses: "Does he employ Amerigo to make love to Maggie, or does he use Maggie to 'rub against' Amerigo?" (157). In both readings, Amerigo's potency is brought under control through his sexual performance for pay. However, while Adam's economic control has reduced Amerigo to a kept man, Adam becomes an accomplice in his own cuckolding—this form of masochism being the price he has paid for the procreative (and recreative) services Amerigo provides. Thus, the two men maintain the reciprocality between sadism and masochism inherent in such relationships.

Amerigo, now reduced to a woman's position through selling his sexual performance, reacts to his sexual and economic objectification by passively accepting Charlotte's advances. In so doing, he temporarily restores a sense of himself as a sexual subject who brutally dominates their relations. However, Amerigo only appears to restore his sense of sexual power in his affair with Charlotte because he is, throughout the adultery, in Adam's employ as his sexual surrogate; he is merely allowed to enact his sexually potent persona for a time. When Maggie recognizes Amerigo's betrayal, she silently effects the separation of the adulterers with her father's equally tacit cooperation.

Such silence between the little capitalist and his daughter is necessary because "Amerigo must remain manly—empowered in a sadistic, masculine pose—because only then does he remain useful" (164).

Maggie's love for Amerigo works for him, just as Charlotte's had during their adultery; the psychic economy among the four remains balanced, but now Maggie provides the desire that transforms Amerigo's actual position as Adam's surrogate into the fulfillment of her "feminocentric sadomasochistic fantasy" (167). Her sense of his absolute power over her sexual desire for him conceals from both of them her actual economic control over him. Thus, Maggie proves herself to be the ideal mediator in the complex relationship between her father and her husband. The more she loves them both, the more she works to disguise her inherited economic power as her father's daughter so that her husband perceives instead his emotional power over her.

Amerigo's male subjectivity has, however, been destabilized over the course of the novel—through his acceptance of his role as Adam's sexual surrogate and then through the permutations that role undergoes once he has given Adam a male heir, cuckolded Adam in an effort to restore his sexual identity, and accepted Maggie's restoration of their marriage, which is also his reacceptance of his role as an sexual/aesthetic object. Person reflects that Maggie is now able to "simultaneously appreciat[e] and control[] his powerful masculine performance. . . . At best, . . . James has established a state of uneasy tension in Amerigo's case between being and performance. . . . the Prince reemerges as a 'congruous whole' . . . but largely because his performance of that part fulfills the job description under which he was hired in the beginning. . . . [Maggie], as the phallic woman . . . lends the phallus to her husband, enabling him to reconstruct himself according to her 'instructions' " (172).

The last two essays in this book deal with James's nonfiction, specifically his literary criticism and *The American Scene*. Sarah Daugherty, in her essay entitled "James and the Representation of Women: Some Lessons of the Master(')s," enhances her reputation as the James scholar who has most comprehensively studied his own literary criticism. Daugherty's formidable grasp of the major and minor Continental, English, and American novelists throughout the entire nineteenth century enables her to give us valuable insight into James's senses of himself, psychologically and artistically, in relation to his predecessors and

contemporaries. She skillfully explores the psychological motives behind James's praise of Ivan Turgenev and Honoré de
Balzac as well as his complaints against a herd of men and
women writers, many of whom James felt were inferior, such
as Louisa May Alcott and Elizabeth Stoddard, and some whom
he acknowledged as good—but only to a degree—such as Anthony Trollope, Nathaniel Hawthorne, George Sand and George
Eliot. Like Michael Wilson in his analysis of *The Tragic Muse*,
Daugherty considers James's fiction as problematic for feminist
analysis and suggests as an explanation of this problematic
character that James learned from Turgenev "to idealize
women in a manner resistant to analytical criticism. And from
Balzac, his chosen master, he learned that a conservative ideology, not a democratic or a radical one, best served the novelist's
primary need—the need for dramatic material" (Daugherty
178). Through a critical survey of works by male and female
writers of women's novels from the 1860s and 1870s on both
sides of the Atlantic, Daugherty proves that James learned how
not to treat these works' "most common protagonist," "[t]he female victim of a patriarchal culture personified by a despotic
father, suitor, or husband" (177). By reviewing these novels,
James learned that their unoriginality lay in their "diffuse, sentimental, amateurishly written, and thematically confused"
treatment of their female protagonists (177).

Daugherty points out that James's greater challenge as a
young author lay not in writing satirical reviews of inferior writers but rather in formulating responses to the acknowledged
masters of fiction. She shows James, in Bloomian fashion, reas-
suring himself about his own creativity by dismissing some of
these writers' gifts through misreadings of their works. Thus,
Daugherty suggests that James's now well-known criticism of
Hawthorne's provincialism was less accurate than it was reas-
suring to the young author whose own ideological conservatism
and psychological uneasiness with earlier writers' successes
prevented him from recognizing Hawthorne as a potent "critic
of patriarchal culture" (177).

Turgenev and Balzac, because James admired both for the
strength of their masculine personalities as well as for their
writing, present James with his most interesting Bloomian dis-
missal/appropriation dilemmas. Turgenev's cosmopolitanness
and Balzac's raw power nearly overwhelm the young James.
Daugherty convincingly shows the reader that James appro-
priates a version of these attributes for himself, thus mastering

his masters by assimilating them into a more cultured, confident version of himself. Ultimately, Daugherty sees James's most significant appropriation from these two as his cultural conservatism. Daugherty then discusses James's response to great women writers. For example, she suggests that because "James learned to see the dramatic potential of women's themes" from George Eliot, this debt then pushed him to "underscore the aesthetic limitations of [her] novels" (184).

Thus, Daugherty concludes that James's limitations as a feminist derive from his psychological and aesthetic allegiance to a conservative, patriarchal society out of which James created his politically incorrect—by some contemporary standards—but obviously great fictional melodramas.

The last piece in this volume, by Mary Esteve, "Anerotic Excursions: Memory, Celibacy, and Desire in *The American Scene*," is a complex, compelling reading of that work's language of memory, desire, and capitalism. Esteve unlocks an understanding of the travelogue's truly exotic, often bizarre imagery through a combination of William James's and Henri Bergson's explorations of memory's functions in relation to consciousness; thus, she reads in James's *American Scene* imagery an "anerotics" or transformed erotics in which desire is located in the memory's recreation of experience.

Esteve begins by comparing *The American Scene* to James's *Autobiography* as explorations of memory. And even though Henry remembered his older brother as always ahead of him— "always round the corner and out of sight" (Edel, *The Untried Years*, 59), Esteve discovers a striking parallelism in their writings about the operations of memory and consciousness. In *The American Scene*, James demonstrates the ubiquitous American traits of being seer and seen; equally crucial to James's dual positions of native and stranger from which he observes America is his duality of tone—simultaneously detached and intimate— that he relishes for the comforting distance it provides him without depriving him of the ability to mingle, imaginatively and erotically, with his countrymen.

While his brother and Bergson "called into question traditional notions of the harmonious, seamlessly self-conscious, and deeply interiorized human subject," Henry "appears (however unconsciously) to put their theories into practice" by creating a complex narratological stance that is simultaneously intimate and impersonal. "[M]emory functions in James's work to point toward what can be called the impersonal limit of a sub-

ject's conscious experience. . . . The more often James pronounces 'I' and the more details he collects from his *personal
history,* the more he reveals the cohabitation 'within' of an *impersonal subject.* . . . reflec[ting] a conception of human subjectivity as constitutively disjoined" (Esteve 197; emphasis mine).

This interiorized, disparate sense of consciousness from
which James narrates *The American Scene* has "specific implications for his representation of desire and sexuality" (197). The
more impersonally James creates his voice, the more destabilized his sexual identity becomes; indeed, "[s]table sexual identification becomes difficult if not impossible to ascertain" in the
book's simultaneously "illuminat[ing] and obfuscat[ing]" "figural flourishes" (197–98). Esteve discovers that, in *The American Scene*'s "libidinal economy," "celibacy circulates as a kind
of positive interruption: infused with anonymity, it functions as
a 'deinteriorizing' plenitude, an anerotic lure that draws subjective identity out of itself" (197). Thus, celibacy in *The American
Scene* is not, as some other current readings of James's fiction
and biography argue, the "locus of renunciation from which
issue dialectically coherent (homo)sexual identifications and
literary productions" (199). Rather, celibacy as the limit-condition of sexuality, performs two functions: it confuses sexual
identity, and it coalesces two economies, that of eroticism and
capitalism, as she will demonstrate in an extended reading of
James's visit to Wall Street (199).

Initially, the crowds disorient James as he strolls down Wall
Street; he responds by "destabilizing through figures of speech
the scene's discrete elements": the crowd becomes "both a
'dense mass' and a 'muddy medium,'" conveying "both 'sounds
and silences' " (211–12). Following suit, "the entity 'Henry
James' differentiates and multiplies into a number of incongruous narrating and observing selves" (Esteve 287). At one point,
"James triply interiorizes [his] observer-self: he is in the midst
of the swarming city that is 'inside' a tower that is 'inside' down-
town" (212).

Thus, James's self, his language, and his perceptions have become multifold: "With a rush of rhythmic, climactic force, a
'muddy medium' of words spills out into the space of writing
like a crowd into the streets: a 'welter of objects and sounds in
which relief, detachment, dignity, meaning, perished utterly
and lost all rights' " (213). Esteve speculates that a "welter of
contiguous nouns and reiterated verbs" indicates that his writing has become the site of "the coincidence in him of [both] cel-

ibate and erotic intensities" (213). Yet Esteve goes further to see that this imagery of sexual instability has Deleuzean economic implications. James "not only disorganizes himself libidinally and narratologically," but he also destabilizes the contemporary, secure conventional wisdom about Wall Street's financial sturdiness. In his hallucinatory vision, the crowd embodies "pure, terrifying, utterly disorganized capitalist desire, desiring for its own sake. . . . unmoored from coherent, exchangist visions of self and society, of monetary obligations and value, of history and future" (214).

This Wall Street scene "invites us to consider how James's *American Scene*" more generally "carries out his 'excursions of memory . . . reckless almost to extravagance' " (215). Esteve's gifted reading of the passage enables us to grasp how closely Henry's operations of memory and consciousness parallel Bergson's concept of memory as external yet immanent to consciousness as well as brother William's notion of consciousness as that which is entering experience and still unnamed.

It is difficult to do justice to the intelligence and complexity of these essays in this introduction, but I hope to have indicated their subject matter and points of view. In this collection readers will, I believe, find much to interest them and stimulate their understanding of James's ways of representing two central aspects of culture and of human nature: gender and sexuality. Finally, I look forward to reading more studies of these crucial aspects of James's writing.

PEGGY MCCORMACK

Notes

1. Leon Edel and Sheldon M. Novick, "Oh Henry! What Henry James Didn't Do with Oliver Wendell Holmes (Or Anyone Else)," *Slate*, 11 December 1996: 8 messages. On-line. Internet. 24 September 1997. Available http://www.slate.com/Concept/96–12–11/Concept.asp

2. The highly charged debate about Philip Novick's *The Young Master* (New York: Random House, 1996) and *Henry James and Homo-Erotic Desire*, edited by John R. Bradley (New York: St. Martin's Press, 1998), on the Henry James List Serv since December 1997, indicates the deeply divided attitudes toward criticism that assumes a priori attitudes toward James's sexuality and his expression of this in his writing.

3. Laura Mulvey, "The Oedipus Myth: Beyond *The Riddles of the Sphinx*," in *Visual and Other Pleasures* (Bloomington: Indiana University Press, 1989), 177–201.

Questioning
the Master

The Janus Faces of James:
Gender, Transnationality, and James's Cinematic Adaptations

PRISCILLA L. WALTON

THE SIGNIFIER "HENRY JAMES" OPERATES ON A NUMBER OF DIVER-
gent levels and offers a profusion of meanings to audiences
around the globe. On the one hand, as a member of F. R. Leavis's "Great Tradition," James enjoys iconic status as an English
writer and receives the cultural sanction accorded to an acknowledged arbiter of literary values and cultural taste. On the
other hand, while James's inclusion in a summarily *British* tradition reflects the author's long sojourn in the United Kingdom,
it also elides his position as an *American* novelist. James, therefore, assumes a cross-national status, which is particularly apparent in his historical reception and in the cinematic and
televisual translations of his writings.

In these translations, the author's cross-nationality is complicated and nuanced by the cross-media transference from novel
to screen. Such an emigration, according to Brian McFarlane,
must be critiqued textually as well as analyzed and placed contextually, if it is to be appreciated fully. The critic explains his
position as follows: "Conditions within the film industry and
the prevailing cultural and social climate at the time of the
film's making (especially when the film version does not follow
hot upon the novel's publication) are two major determinants
in shaping any film" (21). He goes on to stress that "cultural
conditions (e.g., the exigencies of wartime or changing sexual
mores) might lead to a shift in emphasis in a film as compared
with the novel on which it is based" (22).

The recent spate of Jane Austen films offers an exemplar of
McFarlane's thesis, evident in the two main branches of criticism these products have generated, both of which take into account the context of the phenomenon. One branch argues that

37

the Austen films perform a process of containment, confining Austen's writings within the "safe" space of home and family, a space that has especial resonance for an audience living in a time of flux and crisis and thus accounts for the popularity of the ventures. Another branch contends that these cinematic efforts are transgressive moves to bring a female author to the attention of the contemporary mass public. While both of these critical branches pose valid arguments, neither takes into consideration the Austen phenomenon's *overarching* placement within a cultural climate favorable to filmic translations of "classic authors," nor do their contentions open lines of inquiry into the ways in which James seems to be stepping into Jane's shoes as a cinematic draw. Indeed, over the past several years, three major Jamesian films have been produced (Jane Campion's *The Portrait of a Lady*, Agnieszka Holland's *Washington Square*, and Iain Softley's *The Wings of the Dove*). Each of these productions has inspired new editions of James's novels, sporting film stills on the covers and throughout the texts, offered for purchase in such middle-brow venues as the Doubleday Book Club and the Book of the Month Club, and thus marking a class shift in Jamesian appreciation from its traditional high culture placement to a middle ground. Concomitantly, it is rumored that another version of *Washington Square* is in the works, along with a BBC production of *The American*, as well as a third potential Jamesian adaptation from Merchant-Ivory.[1]

Nonetheless, this is not the first time James has proved an attractive prospect for filmmakers. Throughout the twentieth century, more than twenty-nine films have been based on his works, and have emerged from such diverse locales as Hollywood, the United Kingdom, France, Portugal, and Spain, to note only a few. What interests me about these Jamesian productions are the periods in which the cinematic conveyances arise or, in McFarlane's words, their cultural conditions, as well as how their textual meanings have shifted over the ages. Indeed, an adaptation, particularly of James, also requires an act of translation involving, as it does, a movement that is cross-national as well as cross-media. A representation of a representation, a filmic translation of a novel, includes a shift of venue and context and, thus, encompasses, as James Boyd White argues if in a quite different context, neither a mechanical nor a technical process, but rather "a kind of pushing forward of what was written in one text into another." For White, translation comprises a fully paradoxical "space of uncertainty," or a "no-place"

(246). "No-place" resonates in specific ways for James, whose writings traditionally have been a source of mostly ineffectual efforts at nationalist "patriation."

James's works, which reflect cross-national confrontations textually, have also been integral, extratextually, to various narrations of nation. Thus, White's paradoxical "no-place" recalls Homi K. Bhabha's discussion of in-betweenness since, for Bhabha, nation and narration converge:

> The 'locality' of national culture is neither unified nor unitary in relation to itself, nor must it be seen simply as 'other' in relation to what is outside or beyond it. The boundary is Janus-faced and the problem of outside/inside must always be a process of hybridity, incorporating new 'people' in relation to the body politic, generating other sites of meaning. . . . What emerges as an effect of such 'incomplete signification' is a turning of boundaries and limits into the *in-between* spaces through which the meanings of cultural and political authority are negotiated. (4)

If James resides in an "in-between" space, as I think he does, and if translation itself generates a "no-place," then James's cinematic transferrals manifest particularly fruitful grounds for examinations of cross-nationality and the narration of nation.

James's national and cultural positions are difficult to locate, since he is situated in one of those "in-between" spaces that Bhabha emphasizes. Although it is possible to perceive James as a figure of "postcoloniality," his position as an American-born author (whose country of origin undeniably has enjoyed global dominance in the twentieth century) renders that categorization problematic. He might, therefore, best be viewed as a transnational figure, whose writings blur and obscure national distinctions.

Consequently, as the product of a country that was not a social center in his day, James was lured by the cultural capitals of Europe and fled an America he perceived in terms of "lack," a lack to which he drew attention in that famous passage in *Hawthorne,* wherein he describes the United States through a series of negatives (e.g., "No sovereign, no court, no personal loyalty, no aristocracy, no church, no clergy, no army, no diplomatic service, no country gentlemen, no palaces," etc.). While James is not particularly fair to the United States in this observation, and assessments like it did not help to endear him to its citizenry, he nonetheless utilized the lack he perceived in American culture and turned it to advantage in the "international theme" to which his writings often return.

Caught between two worlds, then, James was a figure who belonged to neither. This may be one of the reasons that his status crosses demarcated borders and is used to reinforce contrasting and even conflicting national trajectories. Thus, as a cultural icon, James's decision to become a British subject in 1915 became fodder for anti-American sentiments in England during World War I and worked to solidify his position in the "great tradition" of British authors. Conversely, his European self-exile caused no end of problems for many American scholars. Van Wyck Brooks, for example, was greatly disturbed by the author's expatriation, and argued that James's writings concomitantly lost their American flavor. Critics such as Brooks and, later, Lionel Trilling, whom Andrew Ross has called an historically and politically specific "defender of the faith" (216), focused on James's Americanness and employed the author to endorse American culture as a legitimate object of study. Indeed, contentions such as these foreground the ways in which nation is predicated upon specific ethnocentric lines. As Timothy Brennan points out, the "idea of nationhood is not only a political plea, but a formal binding together of disparate elements. And out of the multiplicities of culture, race, and political structures grows also a repeated dialectic of uniformity and specificity" (62). Brennan's contention here is astute; however, his elision of gender and the ways in which nation is often mapped and narrated over and through the female body is a crucial oversight, since the female body frequently serves as a conduit for the positing of nationality. As Anne McClintock observes in her important study, *Imperial Leather:* "All nations depend on powerful constructions of gender. Despite many nationalists' ideological investment in the idea of popular *unity,* nations have historically amounted to the sanctioned institutionalization of gender *difference*" (353). Accordingly, nation is often narrated through "commonly accepted" gender distinctions, with gender providing the basis for the construction of national difference. The bodies of women habitually serve as the means of speaking nationality, a situation that the American and British visual translations of James's novels illustrate clearly. As a result, the cultural struggle over the iconic national status of Henry James covertly points up how national identity is expressed over the female body, at the same time that Campion's cross-national and postcolonial production of *The Portrait of a Lady* draws attention to this usage of women throughout the narrative movement of her film, and Softley's *The Wings of the Dove* breaks with tradition and posits a transnational view bespeaking the potential of a globalized culture.

Historically, early attempts to nationalize James foreground the imbrications of gender and nation. In keeping with Brennan's formulation, in the United States, the vision of "America" embodied in the writings of Brooks and Trilling relies on unspoken ideological and gendered interstices. For Brooks, in 1925, the problem with James's writings is located in the author's heed of the siren call of the American society circles to which he was exposed, circles that were "so intensely feminine," they served as "an unregarded, but ever so keenly regarding protectorate . . . of the fashionable world of England and France" (20). James, therefore, listens to the fairy tale of Europe and is seduced away from the rough-hewn reality of the United States. In 1940, Trilling attempts to reevaluate James by emphasizing the use-value of the author's otherworldly attributes. He takes issue with those critics who condemn James as irrelevant because he was "debarred" from the "odors of the shop" (11) and argues that this maneuver is indicative of an American fear of intellectuality. For Trilling, James "shows so many of the electric qualities of the mind" (10) that his works demonstrate "a complex and rapid imagination . . . [along] with a kind of authoritative immediacy" (12). Ultimately, Trilling contends, to dismiss James because of his visionary capacities would be to reduce "ideas to details," ideas that are "crucial to the advancement of the liberal imagination in America" (19). Thus, the rough-and-tumble of the national character, if it is to develop, must be refigured through the "feminine" qualities embedded in the writings of the Master.

It is striking how gender constructions propel the above criticisms, apparent in Brooks's condemnation of feminized social circles and Trilling's authorization of those otherworldly and impractical traits that, traditionally, have been associated with "Woman." Accordingly, for Brooks, James is too feminine, and for Trilling, just feminine enough to open the ideological construction of "America." Significantly, here, neither critic looks to women writers to fulfill their objectives.

Nevertheless, it is important to remember that Brooks is writing in 1925, when it was particularly consequential to stress the promise of the United States, given the compelling lure of

Europe for American artists and intellectuals. And in 1940, the year in which Trilling wrote "Reality in America," the rise of fascism in Nazi Germany was posing a very real threat to "the liberal imagination" he championed. In the aftermath of World War II, however, Europe no longer offered the same cultural haven to displaced Americans, and the United States had become "feminized" in ways that cultural advocates such as Brooks and Trilling could not have foreseen.

In the postwar period, wherein the United States wielded an undeniable global influence, the nationalist impetus was assimilated into popular forms such as mainstream cinema, which then converged affirmations of American strength with celebrations of American culture. It is not surprising, therefore, that in 1949, Warner Brothers Studio, a production company noted for its patriotic " 'service' pictures and 'headliner' " films (Bordwell 326), turned to the work of a great American novelist for the basis of a feature production. But this film, William Wyler's *The Heiress*, adapted from Ruth and Augustus Goetz's successful Broadway play based on James's *Washington Square*, provides for an extension of the work of the cultural advocates, since it moves to homogenize sets of common cultural values and shared ideological norms as it contingently displays further twists in the imbrications of gender and nation. Looking back to American history for an affirmation of its project, the film's opening frame bears the words: "One hundred years ago." While this frame duplicates the setting of the novel, the film's location in the past also serves as a guise for its distinctively topical message. Indeed, *The Heiress* demonstrates how, as R. Radhakrishnan, in a different context, aptly observes, " 'woman' becomes the mute but necessary allegorical ground for the transactions of nationalist history" (84).

The dominance of American culture may have been indisputable in 1949, but along with it came a pronounced uneasiness in relation to gender roles. Importantly, *The Heiress* was released during a period when women, who had worked to support the war effort, were being urged to return to their homes to ensure the continuation of the "American way of life." If less explicit in its appeal toward American women than films such as *Mildred Pierce, The Heiress* nevertheless offers the suggestion of a return to a normatively gendered past.

The Heiress stars Olivia de Havilland as Catherine Sloper, a role for which she was rewarded with an Oscar. Her appearance here, however, also recalls her performance as Melanie in *Gone*

With the Wind, wherein she played the good woman who en-
acted her feminine tasks in marked contrast to the "bad girl,"
Scarlett O'Hara. And, in effect, *The Heiress* documents what
goes wrong when "Melanie" refuses to heed her place. Lacking
the ambiguity of James's novel, Catherine's actions in the film
testify to the dangers posed to the normative American family
by women's refusal to heed paternal advice.

Like *Washington Square, The Heiress* dramatizes how Catherine is the victim of an unloving father, yet while the film fore-
grounds Dr. Sloper's problematic treatment of his daughter, its
postwar context nuances its narrative movement. It is significant, here, that Catherine was raised by Dr. Sloper and her surrogate mother, Aunt Lavinia Penniman; she thus lacks a "real"
in-house mother. Consequently, while Dr. Sloper, bereft by the
death of his wife, is a faulty father, the film implicitly attributes
his faults to an inability to perform as a custodial parent.
Filmed and viewed in a postwar period that saw women as unwilling to return to their primary domestic duties as mothers
and housewives after the return of American soldiers, the feature underscores the dangers that ensue when mothers act in
absentia. Aunt Lavinia is clearly unable to serve as a "real"
mother to Catherine, and Catherine, because of her lack of
motherly guidance, follows her own desires to the detriment of
herself and her family.

The Heiress emphasizes Dr. Sloper's well-intentioned efforts
to guide his daughter.[2] He responds to Catherine's request that
she be allowed to marry Morris Townsend by pointing out to her
abrogation of proper gender roles: "You should not plead for
him; he should plead for you." He goes on to urge his daughter
to consider his advice, for "you are a weak young woman with a
large fortune," in need of guidance. Frustrated by Catherine's
refusal to abandon Townsend (played by a particularly winsome
Montgomery Clift), the good doctor despairs that it is impossible to "protect such a willing victim." Certainly, "protection" is
what Catherine needs, for Dr. Sloper's estimation of Townsend
is accurate, and within the cinematic framework, father does
know best.

Although, up to this point, Catherine has been a sympathetic
character, her defiance of her father's wishes engenders a shift
in her character. Her threat: "I can be very cruel; I have been
taught by masters," signals the beginning of her transformation
into a virago. In the final scenes of the film, Catherine is abra-
sive with servants and rude to her aunt. Her character softens

once, in an important scene that flags the film's ideological impetus. In a wide-angle shot, Catherine is positioned behind a
carriage that is overflowing with Townsend's nieces. Happy and
carefree, Catherine accedes to their plea to visit soon and waves
the carriage away. But as it rolls out of the frame, the camera
depicts Catherine, in medium shot, alone and thus focalizes the
solitude of her life. As a result, in the cinematic conclusion,
when Catherine mounts the stairs to the sound of Morris
pounding on her locked door, she ascends to a void. Denied
motherhood, through her own refusal to heed her father's advice, Catherine can only achieve fulfilment through other people's children.[3] The film covertly suggests, therefore, that
children require the guidance and succor embodied in live-in
mothers and stresses that if they defy their fathers and throw
their love away, they will be left with nothing but the solace
granted by surrogate motherhood—a surrogacy that has already
been thrown into question by Aunt Lavinia's inefficacy.

If James was used in the early part of the century, then, to
solidify an American nationalist project, as *The Heiress* suggests, his performance as a member of the British "Great Tradition" also highlights his transnationality. Indeed, in the United
Kingdom, James's novels have been used to confirm the importance of British culture in a world wherein the former imperial
center has increasingly declined in its global influence. Suggesting that the United Kingdom may no longer be the most powerful, the films also assert that it is still the best. Consequently,
James's British productions both emphasize the cultural heritage of *Britain* at the same time that they do so through the bodies of women.

In 1979, a young gay director, James Ivory, teamed with his
partner, Ismail Merchant, to produce one of James's important
early international novels, *The Europeans*. In the hands of these
Anglo-Indian filmmakers, James's text attests to the superiority
of European lifestyles for women. *The Europeans* dramatizes female sexuality and its repercussions on the lives of a group of
puritanical New Englanders. Unstressed, but implicit within
the film, is the supposed freedom granted to women in Europe
as opposed to the strict and doctrinal roles afforded them in the
United States. *The Europeans* documents the transformation of
Gertrude Wentwood (played by Lisa Eichhorn) from Puritan
daughter to Bacchanalian sylph, presumably because of the influence of her European cousin, Felix. When questioned about
her behavior, Gertrude refuses to return to her former (at least

outwardly staid) self, with the words, "I'm not going back. . . . I want to be wicked again. I've been dishonest. It's pleasure that I care for—pleasure and amusement."

Perhaps more importantly, Felix's sister, Eugenia, the Baroness Münster (played by Lee Remick), serves as the personification of European sexuality in feminine form. Making her first appearance in a veil, Eugenia embodies the mystery and sexuality that Mary Ann Doane locates in veiled female figures:

> [T]he veil functions to visualize (and hence stabilize) the instability, the precariousness of sexuality. At some level of the cultural ordering of the psychical, the horror or threat of that precariousness (of both sexuality and the visible) is attenuated by attributing it to the woman, over and against the purported stability and identity of the male. The veil is the mark of that precariousness. (46)

In Doane's view, the veil is indicative of a disruptive female sexuality, and interestingly, within *The Europeans,* Eugenia lifts her own veil, suggesting that it is she who is in control of her desire. In keeping with this signification, Eugenia is flirtatious and opportunistic, and she shrouds her past in mystery and allure. When her efforts to entrance the Wentwoods' wealthy cousin, Robert Acton, go astray, however, she decides to return to Europe, to the one place where her sexuality is accepted—or so the film suggests. In one of the concluding scenes, after Acton leaves Eugenia's cottage for the last time, she turns to her mirror. As Doane suggests, the "intellectual woman looks and analyzes, and in usurping the gaze she poses a threat to an entire system of representation" (27). Accordingly, Eugenia, in possession of the gaze, assesses her own appearance, shakes her head, and walks away from the American system of representation that she has disrupted. The film concludes with long shots of various lovers, and by contrasting Eugenia and Acton with the other couples, *The Europeans* implies that female disruptions of sexual norms cannot be tolerated by American men within the United States.

It is worth turning briefly to a later Merchant-Ivory feature, *The Bostonians,* released in 1984, to detail the ways in which this most American of James's novels can be turned to support a hegemonic view of nation. *The Bostonians* appeared at a time when intellectual and social movements were in the process of questioning the exclusivity of what had comprised the authorized construction of American culture. In Jamesian circles, an example of this contestation can be located in John Carlos Rowe's deployment of James's portrayal as a Native Chief (in Donald Barthelme's famous collage), to inquire: "Who'se Henry James?" *The Bostonians* indirectly provides an answer to Rowe's question, by moving to consolidate a conventional hegemonic view of the United States as a former British colony and to emphasize, at the same time, the ways in which women perform as sites of imperial struggle.

In turn, like *The Heiress, The Bostonians* first moves to homogenize American identity by emphasizing the film's historical context, but the past in which it is located is replete with ideological significations. Opening with the framing words "Boston, 1875," the film's English emphasis is highlighted during a later scene in which Olive Chancellor and Verena Tarrant celebrate the 1876 American centennial. While the "rockets' red glare" of fireworks frame the Stars and Stripes in the sky, the film's soundtrack reverberates with the strains of "My Country 'Tis of Thee." Although the film's soundtrack is historically accurate, since "The Star-Spangled Banner" was not adopted as the American national anthem until 1931, because the words of "My Country 'Tis of Thee" are absent, what is heard here is also the music that scores "God Save the Queen." This merging of American and British culture, in 1984, creates a strange frame for that most American of James's novels, yet it works to highlight the authorized origin of the United States as a former and white British colony.

The bulk of the film suggests, like *The Europeans,* that intellectual women do not fare well in the United States. The educated Olive (played by the cosmopolitan Vanessa Redgrave), with her German philosophy and admiring circle of women, attempts to convince the young Verena that her place is in the public sphere rather than the private.[4] Over the course of the film, she and her cohorts lose out to the macho Southerner, Basil Ransom (played by Christopher Reeve, most noted at that time for his role as Superman, but whose performance here generates an eerie resonance for contemporary audiences). Within the film, Ransom literally and physically removes Verena from the women's presence. Underscoring a conflict between the public and private arena for women in America, then, the cinematic translation suggests that no true female intellectual pursuit can be successful in Britain's former colony.

A response to this construction can be found in the product of an authorized former colony, a current member of the British

Commonwealth. From Australia, Jane Campion's 1996 production of *The Portrait of a Lady* centralizes and hinges upon the
ways in which the female body performs as a locus of international cultural struggle. This film, with its English and Australian financial backing, its New Zealand director, and its
Australian star, globalizes the plight of James's quintessential
American girl. A multinational production on a number of levels, *The Portrait of a Lady* highlights the cross-nationality of its
author and demonstrates, as Bhabha has argued, that "the ambivalent, antagonistic perspective of nation as narration will establish the cultural boundaries of the nation so that they may
be acknowledged as 'containing' thresholds of meaning that
must be crossed, erased, and translated in the process of cultural production" (4). Indeed, Campion's *The Portrait of a Lady*
crosses and translates an Anglo-American text in order to establish different thresholds of meaning. Both in the feature's
transnational production and within the body of the film itself,
The Portrait of a Lady generates other sites of signification,
most notably through its equation of the female body with colonization. Australia may have no national stake in claiming
James's narrations as its own, but Campion's film illustrates
how the author speaks to colonial predicaments, and in this
New Zealand director's hands, *The Portrait of a Lady* explicitly
offers a commentary on imperialism, colonization, and the
mapping of the "dark continent" of female sexuality.

   Although I have discussed this film elsewhere,[5] I would like
to outline my reading of Campion's film before turning to Softley's *The Wings of the Dove*. Indeed, McClintock argues, in *Imperial Leather*, that "three of the governing themes of Western
imperialism" include: "the transmission of white, male power
through control of colonized women; the emergence of a new
global order of cultural knowledge; and the imperial command
of commodity capital" (1–3). Campion's film emblematizes
these themes, for it traces the new global order of cultural
knowledge through its multinational production at the same
time that it dramatizes the ways in which conventional power
is effected over the body of a woman, who herself serves as
commodity capital. To these ends, *The Portrait of a Lady* begins
with voice-overs and then pan shots of contemporary Australian
women discussing the erotics of a kiss. The opening frames emphasize the film's antipodean perspective, and the credit sequence positions the ensuing Jamesian text on and through a
postcolonial screen. The abrupt shift that then takes place from

the Australian women to a close-up of Isabel Archer (played by
the Australian Nicole Kidman), as the young "American girl,"
works to situate Isabel as a colonial heroine in an imperial setting—the spacious grounds of her (Anglo-American) uncle's English estate, Gardencourt. Interestingly, because Mr. Touchett
is played by the notable British actor Sir John Gielgud, the
American origin of the family fortunes are virtually erased, and
instead these vast properties betoken the trappings of "Empire." Isabel, placed in a marginal position in this narrative
since she is a poor relation, must rely on the patronage of her
wealthier relatives, and as she attempts to forge her own subjectivity free from marital involvements, her efforts and her
plight serve as the locus of international struggles to possess
her.

Isabel's attempts to construct subjectivity are dramatized
through various dream sequences. In one, she gives vent to her
sexuality in a hotel room in London, where she engages in an
imaginative scene of sexual pleasure. Within her fantasy, Isabel
makes love to the British Lord Warburton and the American
Caspar Goodwood, as her Anglo-American cousin, Ralph Touchett, watches. Isabel is in control of the situation until she becomes aware of Ralph's voyeuristic gaze (a gaze that replicates
the gaze of the camera), which brings the reverie to a halt by
reminding Isabel that she is an object of scrutiny. Further, as
an object of scrutiny both within and without the film, her efforts to control and develop her subjectivity are subverted and
her sexuality constrained by the times in which she lives.[6]

When Isabel is bequeathed a fortune by her uncle, her status
as a poor relation shifts to that of commodity capital incarnate.
Certainly, the Euro-American, Gilbert Osmond, perceives her
as an asset to be cultivated and seized, and the sexual attraction
he holds for Isabel overwhelms the young American. In the
cloisters of Rome, Osmond proposes and kisses Isabel, and the
striped parasol he twirls figures the dizzying effect his kiss has
upon the sexually naive Isabel (at the same time that the scene
recalls the opening frames' evocation of the erotics of a kiss).
Isabel's physical responses to Osmond are later pictured in intriguing cinematic sequences that imbricate her sexuality with
her travels throughout the British Empire. Filmed in early silent newsreel fashion, this "filmstrip" depicts Isabel against the
pyramids, cross-dressed as an Arab complete with veil, and par-
allels her position with that of the backdrop against which she
is portrayed. Isabel, as an heiress, partakes of imperial spoils,

but concomitantly, as a woman, she is also a "territory" to be mapped and conquered. Although on different footings from the colonized who people the landscape she surveys, Isabel's awakened sexuality (dramatized in various swoons to the voice-over of Osmond's declaration "I absolutely love you") makes her vulnerable to conquest, and her struggle for independence is equated with that of the colonies she surveys. Both are sites of imperial contestation: the land is firmly under imperial control, and Isabel, when she returns to Italy, comes under the control of Osmond, the professional seducer and the notorious collector of fine objects.

While the early parts of the film accent light and airiness, the latter parts are filmed largely in dark interiors, illumined by flickering candlelight, through which the mature Isabel moves, often veiled, trying to hide the "secret" of her disastrous marriage. Campion's depiction of James's heroine as a victim of her own sexuality in an era when female sexuality went unacknowledged and unspoken breaks with the pattern I have outlined thus far in relation to nation and narration.

And so too does Softley's 1997 production of *The Wings of the Dove*. This film, much like Campion's, emerges in a time of intensified globalization and transnationalization of capital, a time that is also contradictorily a period of intense nationalistic fervor (this conflict is suggested by the provocative title of Benjamin Barber's *Jihad vs. McWorld: How Globalism and Tribalism are Reshaping the World*). Softley's translation, moreover, moves along the trajectory opened by Campion's but to different effect. Reflecting both globalization and national insularity, *The Wings of the Dove*, an English production infused with American capital, is itself an "in-between" production that self-reflexively focuses on cross-national themes. Through the relationships of women, particularly that of Kate Croy and Milly Theale (played, respectively, by Helena Bonham Carter and Alison Elliott), *The Wings of the Dove* moves back from the abyss so often associated with contemporary postmodernity and suggests that transnationality can also offer newfound possibilities.

Softley's film is historically placed in 1910 and draws heavily on the atmosphere of London's pre-World War I years. Within it, Kate is fragmented between a potential new life with her Aunt Maud and the old life she has known with her father. The schism between the two is visually apparent in the opposition of Aunt Maud's lifestyle, evoked through an art nouveau atmosphere replete with Orientalist trimmings and hallmarked by paintings from the Vienna Secessionists; conversely, Lionel Croy's residence, located in an early Chinatown, is complete with opium dens and Anglo-Chinese beggars. Focusing on class struggle, Softley's film often depicts Kate caged in elevators, stairwells, and undergrounds. In the opening scenes, Kate enters an elevator in the Tube, and the camera pulls back to frame her in the elevator car; when she turns to her lover, Merton Densher, posited within the film as a left-wing radical, their embrace, filmed as it is through the bars of the elevator cage, brings to mind rats caught in a trap. Indeed, Kate is ensnared, since she is torn between the life of poverty she has known and the expansive wealth offered by her aunt.

The Orientalism of Aunt Maud's, figured in Asian artifacts, lush draperies, and Moroccan furniture, bespeaks a world of decadent opulence and attests to Edward Said's contention that Orientalism "expresses a certain *will* or *intention* to understand, in some cases, to control, manipulate, even to incorporate, what is manifestly different (or alternative and novel)" (*Orientalism* 12). Aunt Maud, played by a wonderfully decadent Charlotte Rampling, veiled and smokily seductive, is undoubtedly in the process of capturing Kate, but her congested salons and crowded mansion must compete with Kate's love for Densher, who himself resides in the equally crowded but dim and desultory environment from which Kate has come. Into this milieu enters Milly, the "American princess," who offers Kate an alternative. Interestingly, the film concentrates on the relationship between Milly and Kate and suggests an erotic attraction between them, which is focalized through a number of shared female gazes. In this film, the love triangle of James's novel takes on a new dimension, and twists Eve Kosofsky Sedgwick's definition of the homosocial, for here Densher is cast as the conduit through which Milly and Kate's love can be consummated.

When the locale of *The Wings of the Dove* moves to Venice, the Italian city provides a contrast to Campion's Rome. Unlike the New Zealand filmmaker's depiction of the Palazzo Roccanera, Milly's villa is airy and light-filled and stands in marked contrast to the smoky and congested atmosphere of London. Further, in Venice, the women and Densher enact various fantasies and attend a carnival in masquerade. Recalling Luce Irigaray's assertion, in her 1977 book, *This Sex Which is Not One*, that femininity itself is a masquerade of female desire (134), the disguises the characters choose are significant: Milly appears as a bride; Kate cross-dresses as a Spanish matador, and Densher adopts the garb of a male flamenco dancer. Masked, and thus seemingly anonymous, Kate and Densher consummate their love in an alley (a scene that surely had James rolling in his grave), but it appears later that Kate's sexual congress constitutes a farewell to Densher, whom she gives to Milly, not so much for the money she may gain but as a substitute for her own love for the American princess.

As in the novel, the affair between Milly and Densher is brought to a halt by the advent of Lord Mark, who, interestingly, tells Milly "the truth" about Kate and Densher at the same time that he gives her a biscuit box bearing a portrait of a pre-Raphaelite Ophelia. This portrait sits in marked contrast to the Klimt painting to which Milly was drawn at Lord Mark's estate. The substitution of Klimt here, for James's Bronzino, is important, for the sinuous, exotic, and decadent Klimt symbolizes Milly's desire to live, and to live all she can. As a result, Milly rejects the construction of the emaciated and wan Pre-Raphaelite portrait but sends Densher away, so that she might die on her own terms, in Venice.

The concluding scenes offer further spins on the Jamesian novel. In their first meeting back in England, Kate brings Densher Milly's posthumous letter and then tries to seduce him. Undressing in his bedroom and lying invitingly on his bed, this erotic display is depicted as an effort to recapture some of the love that Kate has now lost. Densher is unable to perform, signifying both his rejection of Kate as well as his impotence to provide her with the love she seeks. While the film ends on a note of heterosexual impotence, then, Densher and Kate's rejection of Milly's bequest spotlights a refusal of the transference of capital in favor of an exchange of desire, both lesbian and heterosexual. Densher's return to Italy, in the conclusion, not only figures his ability to migrate but also the inability of the women to do the same. Indeed, despite her refusal of the Pre-Raphaelite construction, Milly's transnational adventure ends in death, and she is frozen in that English representation. Kate, presumably, will also be encased as an English artifact in the Orientalist and art nouveau world of her aunt.

Nevertheless, the film's portrayal of transmigration, from the New World to Europe to the Old World of Italy, offers the possibility of an alternatively gendered space, amidst the ruins of Venice. Venice, with its resonance of the Levant, gives Orientalism a divergent meaning, since historically the port city was the locus for various forms of cross-cultural exchange. In this, the potential of the film's Italian setting evokes a nomadic movement that Said suggests is opposed to the "[p]recision, concreteness, continuity, form," all of which, he continues, drawing on the theories of Paul Virilio, "have the attributes of a nomadic practice whose power . . . is not aggressive but transgressive" (*Culture* 332). Softley's feature pictures such a nomadic movement but cannot sustain it; however, at least for a time, the transnationalism it depicts engenders a site of transgressive sexuality, intellectuality, and promise envisioned through the bodies of women.

Much like *The Portrait of a Lady*, then, *The Wings of The Dove* clearly demonstrates the imbrications of nation, narration, and the female body. It goes further than Campion's feature in that it allows for a consummation of female sexuality, although its consummation too is ultimately abrogated. Even so, it continues to attest, as indeed do all of the cinematic translations of James through their disparate trajectories, to the author's transnationality and to the female body's deployment as an object of control in national ventures. Significantly, then, James, as a writer caught between two worlds who belonged exclusively to neither, embodies multiple faces that allow his works to operate to different purposes at different times. Testifying not only to James's cross-national adaptability but also to his perceptive readings of female sexuality, the cinematic translations of the author's works demonstrate how that "in-betweenness" to which Bhabha draws attention creates a space "through which the meanings of [gender,] cultural, and political authority are negotiated." The films based upon James's writings open alternative readings of the written texts, shedding light on divergent cultural endeavors that, to whatever ends they serve, illustrate how nationality is often staked on and through the female body and underscore the importance of gender in the construction of nation.

Notes

1. I've derived some of this information from the manuscript of "A Henry James Filmography," soon to be published in the "Popular James" issue of the *Henry James Review*.

2. Holland's *Washington Square* is much more critical of Dr. Sloper's behavior. This film suggests that Dr. Sloper resents Catherine because her birth de-

prived him of his wife (as in the novel, Mrs. Sloper dies in childbirth). Thus, it is his own lack of love and esteem for Catherine that engenders his distrust of Townsend and leads him cruelly to expose her to her suitor's fortune-hunting proclivities. Unlike the novel, there is little doubt here that Townsend is motivated by Catherine's money.

3. Similarly, in the 1997 *Washington Square*, Catherine ends up running what is presumably New York's first day-care center.

4. This dramatization of the all-female community Olive frequents at Cape Cod constitutes a nod to the possibilities of lesbian relations. But Ransom's plea to Verena: "How much more natural it is to give yourself to me instead of to a movement of some morbid old maid," raises the specter of "naturalness" that haunts the homoerotic scenes between Olive and Verena. Invisible but tangible in the polarization of hetero- and homosexuality, here, is the shadow cast by the AIDS crisis in the 1980s.

5. See "Jane and James Go to the Movies: Postcolonial Portraits of a Lady," *Henry James Review* 18 (1997): 187–90.

6. Holland's *Washington Square* also emphasizes its heroine's corporeality, although to different purpose. Here, Catherine's physicality works to discredit her by indicating her tendency to fleshly excesses. As a child, she is given to overeating, and during an attempted oral recital, she urinates on the drawing-room floor. Painfully awkward, Catherine has no bodily control and is often pictured walking into doors, falling over her feet, and dropping things. Her physicality is also figured in her sexuality: one scene, shot in medium-height close-up, focalizes Catherine's literal swoon when Townsend first kisses her. She learns to control her body and her sexuality as a result of her father and Townsend's mistreatment of her but becomes an asexual spinsterish mother-surrogate in the conclusion.

Editor's note: Because Jones's essay treats the theme of difference or alienation, she has requested that her essay be printed as she submitted it to me, rather than have it reformatted to fit American typography and publishing. Thus, her Englishness, a form of alienation within a collection of essays by Americans, is represented rather than repressed in the publication of her essay exactly as she submitted it to me.

Strange Meetings:
Henry James and *The Siege of London*

ANNY BROOKSBANK JONES

THIS ESSAY CONCERNS HENRY JAMES AND HIS NOVELLA *THE SIEGE OF London*. It starts, however, in a way that might seem rather alien to a British reader, with a word about me.

I'm an English academic, and a reasonably competent user of my own language. Include my work in an American collection, however, and immediately its language seems slightly quaint or alien, even wrong. The language of the essay that follows attempts no compromise between American and British academic English: not for reasons of national arrogance, nor (entirely) from personal stubbornness. Instead the scene is being set for an examination of strangeness in James's novella, and of what it means for a woman to be—or to make herself— "at home".

The novella's opening pages set out its theme even more theatrically. It's September in Paris, and the city is full of foreign visitors. Among them, in the audience at the Comédie-Française, are the story's four main characters—one Englishman and three Americans surrounded by "persons of provincial or nomadic appearance."[1] Rupert Waterville is an American in Paris for the first time. He finds the evening's "antiquated play" a bore and is more interested in scanning the audience for pretty women (103). George Littlemore is more at home with "European civilization" than his compatriot, and fancies the "French capital could have no more surprises for him" (104). He too finds the play tedious: *L'Aventurière* has "no pretension to novelty" and is acted by doublures or understudies (103). It is not until Waterville spies Nancy Headway that the "historic cobwebs" and "the new-looking curtain," and all the other strange and familiar details of the opening scene, come into focus (103/4).

The familiar "drama of transatlantic relations" is under way. Its cast includes a selection of James's best-known characters: Headway is the headstrong American social climber, Littlemore the sympathetic but neutral narrator, Sir Arthur Demesne the reticent English aristocrat, and Waterville the naive young American observer. The recognition and misrecognition of characters is a key element in the novella. When Waterville makes Mrs Headway's acquaintance at the theatre he cannot make out what kind of woman she is. Littlemore knows her of old but is in two minds whether to acknowledge her. His reply to Waterville's " '[d]o you know her?' " simultaneously denies and betrays a previous acquaintance: " '[n]o. she's not respectable' " (105). The next 86 pages will turn on this ambiguity, for it seems that without Littlemore's unequivocal endorsement of her good character the American divorcee cannot achieve her ambition to marry the aristocratic young Englishman, Demesne.

Little has been written about *The Siege of London* since its publication in 1883. In the preface to the New York edition James himself pleads "a blank of memory as to the origin of the tale"[2]. He does, however, record a visit to the Comédie-Française six years earlier to see *Le Demi-monde* by the younger Dumas and his irritation at Olivier de Jalin's denunciation of his ex-mistress, Mme. d'Ange, which forms "the main hinge of the action"[3]. What is at stake for James is whether "a gentleman 'tells' on a lady"[4]. The sense of déjà vu is palpable: De Jalin and Mme d'Ange are the originals of Littlemore and Mrs Headway, who watch as their story is acted out by doublures: Littlemore encounters a familiar play and an over-familiar woman, and Mrs Headway meets a ghost from her past (103). The original theatre-goer now directs the action. Those of us who know the story in advance will be more concerned with the relationship between this aventurier, living on his wits in self-imposed exile, and his leading lady.

It is by no means clear that Mrs Headway is a lady, however. She may not even be an exile. Only Littlemore—himself a "man of the world", equally at home in New York, Paris or London—is empowered to say whether she left, absconded or was effectively expelled from the US (117). He met and became friendly with Mrs Headway in California, when she was still a young provincial, "very pretty, good-natured and clever" and with few social pretensions (113). In his account—we have no other of her early years—she was also "ignorant, audacious, crude, . . . full of pluck and spirit, of natural intelligence, and of a certain intermittent, haphazard good taste" (113). She subsequently married several times ("mainly editors"), became "exceedingly divorced" and, as a result, exceedingly wealthy (112). What preoccupies Waterville, Littlemore's sister (Mrs Dolphin), Demesne, and his mother is whether Mrs Headway acted improperly in the acquiring of that wealth and the divesting of those husbands. Since Littlemore is presented as the only authoritative source of information on Mrs Headway, his testimony will be enough to block or enable his old friend's marriage to her aristocrat. There are, apparently, no doubts as to the probity of the informant who shared her piazza and her society in those early years.

Other exiles enjoy a less ambiguous status. As Secretary to the US Legation in London Waterville can mix business with pleasure by keeping an eye on pretty women and Americans. With the licence and affected inscrutability of the immigration officer he polices the border zone, ensuring that any "beauty" he sees is fit to be looked at by people (like him) of irreproachable character. In such circumstances the identification of "unusual" women is essential (104). Experienced though he is in classifying desirable aliens, Waterville too relies heavily on Littlemore's judgement. "You stare at them all alike" Littlemore observes "except when I tell you that they are not respectable—then your attention acquires a fixedness" (104/5).

Mrs Headway will be subjected to more fascinated stares, penetrating glances and averted eyes before efforts to identify her reach their conclusion. It's not simply the facts of her past that her investigators are trying to establish. They want to know how those facts were viewed, and how she must be viewed as a result: like Waterville, they need a representation of her on which to base their own identification.

Unsurprisingly, critics are also keen to identify Mrs Headway. I have already suggested a link between the author/director and his leading 'lady', but James's tendency to make women the focus of his narratives has a wider resonance. Feminists such as Rosi Braidotti have noted a tendency among contemporary male philosophers to ally themselves with "the feminine"[5]. For Braidotti, this is symptomatic of a loss of faith in the all-knowing philosophical subject, which leads Jacques Derrida and others to turn instead to the philosophical 'unconscious' in search of what the history of philosophy and its binary logic have hitherto repressed. Since no philosophical name is available for what they find, they call it "unrepresentable" or "undecidable", "the other", or "the feminine". Identifying Mrs Headway's place in *The Siege of London* may go some way to illustrate the workings of this "repressed" term in James's narrative.

Stare at her as we might, we don't know what Mrs Headway sees. There is a convention that foreigners have special insight into life in their adoptive home. In Mrs Headway's case this insight is crucial, for, like James, she wants to get to the heart of "English society" (141). She wants to originate there, to become well-bred, and once again this involves doublures: like a voodooist with a doll, she'd "like to have" a little girl and "make her" the "nice woman . . . in another style" that she herself longs to become (126). This self-begetting involves cutting the old umbilical cord. By fleeing from America she hopes to avoid determination by her previous husbands and take revenge on the New Yorkers who humiliated her.

Even in England, however, Mrs Headway has the greatest difficulty cutting her "editors" from her autobiography (112). Reflected in her final questionable success is James's ambivalence towards "English society", and both are linked to the insecurity that another "theorist of exile", Julia Kristeva, a Bulgarian-born linguist working in France, sees as characteristic of the foreigner. In *Strangers to Ourselves*, she describes the "incomprehensible speech [and] inappropriate behaviour" that underlies the exile's insecurity and marginalization[6]. "Your speech, fascinating as it might be on account of its very strangeness, will be of no consequence . . . One will listen to you only in absent-minded, amused fashion, and one will forget you in order to go on with serious matters"[7]. Resonating here is not only the treatment Mrs Headway receives at the hand of her aristocratic acquaintance but also an echo of the way men have always listened to women. Something similar underlies James's concern that his own "conquest of social as well as literary London had been achieved not on the ground of intrinsic charm or literary talent, but because he was yet another freak of nature"[8]. Yet the outsider remains fascinated by exclusive clubs, by their "community of ideas, of traditions [. . . and the members who] understand each others' accents, even each others' variations" (156).

"English society" would not entertain outsiders, however, if it were as self-sufficient as this quotation suggests. In fact its exclusiveness depends on admiring outsiders. Less clear is why outsiders should risk insecurity and humiliation by shoring up what James presents as aristocratic decadence. Kristeva offers one explanation for his ambivalence on this point:

> [the exile] readily bears a kind of admiration for those who have welcomed him [sic], for he rates them more often than not above himself, be it financially, politically or socially. At the same time he is quite ready to consider them somewhat narrow-minded, blind. For his scornful hosts lack the perspective he himself has in order to see himself and to see them. [This detachment] gives him the lofty sense not so much of holding the truth but of making it and himself relative while others fall victim to the ruts of monovalency . . . In the eyes of the foreigner those who are not foreign have no life at all: barely do they exist, haughty or mediocre, but out of the running and thus almost already cadaverized[9].

Though small, recognizable differences seem to pose no threat to these communities, Mrs Headway's variation is of a completely different order. In the company of its members she is at once amusing and unsettling; she "looked foreign, exaggerated . . . She might have been engaged for the evening" (156). Since "civilization begins at home", an exile with a shady past is destined to remain a "freak of nature" or a "barbarian" in this community (144, 170). And like all communities that recognize only the paternal genealogy, this one allows a woman entry only on fulfilment of certain conditions: she has to alienate herself, take the male name and part, pursue his interests in place of her own and guarantee the continuity of his line. The condition of Lady Demesne's inclusion—apart, that is, from the elevated entrance fee paid by her banker father—is that she look "for her own happiness in the cultivation of duty and in extreme constancy to two or three objects of devotion chosen once for all" (167). When her husband died she didn't take up the first of the relict's traditional options and "clear out" of the family home (161). Instead she devoted her abilities to the advancement of the son who now inherited her services. "She never admitted, even to herself, that [Sir Arthur] was not the cleverest of men; but it took all her own cleverness, which was much greater than his, to maintain this appearance" (132).

Wealth alone won't entitle Mrs Headway to exchange an obscure patronym for that of "a fine old race" (181). She waits at the border of a motherland she has abandoned and a fatherland that's not ready to accept her, aware that her physical and financial assets are starting to depreciate. Sir Arthur will never need to protest his identity: he has "the blood of a score of Warwickshire squires in his veins: mingled in the last instance with the somewhat paler fluid" of his mother (132). Money of course can darken what would otherwise be beyond the pale, and the greater the difference between the aspiring lady's "fluid" and the patriarchal blue "blood" the greater the sum required. But the ladies will always screen out the red-blooded outsider, however wealthy, who has no patronym to speak of.

For Lady Demesne and Mrs Dolphin, contaminated blood is a life-or-death affair. While men find Mrs Headway "attractive but dangerous", the ladies find her unequivocally "displeasing and dangerous" (135, 167). Lady Demesne's distrust of the "horrible" interloper is restrained in comparison with Mrs Dolphin's phobia for the "dreadful, disreputable, vulgar little woman": "I was afraid she would know who I was and come and speak to me. I was so frightened that I went away" (180/1). James attributes this to the drawbridge effect: the desire that "the class to which she [now] belonged should close its ranks and carry its standard high" (180). "She deeply desired . . . that Mrs Headway's triumphant career should be checked" and with it further claims on the social sphere Mrs Dolphin had made her own (180).

Yet it is precisely the ladies that Mrs Headway is concerned to win over. As long as she can fascinate every man she meets, "men don't count" (143). Being a beautiful object is not enough: she wants a certain social status and knows that the guardians of that status are female. The French psychoanalyst Luce Irigaray has noted that "the circulation of women among men is what establishes the operations of . . . patriarchal society"[10]. Within a society that denies them the status of subject, it is women who watch over the property to which they are themselves unentitled. They must therefore distinguish themselves unequivocally from the interloper who threatens the value of their investment. They fear her because they cannot identify her or identify with her, and no lady can. "[F]emale relations . . . mother . . . sisters", all refuse to countenance her (143).

Yet Mrs Headway never loses sight of her goal: she wants to be brilliant rather than obscure, and to be seen for what she is or will be, rather than for what she was or might have been. She acknowledges, however, that self-begetting is an ambiguous pleasure. "None of my people are here: and I'm terribly alone in the world" (186). As Kristeva puts it,

. . . the exile has fled from that origin—family, blood, soil—and, even though it keeps pestering, enriching, hindering, exciting him, or giving him pain . . . the foreigner is its courageous and melancholy betrayer. His origin certainly haunts him, for better or for worse, but it is . . . elsewhere that he has set his hopes, that his struggles take place.[11]

The Siege of London narrates Mrs Headway's struggle to reject her origins; in the process it questions the ways in which we relate to ourselves and to each other. By structuring his novella around the interplay of home and exile, the familiar and the foreign, the superficial and the secret, James is being precociously suggestive. Two years after the publication of The Siege of London in the Cornhill Magazine in 1883, Sigmund Freud too was in exile, as a student of Jean-Martin Charcot in Paris. His later interest in the interplay of the strange and the familiar in his discussions of 'Das Unheimlich' (the un-home-ly, or uncanny) are crucial for Kristeva's study. Foreigners, she notes, make us uncomfortable: we simultaneously identify with them and reject them. Using Freud's work on the uncanny, she relates this discomfort to an analogous division within ourselves. Following Freud, she describes how uncanny effects arise when the individual attempts unsuccessfully to repress familiar dangers—whatever does not contribute to pleasure and self-preservation, for example—causing them to erupt in an unfamiliar form. The "narcissistic self . . . projects out of itself what it experiences as dangerous or unpleasant in itself, making of it an alien double"[12]. These uncanny effects are linked to the compulsive "recurrence of the same thing—the repetition of the same features or character-traits or vicissitudes, of the same crimes, or even the same names"[13].

It could be argued that compulsive recurrence is a feature of The Siege of London, as characters bring the most detailed and persistent scrutiny to bear on a secret they cannot or will not reveal. The theme recurs, of course, in other works. Talking of his In the Cage, for example, which turns on the reluctance of the anonymous heroine to expose a scandalous secret, James declares that he neither knows nor wishes to know what that scandal involves. He is similarly blank when asked to describe the genesis of The Siege of London. It's not surprising that some of James's best critics have enjoyed speculating on his own repressed secrets. One of the earliest to do so, James's biographer Leon Edel, has drawn attention to the "gubernatorial" mother and the weighty but rather foolish father; the exceptionally gifted older brother who thought his adoring sibling "vainer and shallower than himself"; the "skeletons in the closets" of James's old US homes, that made the prospect of a return strike him in later years with "a superstitious terror of seeing them . . . stretch out strange inevitable tentacles to draw me back and destroy me"[14].

These secrets, which have been explored more recently and in some detail by others, will not detain us here[15]. In order to say something about James's women, we need to turn from secret relations with Oedipal stock-characters to the structure of secrets themselves. In the preamble to his paper on the uncanny, Freud notes that "the German word 'unheimlich' is obviously the opposite of 'heimlich' . . . [that is,] the opposite of what is familiar; and we are tempted to conclude that what is 'uncanny' is frightening precisely because it is not known and familiar". We would be wrong, of course. An investigation of the terms and their uses reveals that 'heimlich' moves "in the direction of ambivalence" from "mystical" through "inaccessible to knowledge" to "hidden and dangerous"—at which point "it finally co-incides with its opposite": 'unheimlich'[16].

Irigaray would find this process oddly familiar: in her view there is no possibility of genuine difference within Freud's system. She illustrates this point with reference to his description of the moment when the little girl becomes aware of her anatomical difference from her male companion.

> At the "sight of the genitals of the other sex," girls "notice the [sexual?] difference" and, it must be admitted, its significance too. They feel seriously wronged, often declare that they want to "have something like it too" . . . and fall victim to "envy for the penis" which will leave ineradicable traces on their development and the formation of their character"[17].

Her ironic asides and inserted emphases make Irigaray's distance from Freud clear. What concerns her about this account, and about Freud's work in general, is that the male is taken as a norm in relation to which the female is seen as deviant or lacking. Freud's little girl is not a little girl at all but a defective boy, a "disadvantaged little man . . . [w]hose needs are less catered for by nature and who will yet have a lesser share of culture . . . A little man who would have no other desire than to be, or remain, a little man"[18]. For Irigaray the inauguration of heterosexual relations is simply another moment in the drama of homosexual relations. The little girl is not different, she is a doublure, an uncanny, defective version of the male. For Irigaray, the implications of Freud's scenario are clear: with that first envious gaze women acknowledge their inferiority, and assume their role as the mirrors and magnifiers of men.

Freud links women and uncanny secrets explicitly when he registers the "connections which the 'double' has with reflections in mirrors" and the uncanny effects that result when the subject identifies himself with someone else[19]. In Irigaray's terms, the male subject always "identifies himself" with someone else, and that someone is always a woman. In this one-way system, however, she can count on no such affirmation herself. With no-one to reflect back her own image, she remains the exclusive and indispensable object of the self-regarding male. James seems indirectly to acknowledge this when he observes in a discussion of George Sand that "[i]t is the ladies . . . who have lately done most to remind us of man's relations with himself, that is with woman"[20].

One effect of specular relations with men is to rule out the possibility of genuine dialogue. Women who refuse to play the game will find intelligibility itself at risk. When her compatriots conspire to prevent her entry into society Mrs Headway is unable to speak in her own defence. Instead she is "always appealing or accusing, demanding explanations and pledges" (128) or, as Margaret Whitford puts it, seeking "proofs of affection or validation of her existence from the male subject" (128)[21]. Waterville and Littlemore seem to agree that Mrs Headway talks obsessively and "her motives, her impulses, her desires [are] absolutely glaring" (141). And yet they fail to grasp her meaning. When she insists, Littlemore laughs and withdraws: when she tries to present her own account of herself in opposition to his, he can't see it. "You don't know me" she tells him, "you don't understand me. You think you do, but you don't" (184). Her protestations are neutralized and she is defined, once again, in a word. It is his word, "[t]he last word of all": she is a "nuisance, an embarrassment, from the moment anything more than contemplation should be expected of him" (124/5). That point has now been reached: she is a danger to the community, and doesn't "deserve to be spared" (184).

As this exchange demonstrates, there is no safe haven for aliens who are trying to cross borders without security or precedents. Instead Mrs Headway shifts between the new and the

old, between unintelligible self-assertion and pleas for male validation. What results is an aura of dislocation and vital unpre-
dictability that those around her find exciting, exasperating,
and unsettling. Their interest does little to advance her case
however. When (as in the exchange cited) she is too unsettling,
her ally is revealed as a neglectful adversary. While she remains
more exciting than unsettling there is no reason why Littlemore—"[a]verse" as he is "to active pleasures"—or any other
man should help her (106). Like the aristocratic society she
yearns for, her male admirers find a degree of novelty attractive. For them she is a "child of nature" seeking women's conventional status as social object, and she'll remain desirable
only as long as she stays in the no-man's land between the two:
as long as she's "not respectable", her male companions will
find her "adorable" (129, 105, 128). "If she wished to get into
society" Littlemore reflects "there was no reason why her bachelor visitors should wish to see her there; for it was the absence
of the usual social incumbrances which made her drawing-room
attractive" (129). For him, Mrs Headway's "salvation" lies in accepting her place as a marginal, desirable object. Her refusal to
accept this role appears, quite understandably, "to irritate him"
(129).

Mrs Headway has had enough of male company in no-man's
land. She wants a home now, even if it's someone else's, and
she wants female relations of her own, even if it means burying
her past in a man's. In a genealogy that excludes women with
pasts in order to make male futures more secure, this might
prove difficult. One reason why this genealogy "is in a rather
bad way", however, may be that its obsession is also its blind
spot (124). Irigaray characterizes the male genealogy as conflat-
ing woman and mother in a "maternal feminine", a "female
identity" that men use to symbolize their own lost origins, leaving women with no way of representing theirs[22]. Mrs Headway
can reveal "everything" "fifty times over" without giving herself away (119, 177). In a domain that doesn't recognize non-
male origins she can talk compulsively about the past she wants
to obscure and it will not be identified. It seems that only a man
can give her away.

Mrs Headway doesn't want to give her past away, of course,
or to have it "identified" by others. There is no attempt to help
Lady Demesne's solicitor to assemble data on it for presentation as a more or less respectable history. As Littlemore notes,
his compatriot will never be more than "half-right" as long as

she's determined "to be different" (128, 120). She wants to specify the headings and the detail, of her past in her own language, and to edit them on her own terms. Yet the language and the symbols available to her all play into the hands of Lady Demesne's solicitor. What the uncomprehending Littlemore witnesses—the "inspiration", the "anxiety and egotism", the excitement, the "flushed face" as she becomes "violent . . . angry . . . passionate . . . incoherent" by turns—is indistinguishable from hysteria (184–86). It could equally be frustration, however, symptomatic of the difficulty women have "in speaking and hearing as women. Excluded and denied by the patriarchal linguistic order they cannot speak in a judicious, coherent way"[23].

Mrs Headway may prefer the regard of women to admiring men, but she knows neither is dispensable. "I don't want to escape notice", she exclaims: what she wants is "different ways of being looked at" (124). If that includes admiring male glances she'll play along with them, in order to catch the eye of the ladies who have refused to countenance her and to be recognized by them. She continues to shift between wanting to please herself and wanting to please: the "joints and seams" of her negotiations, "where the old and the new [have] been pieced together", are "all of them very visible" (139). For her this is a transitional stage: "[i]f I once get there" she asserts "I shall be perfect"! (144). Littlemore sees things differently: people may change "their desires, their ideal, their effort" but they "don't change their nature" (185). Mrs Headway puts her faith in herself. Littlemore puts his in a transcendental vision of human nature: his vision of her nature. He overrules her once again with a lofty phrase: she won't be perfect but "she won't know when she's wrong, so it doesn't signify" (128).

Littlemore isn't going to be allowed the last word on women's nature nor on men's relation to nature. It is an axiom of feminism that all human functions are not deemed to be present in each individual, but have conventionally been distributed according to sex. Irigaray notes that this "double syntax" enables men to identify themselves with culture, society, reason, and order, for example, and to identify women with "nature", the irrational and the disordered, whatever escapes the categories of culture and the social. Critical though she is of this process, she doesn't deny it a certain self-fulfilling truth, since in her view the paternal genealogy is structured in such a way that no woman can enter it without accepting these definitions. A woman can enter patriarchy, that is, "so long as she is not a 'subject', so long as she cannot disrupt through her speech, her desire, her pleasure, the operation of the language that lays down the law, the prevailing organization of power"[24].

As Mrs Headway recognizes, you can enter the paternal gene-alogy if you are prepared to speak its language. By shifting be-tween unintelligibility and role playing she may be able to "recuperate some element of desire"[25]. An exile "multiplying masks and 'false selves' [she] is never completely true nor com-pletely false"[26]. This "masquerade of femininity" will permit her to become what Freud termed a "normal" woman, by giving her "entry into a system of value that is not hers, and in which she can 'appear' and circulate only when enveloped in the needs/ desires/ fantasies of others"[27].

It may be James's interest in "the feminine sensibility" that leads him to confront this repressed aspect of patriarchy, its structural alienation of women. There is always ambivalence, however, something compulsive about his pleasure in the sight of women struggling, and his loss of interest when they meet their inevitably bad ends. If loss of interest equates with loss of pleasure we can, as suggested, read the close of *The Siege of Lon-don* as an abandoning of the 'unheimlich' figure when it be-comes too insistent. Until this point Waterville and Sir Arthur Demesne can't see enough of her; Lady Demesne and Mrs Dol-phin can't stop talking about her; and Littlemore, like James, neglects to resolve the question for as long as "the spectacle might be entertaining" (124).

Reading James one might think there was something inevita-ble about this displacement of male anxiety onto a female dou-blure. There are however, as Mrs Headway insists, different ways of looking of looking at women. *The Siege of London* offers a range of models, and underlying each is the question of how we are to deal not only with uncanny strangers, but with the un-canny within ourselves. We could:

- speculate on her obsessively from a distance, interrogate and spy on her, so as expose her (Waterville);

- invite her into our home, inspect her on our own terms and quiz others about her (Sir Arthur and Lady Demesne);

- defame her, refuse to face her, turn away (Mrs Dolphin);

- wait for her to make herself known, casually and unobsessively enjoy her presence, exploit her and, when the time comes, abandon her (Littlemore).

This list may look exhaustive, but there is one notable omission: there is no model for coming to terms with difference—not in order to smooth it over and assimilate it, but in order to recognize and value it. Mrs Headway, the alienated subject, takes the only course available to her: act out what you can, and illuminate in fitful flashes what you can't. The end result is only marginally more promising: Littlemore's final "I don't think Mrs Headway respectable" comes too late to prevent her from marrying Sir Arthur, but ensures that her new life will be defined according to one (male) account of her old one (190).

Unless we acknowledge and come to terms with strangeness there will be no living with ourselves or each other. This is a political point, addressing the alienation of women in patriarchy and of all marginalized groups, at a time when communities are being conceived in global terms and we are increasingly among strangers. As *The Siege of London* indicates, books can participate in this process by helping us to recognize and analyze our symptoms. Those of us who choose this form of feminist critique, however, need to be sure that we're not complicitous with texts' tendency to neutralize uncanny effects by making them more pleasurable than dangerous.

My reading suggests that James will have derived considerably more pleasure than danger from the writing of *The Siege of London*, but that need not necessarily influence whether we recuperate him for feminism or whether we reject him. My own view is that it really doesn't matter which we do. James will never be more than half right, but that might be enough: it rather depends on what we want from him. There's no reason why we shouldn't play around with him if it suits us: we can exploit him as Littlemore exploits Mrs Headway, speculate on him as long as it's "entertaining", and then abandon him. But though rhetorical revenge is unquestionably sweet, it is not enough. Re-reading James, however sceptically, can only advance the causes of feminism if in the process we come to recognize each other and acknowledge our differences. Only then will there be any possibility of genuine exchange between us.

Notes

1. Henry James, *The Siege of London,* in *"In the Cage" and Other Stories,* (Harmondsworth, England: Penguin, Harmondsworth, England, 1972, 103–

91, 103. Hereafter page numbers will be given in parentheses in the body of the text.

2. *The Complete Tales of Henry James,* vol. 14, (New York: Charles Scribner's Sons, 1936), xvi.

3. Ibid.

4. *The Complete Tales of Henry James,* ed. Leon Edel, vol. 5, 1883–84 (London: Rupert Hart Davis, 1965), 10.

5. For the development of this argument see Braidotti's *Patterns of Dissonance: A Study of Women in Contemporary Philosophy,* trans. E. Guild (Cambridge: Polity Press, 1991), 278–84. Margaret Whitford reinforces this point in her *Luce Irigaray: Philosophy in the Feminine* (London: Routledge, 1991), 29–31.

6. Julia Kristeva, *Strangers to Ourselves,* trans. L. Roudiez, (Hemel Hempstead, England: Harvester Wheatsheaf, 1991), 6.

7. Ibid., 20–21.

8. Edel, *Complete Tales,* 9.

9. Kristeva, *Strangers,* 6–7.

10. Luce Irigaray, *This Sex Which is Not One,* trans. C. Porter with C. Burke (Ithaca: Cornell University Press, 1985), 184.

11. Kristeva, *Strangers,* 29.

12. Ibid., 183.

13. Sigmund Freud, "The 'Uncanny,' " in *The Standard Edition of the Complete Psychological Works of Sigmund Freud,* vol. 17, *An Infantile Neurosis and Other Works,* trans. J. Strachey, A. Freud, A. Strachey, A. Tyson (London: Hogarth Press and the Institute of Psycho-Analysis, 1973), 217–56, 234.

14. Leon Edel, "The James Family," *Henry James Review,* 10, no. 2 (spring 1989): 90–94.

15. See in particular Alfred Habegger's compelling study *Henry James and the 'Woman Business',* (Cambridge: Cambridge University Press, 1989.

16. Freud, "The Uncanny," 220, 226.

17. Luce Irigaray, *Speculum of the Other Woman,* trans. G. C. Gill (Ithaca: Cornell University Press, 1985) 55.

18. Ibid., 26.

19. Freud, "The Uncanny," 234–35.

20. Henry James, *Notes on Novelists with Some Other Notes* (London: Dent, 1914), 237.

21. Whitford, *Luce Irigaray,* 44.

22. Irigaray, *Speculum of the Other Woman,* 71–72.

23. Irigaray, *Je, Tu, Nous* (Paris: Grasset, 1990), 23. Translation my own.

24. Irigaray, *This Sex Which is Not One,* 95.

25. Ibid., 133.

26. Kristeva, *Strangers,* 8.

27. Irigaray, *This Sex Which is Not One,* 134.

The Functions of Women in the Art Tales of Henry James

BRUCE HENRICKSEN

THE ART TALES OF HENRY JAMES OFTEN DEAL WITH THEORIES CONcerning the production and reception of art, the relationship of the artist to the world, and the nature of aesthetic experience. The tales not only speculate upon the social consequences of such theories and concerns but upon the way that talk about the arts often works as an alibi in struggles for power and domination. The theory of art is not, for James, an autonomous and self-justifying realm but is always, in a loose sense of the current phrase, ideologically freighted.

"The Real Thing," for instance, seems at first reading to be merely about how the demands of artistic mimesis must not be allowed to stifle the artist's imaginative freedom. In that tale, a painter who is doing illustrations involving aristocratic characters for a magazine is confronted by an apparently aristocratic couple, down on their luck, who offer to sit for him. He gives them a try but discovers that his working-class sitters actually serve his turn better than "the real thing." He is forced to dismiss Mr. and Mrs. Monarch. As I have argued elsewhere, the painter-narrator, who works in a time when artists are no longer dependent upon aristocratic patronage, is actually using a theoretical cliché as an alibi for exacting revenge upon a vanishing aristocracy. He and his theories of art are a conduit for society's discourse upon the irrelevance of an older social formation.[1]

In other art tales, the social subtext often concerns gender relations. As theories of art and the lives of artists are ostensibly discussed in the discourse of his inevitably male narrators and dramatized in their stories, woman is constituted as a subject—fixed and defined within a discourse she does not produce. The current debate about James's representations of women is complex, since women are positioned in a wide variety of ways

in his fiction and since the male narrators who do the positioning are themselves conceived by their author with an unstable
irony—unstable at least in this particular area of gender attitudes.[2] Many of our great canonical writers are at once hegemonic and oppositional, and this may also be true of James's
representations of women. As Mikhail Bakhtin has asserted, all
novelistic discourse is essentially conflicted or heteroglossic.
Therefore, rather than try to approach final judgments about
James and "the woman question," I will offer a typology of the
representations of women in the art tales. This typology describes the "functions," with a nod to Vladimir Propp, of women
in the plots of these tales.

According to Propp, in *The Morphology of the Folktale,* "function is understood as the act of a character, defined from the
point of view of its significance for the course of the action."[3]
Functions are the fundamental components of folktales. They
exist prior to characters and bring characters into being, as perhaps the function of betrayal gave birth to the character Judas
in the Gospels. A finite number of functions recurs from folktale to folktale, and the definition of a function is independent
of the specific personage who carries out the function in a given
tale. Concepts such as the function help us discern a basic structure, something like a grammar, out of which individual tales
are produced. In James's art tales, the functions I see for
women are: (1) women as artists, (2) women as subjects of art,
(3) women as prizes, and (4) women as gatekeepers. In the first
and last of these, women are active; in the second and third,
passive. Each of these functions can be presented so as to encourage in the reader either a positive, negative, or ambivalent
evaluation (gatekeepers, for instance, are not inevitably good or
bad), and it is possible for a specific character to perform more
than one function. The significance of these functions can be
evaluated in relation to a larger myth or metanarrative described by Jacques Lacan.

Margaret Homans observes that "in virtually all of the founding texts of our culture we can find a version of this myth: the
death or absence of the mother sorrowfully but fortunately
makes possible the construction of language and culture."[4] As
Homans says, Lacan offers a psychoanalytic explanation of this
myth. In his narrative, the infant's relationship to the mother
is immediate and prelinguistic. But soon the intervening father,
who possesses the phallus, introduces the child to language and
the symbolic order. While Lacan's "symbolic father," who is the

agency of the law, does not refer literally to individual biological fathers, Lacan's metanarrative structures real family and interpersonal relationships in terms of functions. In this metanarrative, the phallus is the symbol both of sexual difference and of language, while the mother, exiled from the "Law of the Father," occupies the place of the absent signified. The child enters the symbolic order reluctantly, however, and life becomes a search for substitutes for the lost mother. This explains the privileging in patriarchal culture of figurative language, which enacts a series of substitutions along chains of signifiers that refer to other signifiers without fully embracing the absent signified. Figurative language is structured like desire, which is always masculine within these metaphorics.

This Lacanian myth offers an explanation of the ideological positioning of women in language and in patriarchal culture. To the extent that the narrators of James's art tales make women the subject of their discourses, the Lacanian myth is the metanarrative upon which the art tales rely and upon which they sometimes seem to comment.[5]

Because each story contains more than one function and because multiple functions are sometimes fused in a single character, there will be some cross-referencing and some slippage in my attempt to treat these functions separately without unduly splintering the discussion of individual stories. I have not tried to count the frequency of each function across the corpus of tales, but the gatekeeping function seems most prevalent. My ordering has no great significance—I simply reserve until last the one about which I say the most.

Women as Artists

Some of James's narrators treat women in the function of artist, a position gendered male in the patriarchal myth. Women were a powerful force in the nineteenth-century publishing industry, and James is known to have looked down his nose, probably with secret envy, at best-sellers by women.[6] Of course, women who were not writing for the commercial market often felt obliged to adopt male pen names. In "The Death of the Lion," a female author who is committed to "the larger latitude"—vaguely progressive political attitudes—goes by the name of Guy Walsingham. There is a social gathering conducted by Mrs. Weeks Wimbush, the cultural gatekeeper, in which Walsingham meets Dora Forbes, a male writer who has also seen the advantages of cross-naming. In "Broken Wings," the deceptive aura of economic success that surrounds a female novelist nearly destroys her most cherished personal relationship.

Greville Fane, in the story by that title, is also a female author whose financial situation is central to the plot. Her other name is Mrs. Stormer (both names reveal the stamp of patriarchal authority, and her "true" name remains effaced). She writes "romances" filled with "passion" for the easy consumption of an unsophisticated audience (155).[7] The narrator of the tale, a reviewer and failed novelist, is condescending toward her work, which he finds crude in style, form, and thought, but he sympathizes with her as a person. Her husband is dead, and her burden is to support two ungrateful and parasitical children. Determined to raise the son, Leolin, to be a novelist, Mrs. Stormer pampers him in his young adulthood, allowing him simply to travel and absorb "life" as she works harder and harder (now that her books earn less and less) to pay the bills. In the end, since of course he has no writing talent whatsoever, she allows him to pretend that he is her coauthor because he brings home anecdotes from his club and his parties.

In this story, the Lacanian or patriarchal myth is subverted. It is not the mother who dies or withdraws to allow the son to enter the Law of the Father. Instead, the father is absent. In Lacanian terms, the absent father in fiction perhaps represents anxiety over reality's swerve from the norms of the myth, which assumes the primacy of the father's Law.[8] Here, Mrs. Stormer fuses the maternal and paternal functions; *she* represents the symbolic order to which the son would gain access. On the other hand, from the narrator's point of view, there is a still higher symbolic order of serious literature, and from this order the mother is excluded. Indeed, toward the end of the story the narrator, in his capacity as character, tells Mrs. Stormer that he intends to write about her son. This male narrator, then, has the final say and—in his moralistic criticism of Leolin— reinstates the Law of the Father that was absent on the story's literal level. The female novelist and her son become the "subjects" of a fictional male novelist's discourse.

Another important female novelist who also becomes the subject of a male narrator-critic's discourse is Gwendolen Erme in "The Figure in the Carpet," but I will discuss her under the function of gatekeeper.

Women as Subjects

The way women become subjects of a male writer's discourse is thematized to a degree in nearly all of the art tales, since James so often exposes the biases and allegiances of his narrators in the act of representing their characters. An especially direct but complex confrontation with the theme of males representing women is found in "The Madonna of the Future," in which the woman in question is not only the intended subject of a male painter's art but in turn becomes the subject of a male narrator's verbal art.

As in "The Real Thing," there is a certain amount of theorizing about art in the foreground of "The Madonna of the Future" in the conversations between the narrator and the would-be painter he befriends. Both are Americans—the narrator a tourist in Florence, the artist a permanent exile. They meet on the streets on the night of the narrator's arrival, and in their first conversation, as they express their admiration for the great art of the past, it is apparent that the painter suffers under an anxiety of influence. The story raises the question, as T. S. Eliot was to formulate it, of how original talents position themselves in relation to the monuments of the past. This general question is particularized in two ways. First, is there an authentically American artistic vision that the artist is failing to realize in his worship of European art of the past? In this regard, the story enacts a familiar theme in James, that of the American who has been Europeanized to his own detriment. A second problem arises from the artist's decision to paint a Madonna. The narrator asks whether great Madonnas can be produced by a secular artist in a secular age. In addition to these questions of influence and originality, the story concludes by posing questions concerning the ontology of the work. The narrator visits the artist's studio and discovers only a blank canvas. In what sense can the work be said to exist if it has not been given material form—if it exists only in the mind and aspirations of the artist?

But also as in "The Real Thing," there is a political subtext to this overt theorizing, this time a subtext concerning the representation of women. The woman whom the artist takes as the model for his unpainted painting first met the artist twenty years ago by asking him for money on the street; she was an unwed mother with a small child. This fact makes the title of the story into a dark commentary on James's own time if, from the point of view of the Christian past, the time of the story *is* the future. But if some confluence of male exploitation and societal blindness has swept this woman and her child onto the streets, this is a story that is not told by either painter or narrator. Nonetheless, the brief allusion to her plight suggests that history, as Fredric Jameson might say, is the "absent cause" of this tale's plot; woman's economic circumstance is the base upon which the would-be artist's cultural and aesthetic ruminations rest.[9]

When the would-be artist introduces the narrator to the woman, the narrator is shocked to see that she is middle-aged, a far cry from the magnificent beauty the painter had led him to expect. Later the narrator says as much to the artist, precipitating the artist's realization that he has failed to act (her beauty has faded before he can represent it artistically)— another variation of James's theme of the unlived life. When the narrator returns alone to visit the model, he finds her with another man—a lowlife who sculpts cats and monkeys to sell to tourists. In the narrator's first glimpse of this couple, the woman is gorging on macaroni.

Whoever she is in reality, we encounter her only in these antithetical male representations: in the verbal idealizations of the failed painter and in the vulgarization of the narrator, who tells us "in plain prose, she was growing stout" (36). The Christian story of the Madonna is itself a version of our patriarchal metanarrative, a story told by a male-dominated church about a mother who must efface herself so that her son can enter the Law of the Father. Artistic idealizations such as those found in conventional representations of the Madonna serve the ideological function of making subjected positions appear attractive. Within James's story, the question of whether an artist should attempt to rival the idealizing forms of the past is answered by the narrator's "plain prose." The woman will be represented either as Madonna or Dark Lady. Ironically, the narrator criticizes the vulgar art of the woman's companion, his cats and monkeys, but the narrator's own vulgarization of the woman is equally appropriate to an age of tarnished ideals.

"The Madonna of the Future" employs a framing device. The primary narrator delivers his tale orally at a social gathering, and the framing narrator, before turning the story over to the primary narrator, tells us that at story's end the hostess "showed me a tear in each of her beautiful eyes" (18). She, too, seems to be a cliché of male discourse, the beautiful and sentimental woman moved by a tale of an artist's failed dream. But the hostess comes to us through a patriarchal hookup between a real author, an inferred or implied author, and a framing narrator, and she is the docile narratee to another male narrator. The hostess remains subjected by the discourse of this four-tiered priesthood; whatever other knowledge or story concerning the unnamed Madonna that may haunt her tears eludes representation.

Women as Prizes

Perhaps the least complimentary role women can play in a male-dominated cultural establishment is that of the artist's prize, recalling the exchanges of women Claude Lévi-Strauss describes in primitive societies.[10] In "The Lesson of the Master," patriarchal order dominates. Here an older novelist, the "master" who has not realized his full potential as an author, counsels a younger, promising writer to avoid marriage because it will inevitably lead to entanglement with "the mercenary muse" (133). Exhorting the young writer to follow true art, rather than the compromised art that would result from marital responsibilities, the master says: "That's what I want *you* to go in for. I mean the real thing" (134).

The young writer, Paul Overt (his name perhaps suggests his inability to see motives behind theories), follows his advice and retires to Europe for two years to pursue his career. Upon his return to England he finds that the master, Henry St. George, has, after the death of his first wife, married the young woman Paul had loved. Paul feels deceived and cheated, but St. George protests that in no way could he have anticipated his good fortune and that his advice had been sincere. Although James leaves the question of conscious intention in doubt, propositions concerning the artist's necessary freedom have worked to St. George's advantage. The belief that artistic perfection can be obtained only through renunciation serves to dispatch the young writer, leaving the social arena free for the master.[11]

In all of this, women occupy two entirely conventional roles. Mrs. St. George is the burdensome wife, suggesting the "prize" under a negative evaluation—the prize turned burden. Like Mark Ambient's wife in "The Author of Beltraffio," Mrs. St. George once made her husband burn a "bad Book"; and like Ambient's wife, who dies soon after the death of her son, Mrs. St. George is conveniently killed off. The younger woman is the conventional object of male desire—the prize for which men compete. Neither woman is individualized to any degree. Of course, the irony is that the apparently inferior writer wins the prize; it would seem that gaining the prize, be it sexual, marital, or monetary, entails compromise if not outright deceit.

In "Broken Wings," the function of novelist and prize are fused. Mrs. Harvey, a widow, has enjoyed a certain success as a novelist but has earned less money than people assume. The same is true of Stuart Straith, a painter. Each has therefore misinterpreted the other as being arrogant, and the potential romantic attachment has been deferred for ten years. Only when they come to realize one another's relative poverty does the love blossom. Each is a prize for the other, but the prize ironically depends on the artists' *lack* of commercial success.

Women as Gatekeepers

In "The Death of the Lion," the "serious" writer, Neil Paraday (parody?), is taken up by Mrs. Wimbush, who functions as the gatekeeper by staging social occasions that grant her guests access to fashionable writers, a scene repeated in many tales. Paraday is quickly discarded by her and her fashion-hungry guests. In fact, he dies at her home as the guests are moving on to other interests; they have lost his final manuscript. If one adopts as a standard the patriarchal myth described by Lacan, "The Death of the Lion" shows us a topsy-turvy world in which the male power of the pen—the Law of the Father—languishes and dies in a system of cultural consumption that is gendered female by virtue of the function of Mrs. Weeks Wimbush—her first name perhaps suggesting the outer limits of her commitment to any single author.

The wife in "The Author of Beltraffio" is a gatekeeper in a story that even more directly invokes the patriarchal myth. "The Author of Beltraffio" is clear in giving shape and form to patriarchal desires concerning the position of women in relation to language and culture and to patriarchal paranoia concerning the results of women escaping this position. Thus the tale lends itself either to charges of misogyny or to admiration for exposing the workings of a patriarchal cultural establishment—depending on just how one characterizes the irony of the inferred author.[12] But like the narrator of "The Real Thing," the narrator of "The Author of Beltraffio" does not realize that such fundamental ideological issues are at stake in his story. His own discourse privileges art and aesthetics to a degree that blinds him to other matters. He sees the conflict between the author, Ambient, and his wife only as a conflict between the artistic imagination and those voices of morality and orthodoxy that would stifle that imagination. The narrator even aestheticizes the couple's son to the point of making him a symbol for the work of art itself, which cannot survive in a world controlled by prudery. But James may have more in mind than the commonplaces implied in the indignant discourse of the narrator.

The family depicted in this story is the site of a primal struggle, anticipating with uncanny accuracy the Lacanian revision of Freud outlined above. Ambient, a sort of bourgeois Decadent, lives conventionally but writes novels that are apparently scandalous from the view point of conventional morality, represented by his wife; she functions as a gatekeeper in relation to her son, denying the son access to the father and his allegedly immoral writings. It should be recalled that if, in Lacan's metanarrative, the father is to be recognized as the founder of the law that institutes humanity, it is crucial that the mother acknowledge the father's *language*. For our purposes the distinction between speech and writing and the questions Jacques Derrida has raised about it are not important. Lacan writes:

> The father is present only through his law, which is speech, and only in so far as his Speech is recognized by the mother does it take on the value of Law. If the position of the father is questioned, then the child remains subjected to the mother.[13]

Ambient's wife is so concerned about the dangers of her husband's writings, which she has never read, that she in fact attempts to deprive him of all contact with their son. Her worst fear is that one day the boy will read his father's words—will enter the symbolic order his father's words help to create.

The young American critic (also male) who narrates the story has taken a train from London to visit the great author for the weekend in his country home. His first encounter with the family is as follows:

> "Ah there she is!" said Mark Ambient; "and she has got the boy." He noted the last fact in a slightly different tone from any in which he had yet spoken. I wasn't fully aware of this at the time, but it lingered in my ear and I afterwards understood it.
> "Is it your son?" I inquired, feeling the question not to be brilliant.
> "Yes, my only child. He's always in his mother's pocket. She cod-

dles him too much." It came back to me afterwards too—the sound of these critical words. They weren't petulant; they expressed rather a sudden coldness, a mechanical submission. We went a few steps further, and then he stopped short and called the boy, beckoning him repeatedly.

"Dolcino, come and see your daddy!" There was something in the way he stood still and waited that made me think he did it for a purpose. Mrs. Ambient had her arm round the child's waist, and he was leaning against her knee; but though he moved at his father's call she gave no sign of releasing him. A lady, apparently a neighbor, was seated near her, and before them was a garden table on which a tea-service had been placed.

Mark Ambient called again, and Dolcino struggled in the maternal embrace; but, too tightly held, he after two or three fruitless efforts jerked about and buried his head deep in his mother's lap. (56)

Midway through the story the boy has taken ill, and shortly thereafter the meddlesome narrator persuades Mrs. Ambient to read her husband's latest manuscript. Subsequently, she locks herself in a bedroom with Dolcino and the manuscript— becoming a gatekeeper in a literal sense—and refuses to admit the doctor. The child dies. When we recall that death is an ancient metaphor for orgasm, the subtextual theme of incest is apparent. The narrator had momentarily felt that he had prompted Mrs. Ambient to take a more tolerant view of her husband's writings. But the husband's sister, also on the scene, offers an interpretation by which Mrs. Ambient was so shocked at what she read that she chose to let her son die rather than be corrupted by the father's novels. Although James's novels often question the privileging of art over life, here we have the dominance of life by a moralistic *interpretation* of art.

Thus the resolution of the Lacanian narrative is reversed or disallowed. The mother's original bonding to the child is a stronger "law" than that of the father, and the child is prohibited from entering the symbolic, which is to say from living. Such a negative representation of unchecked maternal bonding—turning it into a death force—can certainly be read as blatant patriarchal propaganda, as problematical on this small, domestic canvas as, say, Charles Dickens's depiction of the Terror as feminine in the figures of Madame Defarge and "La Guillotine" on his much larger, historical canvas. (When one recalls that Dickens's story begins with a rape, the knitting by which Madame Defarge inscribes the names of her victims seems today to be a demonic parody of the notion of a specifically feminine and therefore liberational writing.)

In the narratological distinction between story and discourse, story is the sequence of events that supposedly "really" happened. Discourse, on the other hand, refers to all the various enmeshed effects of telling—the main ones being plotting (which may reorder events, omit events, and so on), point of view, and narrative voice.[14] In Lacanian terms, we may say that discourse is the realm of the symbolic and of masculine desire, whereas story is the absent and feminine real—the object of discourse's desire. But this analogy may seem strained, since the "real" is always absent in Lacan—is that which escapes signification—whereas the story, we say, is present *in* the discourse. But of course it is only present in a very problematical sense, and Jonathan Culler has demonstrated that events often taken to be indisputably "in" the story are in fact effects of discourse.[15]

What we are told about what went on behind the locked door in "The Author of Beltraffio," where mother, son, and manuscript are sequestered, is just such an effect of discourse. It is curious that in her most egregious moment of gatekeeping, she herself is locked behind a gate; she is not directly observed by the narrator, and her behavior is at best an inference. It is an interpretation or guess offered by Ambient's sister and accepted by a misogynistic narrator whose homoerotic temperament seeks the exclusion of women according to its own agenda. The narrator's desired object is Mark Ambient and also, metonymically, his son, who is "extraordinarily beautiful" (57). When the mother takes Dolcino out of the narrator's presence for the last time, the narrator laments: "So I never laid a longing hand on Dolcino" (86). Indeed, the narrator aestheticizes everything associated with Ambient, and at least in relation to his discourse the old saw about the aesthetic category being a repository of displaced sexuality seems entirely appropriate. The homoeroticism suggested in the narrator's words reflects his longing to replace the woman, and its alibi—or the closet it has not come out of—is his discourse on art and beauty. Thus the narrator, a critic, is in competition for the function of cultural gatekeeper, and this gatekeeping floats upon a subterranean stream of desire.

Ambient's sister, who makes the guess the narrator so wants to credit as an event in the story, is herself a mere effect of male discourse, or at least she is ironically portrayed as such by the narrator. "She had no natural aptitude for an artistic development, had little real intelligence" (65). She dresses herself like a figure from a Rossetti, apparently also achieving the impression of a disreputable woman from one of her brother's novels. "As there were plenty of people who darkly disapproved of him they could easily point to his sister as a person formed by his influence. . . . He was the original and she the inevitable imitation" (65). By portraying the sister as a "typically" shallow and fashion-conscious woman, the narrator discredits the source of the climax of his own story. If we see this as a stable irony—an effect intended by our inferred author—we would probably not attribute the sexist attitudes of the narrator to that author.

If the extent of James's irony is unclear, we also receive a very unclear impression of Ambient's novels. They are absent signifieds that are themselves signifiers, links in the metonymic chain of desire. Wolfgang Iser's way of figuring the text as a place of gaps and holes that must be filled by the reader's interpretive activity and Stanley Fish's even more imperial and total domination of the text by the reader's desires set up a masculine-feminine relationship between reader and text, masculine and feminine being construed according to patriarchal habits of mind. In James's story, it is the woman who refuses to read and the male narrator for whom reading is such an obvious conduit for desire. With both the aestheticized Dolcino and Ambient's novels as convenient loci of desire, there is no need for woman. And, of course, the narrator assumes that his readers are male: "My story gives the reader at best so very small a knot to untie that I needn't hope to excite *his* curiosity by delaying to remark that Mrs. Ambient hated her sister-in-law. . . . I shall perhaps not seem to count too much on having beguiled *him* if I say *he* must promptly have guessed it" (65, my emphasis). The male pronoun was a convention of speech, but the ideology beneath the convention, as male narrator and male reader gaze at these hopeless women, is especially apparent here. If art is the ostensible subject of the discourse that passes between them, it is woman who is subjected.

James's story illustrates the thesis that Culler has argued using other examples—the thesis that story often seems to be produced by discourse rather than the other way around. Here discourse is the set of ideological assumptions concerning woman, together with their aesthetic alibi, which are shared between the narrator and his readers, and the discourse positions the woman as a demonic gatekeeper who in turn positions her son forever outside of culture by letting him die. Thus language and culture—the language and the cultural event the narrator's discourse constitutes—conspire in exactly the way Lacan has described. "The Author of Beltraffio," then, depicts a dark inversion of patriarchal power arrangements; it expresses patriarchy's anxiety over society's possible rewriting of the Law of the Father. The narrator's unconscious intention is to offer a warning concerning unbridled feminine influence; one may infer an author who intends to critique the narrator's misogyny and thus to show how such attitudes can be couched in discourses upon the arts. In fact, the narrator could be seen as an early depiction of a character type associated with the aesthetic movement; cartoons in *Punch* in the years following this story make it clear that the homoerotic and pederastic disposition of the aesthetes was taken for granted by the public. But various readers will no doubt infer different authorial intentions in this regard, and whatever irony James intends concerning his narrator's gender attitudes might best be called unstable.

An equally interesting case is "The Figure in the Carpet." The first gatekeeper is Lady Jane. Like Mrs. Wimbush in "The Death of the Lion," she arranges the social event that provides others, including the narrator, access to the famous author. Vereker's wife, lurking in the background of the story, then becomes a shadowy gatekeeper in that her illness denies the narrator access to his beloved author. But more centrally positioned is Gwendolen Erme, who fuses the functions of novelist, prize, and gatekeeper. She is the critic's prize, not the novelist's, and she is comically passed from critic to critic. She is also a novelist; thus the critic's desire is gendered masculine and the cultural object of desire together with its gatekeepers are feminine. But the critic, Corvick, already *has* his knowledge of Vereker's secret (or convinces everyone he has, which comes to the same thing in the tale's exchange system), and he uses this knowledge as his bargaining chip with Gwendolen. She gains the knowledge by consenting to marriage, after which the gatekeeper function passes from Corvick, who is promptly killed off, to her.

In Honoré de Balzac's *Sarrassine*, the proposed exchange between narrator and narratee is more bawdy—a good story for a quick tumble. But in his more refined way, James too links cultural knowledge with sexual, the pleasures of the text with those of the body. In Lacanian terms, the symbolic order is a metonymic chain of desire originating in the primal loss of the mother. And like sexual knowledge, the knowledge of Vereker's "trick" seems not to be paraphrasable—Gwendolen hints to the obtuse narrator that it is an experience that transforms one, not a verbalizable concept or device. It is knowledge that exists outside of the symbolic, which is to say outside of the language and Law of the Father. The narrator wonders: "Was the figure in the carpet traceable or describable only for husbands and wives—for lovers supremely united?" (306). And J. Hillis Miller pursues the meditation:

> What *is* revealed in sexual knowledge? Is it nothing at all? Is sexual experience a figure of death, an absence, the absence of any healing power, any law able to put dots on the i's, or is it rather some ultimate presence, capital source or phallogocentric origin, yarn beam, loom (*istos*), on which is woven the figure in the carpet? Is that figure the figure of nothing, or is it the figure of the logos?[16]

Within these metaphorics, it is appropriate that the woman novelist should function as prize for the successful critic and as gatekeeper for the critic whose "impotence" (310) dooms him to perpetual outsider status. But unlike the wife in "The Author of Beltraffio," Gwendolen's gatekeeping invites a positive evaluation. If cultural knowledge is gendered feminine, the reprehensibly lethal gatekeeping of Ambient's wife (but we say this under erasure—this is a story created only in the suspect discourse of the sister and the narrator) originates in a sort of displaced sexual jealousy. But in "The Figure in the Carpet," the consequences of Gwendolen's gatekeeping are less dire. We consent to it because the narrator *is* a fool (James's irony is entirely stable here) and because we know, despite all our reservations about cultural elitism, that there must always be insiders and outsiders. In *The Genesis of Secrecy,* Frank Kermode shows how outsiders are produced not only by texts but by the institutions that oversee their interpretation and transmission, and "The Figure in the Carpet" nicely traces this process.[17]

A variation on these "functions" and these themes occurs in "The Aspern Papers," in which another of James's deeply flawed narrators—this time a literary historian—seeks to gain access to the papers of the deceased poet Jeffrey Aspern. This Publishing Scoundrel (we will refer to him as Juliana Bordereau does, since his duplicity withholds his true name even from the reader) is associated with Satan, working in the garden being part of his scheme to dupe the Misses Bordereau. He also exploits their economic need by paying a handsome rent, thereby crashing their gate. In his eyes, the aged Juliana, the gate-keeper, is like a folkloric hag guarding a treasure. She has also, apparently, functioned as the subject of Aspern's poetry. Per-haps, like Shakespeare's Dark Lady, her reputation was even compromised by Aspern's immortalization of her. These points, however, are only matters of the Publishing Scoundrel's specu-lation; they are story elements to which the unreliable dis-course does not give us full access. We, too, remain outsiders.

Like the narrator of "The Figure in the Carpet," the Publish-ing Scoundrel is unmarried, and, as in that story, access to the cultural inside—to Aspern's private papers—is associated with matrimony. In this case, the implicit bargain is that if the Scoundrel will marry Juliana's daughter, Tina, he will receive the papers. The possibility exists that Tina is the illegitimate daughter of Aspern and Juliana, but again the discourse only tantalizes us with possibilities. At any rate, rather than opting for marriage, the Scoundrel makes a direct attempt to break into Juliana's desk and is caught. In an image worthy of Freud's "dreamwork," she sews the treasured papers into the mattress of her bed, and after her death they are burned by Tina. As in "The Figure in the Carpet," the gatekeeping function has been passed on because of a death—the sought-after object dies not with the original gatekeeper but with an heir to the gatekeeping function.

Thus, although the producer of the valued cultural object is male, society's gatekeeping is again gendered female. "The Au-thor of Beltraffio" dramatized a swerve from the Lacanian nar-rative, which associates access to culture—to the symbolic order—with the death of the mother. In "The Author of Beltraf-fio," instead, the mother breaks the chain of cultural transmis-sion by bringing about the death of her child, the next generation of culture's consumers and subjects. In "The Figure in the Carpet," the cultural treasure, Vereker's secret, dies a natural death with Gwendolen, while the would-be consumer licks his unreal wounds beyond the gate. Like the man in Franz Kafka's parable, the gate that may have been his is now closed forever. In "The Aspern Papers," the physical cultural object is intentionally destroyed by the gatekeeper with whom the male seeker might have united. Perhaps the cultural object—Vereker's secret or Aspern's papers—is not the true object of the quest. The true object may be the gatekeeper herself. She is a potential substitute for the lost mother, and uniting with her—an act always deferred—would end desire's story.

In no case in James's transformations of the patriarchal myth does woman simply die or step aside in order to allow access to the symbolic. If, then, the Lacanian myth described by Homans is as basic to our culture—or to patriarchal society—as she claims it is, a look at the various "functions" of women in the art tales suggests a deep ambivalence on James's part concerning this myth—perhaps a rejection of the myth, perhaps fear over the consequences of rejecting it, or perhaps both. The roles he assigns to women are more active and more powerful than the Madonna-like one assigned by the myth. In the patriarchal myth, the mother resigns her function as potential gatekeeper, allowing the son to enter the symbolic order, which is itself always a product of male activity. This, the myth tells us, is the necessary and natural order of things. Similar archetypal events and functions lurk behind James's art tales—culture must be produced, mediated, and transmitted.

But in James, the gender values assigned to different functions in the traditional patriarchal myth are blurred and transgressed—his artists are often maternal, his questers and consumers often impotent, his gatekeepers often aggressive. And the stories reveal a firm grasp of the exploitative economic conditions under which women have lived. Readers must create their inferred author with these facts in mind, together with the general recognition that literary texts are places where opposing voices blend and clash and where monologic intentions frequently become conflicted in the act of writing.

Leon Edel makes an interesting inference about the James who wrote, from 1896 to 1899, a series of five novels and tales dealing with young girls. This was the period immediately after James's failure as a dramatist, and Edel infers that James expresses his own sense of powerlessness in the "safety-disguise of a little girl."[18] In this metanarrative, the series would constitute a sort of wish fulfillment, as the heroine of *The Awkward Age*, Nanda, finally achieves a degree of power. Peggy McCormack extends this series to include *The Golden Bowl*, written in 1903–4.[19] This analysis is worth noting because my own synchronic categories obscure the question of diachronic change. Most of the tales I have discussed predate the period of James's intense artistic disappointment, so one would not expect a diachronic analysis of these tales specifically to confirm the Edel-McCormack model of the late 1890s and early 1900s. The earliest of the tales discussed here, "The Madonna of the Future" (1873) and "The Author of Beltraffio" (1884), offer a stark contrast between female powerlessness and the apparent abuse of maternal power. On the other hand, Gwendolen's gatekeeping in "The Figure in the Carpet" (1896) seems at once wise and gentle, the product of personal fulfillment. So perhaps one could see a pattern of change or development in the depiction of women in the art tales. But as the dying author of "The Middle Years" realizes, the second chance to make the text say what one would have it say always belongs to the reader, and I will leave to other readers the question of what a diachronic analysis might say.

Notes

1. Bruce Henricksen, "'The Real Thing': Criticism and the Ethical Turn," *Papers on Language and Literature* 27, no. 4 (fall 1991): 473–95.
2. Wayne Booth defines stable irony as being intended, fixed, and finite in its applications. Once readers discover it they are "not then invited to undermine it with further demolitions and reconstructions." Unstable ironies occur when the author "insofar as we can discover him, and he is often very remote indeed—refuses to declare himself, however subtly, *for* any stable proposition." Booth, *A Rhetoric of Irony* (Chicago: University of Chicago Press, 1974), 6, 240.
3. Vladimir Propp, *The Morphology of the Folktale,* trans. Laurence Scott (Austin: University of Texas Press, 1968), 21.
4. Margaret Homans, "The Name of the Mother in *Wuthering Heights,*" in *Wuthering Heights,* by Emily Bronte, ed. Linda H. Peterson (Boston: St. Martin's Press, Bedford Books, 1992), 341.
5. An excellent collection of essays on how the Lacanian metanarrative informs fictional texts is Robert Con Davis, ed., *The Fictional Father: Lacanian Readings of the Text* (Amherst: University of Massachusetts Press, 1981).
6. Alfred Habegger studies the question of James's attitude toward women's fiction in *Henry James and the "Woman Business"* (Cambridge: Cambridge University Press, 1989).
7. Parenthetical page references are to Henry James, *Stories of Artists and Writers,* ed. F. O. Matthiessen (New York: New Directions, 1965).
8. Davis asserts that in Lacanian thought "the question of the father in fiction, in whatever guise, is essentially one of father absence." *The Fictional Father,* 3.
9. Fredric Jameson posits history as "absent cause," always receding beyond the horizon of the representable, in his discussion of Althusserian structuralism. Jameson, *The Political Unconscious: Narrative as a Socially Symbolic Act* (Ithaca: Cornell University Press, 1981), 23–29.
10. Peggy McCormack has studied how economic language informs the exchanges between the sexes in James's fiction. See McCormack, *The Rule of Money: Gender, Class, and Exchange Economics in the Fiction of Henry James* (Ann Arbor: UMI Research Press, 1990).
11. Even in texts where the explicit discourse is not artistic, renunciation is a value that works to exclude or position women. The rejection of women

by such characters as Strether, Marcher, and Winterbourne are obvious examples.

12. In narrative theory, "implied author" is the more usual term for that shadowy being lurking in the spaces between real authors and fictional narrators. But this term has a deceptively objective ring to it, and I prefer to emphasize the extent to which this creature is a product of readers' inferences. Of course it works both ways—texts imply and readers infer.

13. Quoted in Anika Lemaire, *Jacques Lacan*, trans. David Macey (London: Routledge and Kegan Paul, 1977), 83.

14. See Seymour Chatman, *Story and Discourse: Narrative Structure in Fiction and Film* (Ithaca: Cornell University Press, 1978).

15. Jonathan Culler, "Story and Discourse in the Analysis of Narrative," in *The Pursuit of Signs* (Ithaca: Cornell University Press, 1981), 169–87.

16. J. Hillis Miller, "The Figure in the Carpet," in *Modern Critical Interpretations: Henry James's "Daisy Miller," "The Turn of the Screw," and Other Tales,* ed. Harold Bloom (New York: Chelsea House Publishers, 1987), 72.

17. Frank Kermode, *The Genesis of Secrecy: On the Interpretation of Narrative* (Cambridge: Harvard University Press, 1979).

18. Leon Edel, *Henry James: The Treacherous Years* (New York: J. B. Lippincott Co., 1969), 261.

19. McCormack, *The Rule of Money*, 70–71.

Working at Gender: *In the Cage*

JOHN CARLOS ROWE

CRITICS HAVE OFTEN BASED THEIR INTERPRETATIONS OF *IN THE CAGE* on the telegraphist's thorough mystification by both the dazzling aristocrats who send their messages through her and the technology of the telegraph, which appears to direct *her* far more than she commands it.[1] For these critics, she fits too neatly the stereotype of the working-class woman incapable of overcoming her imprisonment by gender and class; her pathos is the motive for James's social criticism, but she must thereby remain desperately trapped for the sake of his fictional argument. Like other working women in James's fiction, the telegraphist is primarily occupied with a system of representation and thus with symbolic relations. Naomi Nioche's museum copies in *The American,* Verena Tarrant's oratory in *The Bostonians,* and Henrietta Stackpole's journalism in *The Portrait of a Lady* seem the precedents for yet another woman in James who is tricked into thinking that command of her own labor is a way out of the subtler entrapments of romance and marriage. The "mistake," of course, is usually understood as James's identification of the limitation of a discursive mode that is not yet (or never can become) "artistic representation." Such art is finally, according to this argument, the province of the Master, for whom the "feminine" has once more served a purpose in an aesthetic ideology operating still according to the old patriarchal authority.[2]

Throughout *In the Cage,* there are hints that James no longer follows this familiar rhetoric. In my view, this departure of the novella from the pattern accounts for the relative eccentricity of the work within the James canon. It is a change in view and thus technique of social representation occasioned in large part by James's uncertainty before new kinds of work, including the growing number of service-sector jobs employing women. Whereas James had previously represented nonartistic modes of communication as, at root, the same: lacking the figurative complexity requiring active interpretation and thus social in-

86

strumentalities, he views the telegraph as a mode of communication that marks an important difference in the usual conduct of social relations and thus conventional class distinctions.

I do not wish to take social effects for their causes; technological innovation tends to be the consequence of new social needs. The telegraph responds to the demands of industrial, urban, densely populated societies in which market forces drive values (from wages to ethics) and the privacy of the individual is increasingly a lost illusion. The telegraph responds to a world in which the old boundaries between public and private, the industrial economy and household economics, "society" in the sense of the nation and "Society" in the sense of culture, have broken down. The secret world of the ruling class is increasingly open to view. The uncle in *The Turn of the Screw* can command the governess " 'never [to] trouble him . . . neither appeal nor complain nor write about anything' " with some expectation that the class divisions of his world will support this taboo (*The Turn of the Screw*, 156). Servants such as Peter Quint and Miss Jessel are presumed to carry their secrets to their graves, however much they might embody the corruption of their masters. But the private world of the Bradeens, Captain Everard, and Lord Rye in *In the Cage* is full of traffic from the outside world. Not only are their messages open to the view of the counter-clerks and telegraphists at Cocker's Grocery, but the telegraphist's friend and confidante, Mrs. Jordan, arranges the flowers for their parties, in place of the invisible and discreet servants of the previous generation; the telegraphist thinks of her as "a friend who had invented a new career for women—that of being in and out of people's houses to look after the flowers."[3] In earlier times, the servants gathered flowers from the vast gardens of the country estate; now Mrs. Jordan can imagine expanding her business to include the telegraphist, to whom she proposes taking over the accounts of all the "bachelors." Still dazzled by the upper classes, dreaming of a "match" out of a "hatpenny" romance, neither Mrs. Jordan nor the telegraphist understands what James makes explicit—the new powers of the working classes to understand and perhaps even seize what James had always understood as the primary mode of social production: discourse.

In order to encourage scholars of James to pay more attention to how textual questions are related to modes of socioeconomic production in his works and times Jennifer Wicke warned us several years ago that "the realm of language is not privileged, not exempt, and certainly not related to political economy in merely metaphorical ways."[4] Dale Bauer and Andrew Lakritz have shown us how Taylorism rationalizes, systematizes, and mechanizes both the telegraphist's work and sexuality to the point where both she and the words she counts fail any longer to "count" in the sense of social significance or intellectual meaning.[5] Keeping their insistence upon the material conditions of production in the late-Victorian period, we must also remember that the telegraphist's "cage" differs importantly from the smokestack factories or the sweatshops where women and children had wasted their vision, minds, and lives in the earlier phases of industrialism.

Just who "owns" the words and the flowers is less definite in this changing urban world than it was for the children, the governess, or Mrs. Grose at Bly. The telegraphist understands dimly what James knows with perfect clarity—that in this new age the "values" come not from accumulated possessions, not from the hoarded wealth, but from the "combinations" and arrangements compatible with this exchange economy: "Combinations of flowers and greenstuff forsooth! What *she* could handle freely, she said to herself, was combinations of men and women" (2:178). For someone who counts words every day in terms of their monetary value, she knows well enough that textual combinations are the new sources of value. At one point, prompted by Mrs. Jordan bragging about her ability to arrange a "thousand tulips" for her clients, the telegraphist reflects: "A thousand tulips at a shilling clearly took one further than a thousand words at a penny" (7:193). But the narrative suggests there are other ways for words to be worth vastly more than the coppers she counts out at Cocker's.

In Regents' Park with Captain Everard, the nominal aristocratic hero and rogue, she surprises, puzzles, and probably frightens him with her combination of independence, frankness, and familiarity. Above all, she disturbs him, like some uncanny ghost of his own worry, with her claim to knowledge of his complicated, trivial liaisons. Whatever she thinks she knows and however wrong it may be, she nonetheless has touched the one region in which the ruling class is vulnerable— its control and command of language. It is when she says, "'Yes, I know,'" that "[s]he immediately felt him surprised and even a little puzzled at her frank assent; but for herself the trouble she had taken could only, in these fleeting minutes . . . be all there like a little hoard of gold in her lap" (15:219, 220). Whatever she claims to "know" comes from messages sent through her tele-graphic post and "sounder"; what she claims to know is the dis-course of high society. From the first chapter of *In the Cage* to the last, the telegraphist experiences fitfully the glimmers of a class consciousness that she mistakes most often for her own "genius" or for the "love" she imagines draws her to Captain Everard. Whatever class consciousness emerges, however, will not be of the traditional Marxian sort, nothing like what James has already ridiculed in Hyacinth's decorative labors in *The Princess Casamassima*. For James, such awareness must be in-tegrally connected to the new productive value of language in the emerging economies of information and communication.

There are hints in the narrative that a new working-class soli-darity might be built by service workers such as Mrs. Jordan, the telegraphist, and even that late arrival, Mr. Drake, butler to Lord Rye and then Lady Bradeen, affianced at the very last to Mrs. Jordan herself. The offer Mrs. Jordan makes to the teleg-raphist to join her business is an unusual one in James's fiction. It differs from Olive Chancellor and Verena Tarrant's working relations in *The Bostonians,* even though Mrs. Jordan is "ten years older" than the telegraphist and inclined to brag shame-lessly and domineer, just as it departs significantly from the final withdrawal of Mrs. Gereth and Fleda Vetch in *The Spoils of Poynton*. Beyond the interest we should take in the idea of two working-class women starting their own business, we ought also to note how Mrs. Jordan flatters the telegraphist about her spe-cial qualifications for the job: " 'One wants an associate of one's own kind, don't you know? You know the look they want it all to have?—of having come, not from a florist, but from one of themselves. Well, I'm sure *you* could give it—because you *are* one. Then we *should* win. Therefore just come in with me' " (6:190–91). To be sure, James informs us early in the narrative how the telegraphist, her elder sister, and their mother were "ladies, suddenly bereft, betrayed, overwhelmed," who "had slipped faster and faster down the steep slope," not entirely un-like Mrs. Jordan, the pastor's widow, who is dignified enough, except for her "extraordinarily protrusive teeth" (1:176; 6:192). On the other hand, both Mrs. Jordan and the telegraphist have learned most of what they know about the upper classes from their respective jobs. Mrs. Jordan claims that "in the practice of her fairy art . . . she more than peeped in—she penetrated"; the telegraphist is perhaps a bit behind her, "educated as she had rapidly been by her chances at Cocker's, there were still strange gaps in her learning" (6:192).

The romance of a co-owned business by two women is, alas, brought back to earth by Mrs. Jordan's proposal that the telegraphist take on the bachelors' accounts and the telegraphist's own obsession with Captain Everard. But the ideal of cooperative labor as an alternative to the alienation and thus victimization of workers under industrial capitalism seems more realizable in the service- and information-intensive economy of *In the Cage*. Mr. Buckton may be found most often at the "sounder," but the telegraphist and other counter-clerks know how to use it. Labor at Cocker's Grocery and Post-Telegraph is not strictly divided, and thus the workers are not fundamentally alienated from the total process of production. Selling stamps, counting words on telegram forms, sending transmissions, and perhaps occasionally filling a grocery order may not amount to thrilling work, but the variety of tasks suggests also the new cooperative possibilities of the workplace.

In this regard, there is considerable evidence that some such symbolic resolution is what James offers and then withdraws from the telegraphist, whose "education" at the end remains distinguished by its "strange gaps." In the end, it is Mrs. Jordan's "Mr. Drake," Lord Rye's former butler, now "going to Lady Bradeen," who can fill those gaps in the reader's and telegraphist's knowledge regarding the fate of Lord and Lady Bradeen and Captain Everard (25:256). We know that conclusion: how " 'something was lost—something was found' " and " 'it all got about' " to " 'a point at which Lord Bradeen had to act,' " were it not for his " 'most sudden death,' " giving " 'them a prompt chance,' " since " '[s]he just nailed him' " for the " 'injury . . . he [had] done her,' " which is to say, " 'He *must* marry her, you know' " (27:265). Phew! We feel a bit as the telegraphist does on leaving Mrs. Jordan's little flat in Maida Vale, on the Paddington canal: "It was strange such a matter should be at last settled for her by Mr. Drake" (27:266).

Strange, indeed, unless what she has missed all along is just the cooperative work that Mrs. Jordan has proposed clumsily and for which each of them in turn—Mrs. Jordan (the clergyman's widow), the telegraphist (a "lady" fallen down the steep slope), and Mr. Drake (a butler in the service of the rich and powerful)—has part of the talent to solve the puzzle, a piece of real message coded in the telegram that the frightened Lady Bradeen sends and the anxious Captain Everard tries to check.

If the cooperative labor required by the new information technologies is an alternative James holds out to the telegraphist in *In the Cage*, then we must wonder why she has so much difficulty accepting Mrs. Jordan's proposal, working with her fellow workers at Cocker's, or accepting the fact that the mystery has been nominally "solved" by Mr. Drake. In each case, strict distinctions between Victorian gender roles account for her reluctance to work with others. The persistence of such gender stereotypes is all the more noticeable in the new workplaces, in which men and women share many of the same tasks, unlike the common segregation of men and women according to the physical demands of heavy industrial labor. There are two reasons the telegraphist refuses Mrs. Jordan's offer of a share in her floral-arranging business: Mrs. Jordan's meretricious proposal that the telegraphist take the bachelors' accounts, thereby vaguely hinting at some sort of coquetry in the merchandising of services; and the telegraphist's infatuation with Captain Everard and vain hope that her continuance at the "PO," as Mrs. Jordan calls Cocker's, might lead to a genuine romance.

Gender stereotypes are also at the heart of her alienation from the other workers at Cocker's, and here we must grant James an extraordinary sensitivity to the woman's vulnerability to harassment in the late-Victorian workplace. One reason she detests the telegraphic "sounder," in its "ground-glass" cage within the cage, is that Mr. Buckton employs "devilish and successful subterfuges for keeping her at the sounder whenever it looked as if anything might amuse" (3:180). The meaning here is deliberately ambiguous, suggesting either that Buckton assigns her to the sounder whenever interesting clients arrive or that he takes advantage of her in the privacy of the sounder room. In either case, she must endure his "devilish and successful subterfuges" as well as the counter-clerk's "passion for her," whose "unpleasant conspicuity . . . she would never have consented to be obliged to him" (3:180).

It is little wonder, then, that the telegraphist finds no solidarity with the other workers at Cocker's; what interferes is just what prevents her from recognizing in Captain Everard their common poverty and dependence on others who can "nail" them. Of course, James renders ambiguous as well the precise "poverty" of the good Captain. Mrs. Jordan tells the telegraphist that " 'he has nothing,' " but in reply to her " 'Isn't he rich?' " reflects, " 'It depends upon what you call. . . . ! What

does he bring? Think what she has. And then, love, his debts' "
(27:262). Of course, Captain Everard's real poverty is not so
much financial as moral. Beyond his different identities on the
telegrams—Everard, Captain Everard, Philip, Phil, "the
Count," William, "the Pink 'Un," he has little to recommend
him. Beyond his stylish smoking, there is a certain emptiness
that is revealed all too tellingly in the telegraphist's meeting
with him in Regents' Park. Despite her boldness, she elicits little from him beyond, " 'See here—see here' " (17:228).[6]

By the time the telegraphist must write the crucial numbers
of his errant telegram on the back of his calling card, well before Mrs. Jordan announces that he has been "nailed" by the
compromised Lady Bradeen, Captain Everard has lost much of
his military and masculine authority, at least as far as the conventions of Victorian gender roles are concerned. Whatever the
"mistake" the telegraphist may have made in transcribing or
transmitting that telegram, she has at least in some way contributed to Lady Bradeen's success in "nailing" him. But this is
hardly the sort of collaboration that appeals to the telegraphist,
even if it suggests that women working together might cross
class lines to reverse the patriarchal authority of the dominant
culture.

It is not, however, the reversal of conventional gender roles
that James has in mind, although this seems nearly the point of
the telegraphist's bold conversation with the shrinking Captain
Everard—" 'See here—see here!' "—in the park and her triumphant recollection of the crucial numbers in a scene that concludes with her not only explaining the mystery to the confused
counter-clerk but also answering Mr. Buckton's rude inquiry—
" 'And what game is that, miss' "—with the "reply that it was
none of his business" (23:251). Much as the novella revolves
around a certain feminine empowerment at the expense of conventional masculine authority, this reversal seems finally to be
a kind of illusion. After all, James must introduce Mrs. Jordan's
"Mr. Drake" in the final chapters to "explain" it all.

Yet, one of the consequences of the new working relations of
men and women in work sites where the conventional physical
differences between masculine and feminine labor power are
no longer self-evident is that gender boundaries are transgressed, even if many of the same behaviors persist (as in the
harassment the telegraphist must endure variously from Buckton and the moonstruck counter-clerk). By this late date in our
postmodernity, it has become something of a commonplace to

acknowledge the sociohistorical forces determining gender. As Judith Butler has written: "If the inner truth of gender is a fabrication and if a true gender is a fantasy instituted and inscribed on the surface of bodies, then it seems that genders can be neither true nor false but are only produced as the truth effects of a discourse of primary and stable identities."[7]

Beyond the veneer of conventional class and gender distinctions, James offers us peeks at an extraordinary diversity of new class and gender possibilities. Once again, the technology of the telegraph has not *caused* these new possibilities, not all of which are emancipatory, but it has some coincidence with the socioeconomic conditions informing such alternatives. Perhaps the most obvious example of such an alternative is Mr. Mudge, who is dismissed by critics almost as summarily as Napoleon was reputed to have defeated the English with the judgment, "A nation of shopkeepers." To be sure, Mr. Mudge's courtship of the telegraphist appears only slightly more agreeable to her than the counter-clerk's idiotic "passion," and his values seem to be utterly commercial. Nothing is valuable unless it "pays" a material return, and everything in their relationship is as managed as a Taylorized factory. Worst of all, perhaps, Mudge defends the class hierarchies in the manner of a classic petit bourgeois and what survivors of the Reagan-Bush years recognize as the tiresome rhetoric of "trickle-down" economics (10:203). What benefits the upper classes is likely to be good for the shopkeeper's "business," as far as Mr. Mudge is concerned. Selling tomatoes or telegrams is one to him: "Above all it hurt him somewhere . . . to see anything *but* money made out of his betters" (10:203).

Yet, he does differ from the caricatures of the Victorian bourgeois patriarch. When the telegraphist candidly tells him of her meeting with Captain Everard in Regents' Park—" 'I went out the other night and sat in the Park with a gentleman,' "—he does not go to pieces as does the jealous husband in Anthony Trollope's *He Knew He Was Right* (19:232). When she challenges his masculinity by telling him, " 'You're awfully inferior' " to Captain Everard, he can say both with humor and pride in her, " 'Well, my dear, you're not inferior to anybody. You've got a cheek!' " (234). When she tells him she hasn't seen "the gentleman" since, Mudge can judge him with little consideration for his own "inferiority": " 'Oh what a cad!' " (235). Showing no regard for "his honor," Mudge expresses a quiet "confidence in her" that "only gave her ease and space, as she felt, for telling him the whole truth that no one knew" (232). In what other fiction of the late-Victorian period do we find a man giving a woman psychic "space" while she tells him of her meeting with another man?

Let me not overdo this idealization of Mr. Mudge, with his concern for order, his pocket full of chocolate creams, and his acceptance of upper-class rule as if it were a law of nature. Yet, as the only male character with a name escaping the phallic aggressiveness of those Bucktons, Drakes, Everards (and such sites as "Cocker's"), he better approaches understanding of the telegraphist than any other character, including Mrs. Jordan. What he offers may be his petty ambitions, a move from fashionable Mayfair to the dreary suburb of Chalk Farm, and "savings" of "three shillings" a week on lodgings. Chalk Farm is the suburb where swells like Captain Everard gamble at the races, but it is also the neighborhood of "clerks and railroad men and electrical workers."[8] Thus, he offers her a community of other workers, especially those in the newer communications and transportation industries.[9] Of all the people she knows, Mr. Mudge is the only one who gives her mother any recognition, and he does so in an exchange that shows he is not without imagination: "The little home . . . had been visited, in further talk she had had with him at Bournemouth, from garret to cellar, and they had especially lingered, with their respectively darkened brows, before the niche into which it was to be broached to her mother that she must find means to fit" (22:244).

Hardly a revolutionary, Mr. Mudge nonetheless represents a different role for men in his times, reflecting perhaps necessary adjustments to the frank, independent, often bold behavior of the telegraphist. Perhaps James hesitates before Mr. Mudge in his usual caricature of the petit bourgeoisie, even though he details the customary dullness and a commercialism as thorough as Maud Lowder's in *The Wings of the Dove*. It may also be that what James treats with some wry affection in this characterization is on closer examination something like the regard Trollope accords his new bourgeois heroes, such as Johnny Eames in *The Small House at Allington* or Phineas Phinn from the Palliser novels or others in a long list of other good-natured, not particularly dashing, often clumsy, but steady and true young men (who generally endure to win the women who have first declined their offers of marriage for the sake of someone grander). We should recognize this as a strategy of class and

gender legitimation that works by demonizing an illusory aristocracy, so we must be cautious in identifying too readily with
Mr. Mudge. The suburban Chalk Farm where he will settle with
the telegraphist and her mother may turn out, after all, either
to be a neighborhood of like-minded workers or an urban ghetto
of exploited victims.

Suffice it to say that Mrs. Jordan is not Olive Chancellor or
Henrietta Stackpole; James has changed the caricature of the
professional woman to render her with some seriousness. Mr.
Mudge is not, as the name at first suggests, simply the blot on
the otherwise finely written page of Mayfair. Among his other
noms de plume for his telegrams, Captain Everard once selects
"Mudge," and the accident is not lost on us. Where the captain
can only expose his lack of imagination, his imitation of the
rake, when the telegraphist engages him in Regents' Park—
" 'See here—see here!' "—Mr. Mudge offers a community, a
place for her alcoholic mother, a two-career family, and occasional holidays with "sundries," like those chocolate creams.

I am suggesting that some of Butler's sense of the postmodern constructions of gender through discourse are already present in James's text, albeit not entirely under his control. New
representations of gender establish new relations of gender,
and both are often enough the consequence of new working and
living conditions. All these gender relations have been shaped
even more determinately than in previous Jamesian works by
the conditions of their discursive production, although these
are by no means separable, as Wicke rightly reminds us, from
the material conditions of production (Wicke, 150). Throughout
In the Cage, James makes it clear that telegraphic communication depends on the cooperative labor of sender, technician,
and receiver—a triad that changes drastically the transactional,
intersubjective model for writing and speech. Few if any of the
characters understand this change, which is as radical as the
conflation of public and private spheres instantiated by the simple situation of telegraphic "sending," in which a private message is composed in a public space (such as Cocker's) and then
handed to a stranger for "transmission"—effectively, a translation into a code unfamiliar to the sender. The telegraphist herself remains convinced to the very end that "people didn't
understand her" (2:177), "the immensity of her difference,"
"not different only at one point . . . different all around" (9:198).
But such difference belongs not to the telegraphist alone, "the
betrothed of Mr. Mudge," but to the relations of a complex,

changing social reality. It is a new social reality in which customary gender roles are "mudged," and I turn in this regard to two final examples: the telegraphist as "mother" and the dubious Mr. Drake.

The telegraphic transmitter, the "sounder," aurally dominates Cocker's Grocery and Post-Telegraph, even though it is invisible in its cage within the cage (within the shop). It is like some postmodern fetus ticking away at the center of the new object-relations that determine a subject's identities: "She had made out even from the cage that it was a charming golden day: a patch of hazy autumn sunlight lay across the sanded floor and also, higher up, quickened into brightness a row of ruddy bottled syrups" (20:235). This may be the ironic negativity of a new, denaturalized world, but the positive side comes from the slippage of older "names" from their "proper referents" to a wider range of possible significations. Taking care of her alcoholic mother by working at Cocker's and by worrying in the meantime just where her mother manages to get her bottles, the telegraphist is already "mothering." And it is when Captain Everard arrives at Cocker's most desperate for help that he appears to her "quite, now, as she said to herself, like a frightened child coming to its mother" (22:246). Even in her indulgence of the self-important fancies of her friend, Mrs. Jordan, the telegraphist displays qualities of tenderness and care that too often are attributed by patriarchy to the "mother" and would thus seem inappropriate for the care shown by a woman ten years younger for an older, often deluded woman. There is also the diverse imagery of vaginal, womblike, maternal spaces throughout the text, beginning with the "cage" itself (derived as the word is from its Latin root, *cavea*, meaning "hollow or enclosed space") to the presumably pseudonymous "Miss Dolman," to whom telegrams are routed by Lady Bradeen and Captain Everard. A *dolman* is a Hussar's fur-lined coat, combining thus both the captain's military and amorous exploits in a manner not unlike the uncle's "trophies of the hunt" in his London house in *The Turn of the Screw*.[10]

In the customary Jamesian narrative of feminine limitation, the young woman is incapable of becoming not only Artist but also Mother, especially those characters who pursue careers of their own. On one level, *In the Cage* follows just that rhetoric, so that the "promise" of the telegraphist's marriage of Mr. Mudge is merely a repetition of the pathetic genealogy of working-class families of which the alcoholic mother will remind the young couple. At the other level, which I have characterized as one of "hints" and "peeks," as if James himself is not quite comfortable with its meanings, "mothering" is unmoored from its customary domesticity and its conflict with work and the public sphere. The telegraphic "sounder" need not be merely a grotesque image of the automated "mother" of the new technology; it might also suggest how the proper transmission of generational value resides less in persons (and their fragile bodies) than in the means of communication. This, too, is often enough James's theme, even argument, as he thunders about the "historical consciousness" that can be achieved only through a proper interpretation of the semiotically dense texture of everyday reality. But now he offers an alternative to those otherwise barred from access to such means of communication.

In her extraordinary reading of "The Beast in the Jungle," Eve Kosofsky Sedgwick shows how Marcher refuses the "homosexual plot" of his story and becomes the irredeemably self-ignorant man who embodies and enforces "heterosexual compulsion" as he turns away from the "beast" and what is signified.[11] Sedgwick reads Marcher's encounter in the cemetery with the male stranger—the stranger who is capable of mourning—as Marcher's reenactment of "a classic trajectory of male entitlement":

> Marcher begins with the possibility of a *desire for* the man. . . . Deflecting that desire under a fear of profanation, he then replaces it with envy, with an *identification with* the man in that man's (baffled) desired for some other, presumably female dead object. . . . The loss by which a man *so bleeds and yet lives* is . . . supposed to be the castratory one of the phallus figured as mother, the inevitability of whose sacrifice ushers sons into the status of fathers and into the control (read both ways) of the Law. (211)

All of this presumes that the "woman" remains unchanged, the "figure" of "mother" as the one *without* the phallus, the image of the possibility of being unmanned and thus the motive for repression, both of the castration feared in the Freudian family-romance but also of a fundamental lack of authority that provokes the entire cycle of masculine desire in the first place. Yet, the telegraphist in *In the Cage* is not merely a negative image, the convenient "female, dead object" used (fetishized) for a masculine narrative. The "mother" is no longer just the "medium" of masculine transmission of genealogical authority from father to son. At a certain level, the telegraphist assumes the phallus of a newly empowered "mother," especially as she assumes *maternal* functions outside the conventional and literal roles of "mother" reserved for a young, affianced, working-class girl. As "mother" to Captain Everard, to her own mother, to Mr. Mudge, and even to her friend, Mrs. Jordan, she escapes the strict division of private and public, as well as the presumed "naturalness" of the "mother's" relation to her own "child." "Mothering" has been refigured by association with the powers of communication, and the degree to which the telegraphist dons those powers is some measure of an authority that no longer is *precisely* that of "mother" or "father" but of some "authority" for transmission that exceeds their outmoded and gender-specific roles.

And then there is "Mr. Drake," whose introduction by Mrs. Jordan in the last three chapters (25–27) as her affianced seems merely a clumsy deus ex machina. Despite or perhaps *because of* his very masculine name, Mr. Drake is the occasion for what I shall term James's rhetorical cross-dressing. The novella concludes with a conversation between Mrs. Jordan and the telegraphist that is hilarious in its double entendres involving the "gentleman" Drake. The misunderstandings revolve overtly around Mrs. Jordan's habit of exaggerating her involvement with the aristocracy, so that we assume along with the telegraphist that Mr. Drake is the equal of Lord Rye, Lord and Lady Bradeen, and Captain Everard. The bathos appears to be in his revelation as simply the butler, but we do not "know" this until a certain rhetorical banter has accomplished a very different effect.

> "I think you must have heard me speak of Mr. Drake?" Mrs. Jordan had never looked so queer, nor her smile so suggestive of a large benevolent bite.
> " . . . Oh yes; isn't he a friend of Lord Rye?"
> "A great and trusted friend. Almost—I may say—a loved friend."
> Mrs. Jordan's "almost" had such an oddity that her companion was moved, rather flippantly perhaps, to take it up. "Don't people as good as love their friends when they 'trust' them?" (25:255)

If James has allowed "mothering" to slip somewhat from its conventional referents of mother and biological child, he is here more daringly causing "love" to "slip" from the amours of men and women (those "ha' penny" stories) to the trust and care between people of whatever gender.

The rhetoric is, however, charged with the homoerotic. As the conversation about Mr. Drake and Lord Rye's friendship increasingly becomes explicitly analogous to the telegraphist's friendship with Mrs. Jordan, the homoerotic rhetoric increases in frequency and explicitness:

> "Mr. Drake has rendered his lordship for several years services that his lordship has highly appreciated and that make it all the more— a—unexpected that they should, perhaps a little suddenly, separate"(25:255)

Still confused about the real identity of Mr. Drake as the butler, the telegraphist can only echo, " 'Separate?' Our young lady was mystified . . . and she already saw that she had put the saddle on the wrong horse" (25:255–56). The rhetoric of the conversation between Mrs. Jordan and the telegraphist is far too complicated for me to analyze here; it is one of James's tours de force, operating as it does simultaneously on the following registers: the confusion of "gentleman" to be either aristocrat or servant; confusion of Mr. Drake's sexual preference as either straight or gay; confusion of what amounts to a *ménage à quatre* of Drake, Lord Rye, Lady Bradeen, and Mrs. Jordan with the confused relations of the telegraphist, Captain Everard, Lady Bradeen, and Mrs. Jordan.

All of this is further entangled with the sheer plot function played by Mr. Drake in providing information about the fates of Lord and Lady Bradeen and Captain Everard following the scene of the undelivered telegram. For this purpose, Mr. Drake must leave Lord Rye for the "service" of Lady Bradeen, at which point the telegraphist, still uncertain just who Mr. Drake is (servant, lover, fiancé, gentleman) can only wonder, with the help of Mrs. Jordan, about how " 'immensely surrounded' " Lady Bradeen will be with male admirers (257). And when Mrs. Jordan tries to clarify what she has meant by Mr. Drake "going to Lady Bradeen" (256), she only seems to confuse things:

> "He's 'going,' you say, to her?"
>> At this Mrs. Jordan really faltered. "She has engaged him."
>> "Engaged him?" . . .
>> "In the same capacity as Lord Rye."
>> "And was Lord Rye engaged?" (25:258)

The rhetorical effect of this cross-dressing lasts only a moment, and at the beginning of the next chapter the telegraphist begins to "see" (" 'See here—see here!' ") that "Mr. Drake then verily *was* a person who opened the doors!" (Although it is fair to add parenthetically that it is James opening the door to our repressed fears of homoeroticism.)

As Mrs. Jordan brags that she and Mr. Drake, like the telegraphist and Mr. Mudge, " 'shall have our own' " house " 'too,' " she explains just what caused the breakup of Lord Rye and Mr. Drake:

> "[F]or, don't you know? he makes it a condition that he sleeps out."
> "A condition?"—the girl felt out of it.
> "For any new position. It was on that he parted with Lord Rye. His lordship can't meet it. So Mr. Drake has given him up."
> "And all for you?"—our young woman put it as cheerfully as possible.
> "For me and Lady Bradeen." (26:261)

These are just bits and pieces from a sustained banter of confused gender and class roles that stretches across three chapters at the very end of the novella.[12]

Neither Mrs. Jordan nor the telegraphist has intended such confusions of gender and class, but they have been produced nonetheless by the new circumstances of work, communication, and social relations. One of the venerable biographical anecdotes about the contemporary reception of *In the Cage*, written in 1897, is Andre Raffalovich " 'once teasing' James to know what the Olympian young man in *In the Cage* had done wrong. He swore he did not know, he would rather not know."[13] Marc Andre Raffalovich (1864–1934) was, of course, the author of *L'Affaire d' Oscar Wilde* (1895) and, in 1896, of *Uranisme et Unisexualite* "in which he argued that homosexuality . . . and heterosexuality are two equally legitimate manifestations of human sexuality, rejected the current view that homosexuality was a disease, and advocated a life of chastity, supported by friendship, as the Christian ideal."[14]

In his extraordinarily careful and sensitive biographical account of James's "passionate friendships" with contemporaries such as Morton Fullerton, Howard Sturgis, and Hendrik Andersen, Fred Kaplan shows that what James most desired from male companions in his middle and later years was companionship. Without ignoring or diminishing James's capacity for sexual passion, however repressed or evaded, Kaplan understands that what James most desired was someone with whom he might talk, walk, bicycle, garden, and, perhaps above all, *work*. When Sturgis "made his first visit early in 1900," James "read to him each evening from his work-in-progress, *The Ambassadors*. Sturgis was at work on a new novel, the details of which he shared with his host, who urged him on."[15]

In the furthest reach of the melodrama of *In the Cage*, the telegraphist may forget her dreary life in fantasies of the passionate loves, diabolical murders, and coded messages of the rich and famous. In the sad realism of late-Victorian urban London, she is as trapped by her dead-end job as she will be by the hapless Mudge and the squall of children they will visit on the Malthusian nightmare of London. Mudge's chocolate creams will give way to silent screams.

But in the Jamesian text, the possibilities of the new workplace, the developing service industries, and the emancipatory potential of the new century begin to make a difference. To be sure, it is a difference of which the telegraphist herself is at best dimly aware, trapped as she must remain to the end in her stubborn insistence that no one understands her, that she is "different" from the other workers, especially those men whispering and insinuating as she tries to count the words and sell the stamps. Perhaps it is only possible for such "changes" in gender, class, and identity itself to be registered first in the textual space where a certain liberty has always been possible, where the constraints of convention, of consciousness, even of the "unconscious" need not be taken as final. Certainly, James found it safer to entertain the slippage of gender boundaries that he recognizes in *In the Cage* might accompany the changing social and economic boundaries of the new age, for better and worse. He himself identifies far more consciously with the telegraphist, even down to her trip to Bournemouth echoing his first trip to the southern coast of England that would become his home until the very last at Lamb House, Rye. Whether he knows or not how much he shares the anxieties of Lady Bradeen, Captain Everard, and the others once in "charge" of the symbolic discourse of culture is difficult to determine from the surface of a novella with such depths. Sounding those depths, we do find his own unconscious betrayed, not only regarding his ambivalences with regard to his own sexual preference, but also with regard to his own status as the Master, the figure who had devoted his life to "coded" texts, not so much to prevent detection as to encourage, even provoke it. In that, there is a great difference, all the difference, I would say, to distinguish James from less worthy authorities.

Notes

1. For example, Norrman Ralf, "The Intercepted Telegraph Plot in Henry James' 'In the Cage,' " *Notes and Queries* 24 (1977): 425–27; Dale Bauer and Andrew Lakritz, "Language, Class, and Sexuality in Henry James's *In the Cage,*" *New Orleans Review* 14, no. 3 (1987): 61–69; and Janet Gabler-Hover, "The Ethics of Determinism in Henry James's *In the Cage,*" *Henry James Review* 13, no. 3 (1992): 253–75.

2. The argument that James's feminine characters are sidetracked by forms of representation that approach but never quite attain genuine "art" is one I have developed, most recently in " 'Swept Away:' Henry James, Margaret Fuller, and 'The Last of the Valerii,' " in *Readers in History: Nineteenth-Century American Literature and the Contexts of Response,* ed. James L. Nachor (Baltimore: Johns Hopkins University Press, 1993), 32–53. The different thesis I pursue here is, I think, principally explained by way of James's own changing attitudes toward gender and sexuality in the late 1890s. It is also possible, of course, that the change reflects my own reconsiderations of James's attitudes toward gender.

3. Henry James, *In the Cage and Other Tales,* ed. Morton Dauwen Zabel (New York: W. W. Norton and Co., 1958), chap. 8, p. 177. Parenthetical references are to chapter and page of this edition.

4. Jennifer Wicke, "Henry James's Second Wave," *Henry James Review,* 10, no. 2 (1989): 150–51.

5. Bauer and Lakritz, "Language, Class, and Sexuality," 64.

6. Thus Ralf, "The Intercepted Telegraph Plot," p. 427, concludes that "perhaps Captain Everard did not deserve to be saved, penniless and deglorified as he turns out to be at the end," as if only the wealthy and glorious ought to be saved!

7. Judith Butler, "Gender Trouble, Feminist Theory, and Psychoanalytic Discourse," in *Feminism/Postmodernism,* ed. Linda J. Nicholson (New York: Routledge, 1990), 337.

8. John Rimmey, *Henry James and London: The City in His Fiction,* American University Studies, ser. 4, vol. 121 (New York: Peter Lang, 1991), 117.

9. Telegraph lines were first laid along the railroad lines, so that the first major system of telegraphy was developed in the 1840s and 1850s by the Great Western Railroad Company. Thus, communication and transportation workers had common cause for organization beyond the mere complementarity of the technologies.

10. William Veeder, "Toxic Mothers, Cultural Criticism: *In the Cage* and Elsewhere," reads the imagery and thematics of the maternal in *In the Cage* from a psychoanalytical perspective that leads to very different conclusions. Whereas I view the "maternal" as yet another subject-position capable of change and transformation in the newer social conditions associated with new technologies and new kinds of work, Veeder views the "maternal," espe-

cially in the character of the telegraphist's alcoholic mother, as the secret corruption in the early modern "waste land" of the narrative.

11. Eve Kosofsky Sedgwick, *Epistemology of the Closet* (Berkeley and Los Angeles: University of California Press, 1990), 210.

12. There are too many examples to reproduce in this essay, but the following is one of the best. When the telegraphist informs Mrs. Jordan she knows "one" of Lady Bradeen's set, Mrs. Jordan asks, "He's a gentleman?" The telegraphist answers, "Yes, he's not a lady" (25:257).

13. Zabel, introduction to *In the Cage and Other Tales*, 9; the anecdote was first told in Forrest Reid's *Private Road* (1940), then quoted in Simon Nowell-Smith's *The Legend of the Master* (1948).

14. David Hilliard, as quoted in Richard Dellamora, *Masculine Desire: The Sexual Politics of Victorian Aestheticism* (Chapel Hill: University of North Carolina Press, 1990), pp. 148–49.

15. Fred Kaplan, *Henry James. The Imagination of Genius* (New York: William Morrow and Co., 1992), 455.

"To Feel is Such a Career": Gender and Vocation in *The Tragic Muse*

MICHAEL L. J. WILSON

T*HE TRAGIC MUSE* BEGINS WITH A COMEDIC SET PIECE: AN ENGLISH family—"a mother, two daughters and a son" (HM 8)—abroad in Paris. Deftly drawn, these scenes seem to promise that the novel will take up one of the themes that had established Henry James's critical and popular reputation, the vagaries of cross-cultural méconnaissance. In describing the Dormer family as they visit the annual Salon at the *Palais de l'Industrie,* the narrator limns the variety within the phlegmatic English character. The mother, Lady Agnes, "would have been moved to gaiety only by some force more insidious than any she was likely to recognize in Paris" (HM 8). The son, Nick, by way of contrast, "was the sort of young Englishman who looks particularly well abroad" (HM 9). Mother and son aver differing reactions to the artwork they have just viewed, hinting at more profound differences of temperament:

> "There's a great deal being done here—a real vitality," Nicholas Dormer went on . . . "Some of these fellows go very far."
> "They do indeed!" said Lady Agnes. (HM 16)

Meanwhile, the older daughter, Grace, "not pretty," seeks the attention of her mother and is preoccupied with plans for luncheon. Together the two elder women worry about the possibility of arrival and approval of absent friends, Peter Sherringham and Julia Dallow.

The younger, "very pretty" daughter, Biddy, instead tries to engage Nick in discussion of art and of his own painting in particular. She accompanies him on a further tour of the exhibition, where they are surprised to encounter an old Oxford friend of Nick's, Gabriel Nash, accompanied by two "strange women." Nick is extravagantly attentive to Nash, and Biddy, while finding Nash "unlike any other gentleman she had ever seen" (HM 22), attempts to draw him out. Nash, though, will not be drawn, answering the polite questions of Victorian social intercourse with paradoxical pronouncements. Frustrated, Biddy blushingly asks, " 'Are you an aesthète?' " Nash replies, " 'I've no profession, my dear young lady. I've no état civil. . . . Merely to be is such a métier; to live is such an art; to feel is such a career!' " (HM 31). The luncheon that follows is not a success.

Only gradually does the reader discern that this gently satiric opening has initiated a quite different sort of narrative. Deliberately yet obliquely, the narrator has introduced the novel's major characters and plot lines. The initially unseen Peter and Julia are revealed to be cousins of the Dormers; Biddy nurses a small crush on Peter, a diplomat, and Nick is assumed to have a romantic interest in Peter's sister, Julia, a widow of means. The two women accompanying Nash are later identified as the Rooths; the younger is an aspiring actress, the "tragic muse" of the book's title, and the older is her mother and chaperon. The slight and seemingly trivial differences expressed by the characters' dialogue are also telling. They signal James's interest in representing the misunderstandings and misapprehensions that occur within a culture, within the family, between individuals. Moreover, Nash's lapidary evasions of Biddy's attempts to place him socially serve to announce the novel's central conflict: the tensions between one's being and one's vocation. While the novel ultimately neither affirms nor disavows Nash's assertion that "to feel is such a career," it explores in detail the possible relations between the states of "being" and "doing."

The Tragic Muse is perhaps the most critically neglected of James's novels. Readers at the time of the book's publication and since have found much to fault in its shambling, diffuse narrative, its oddly retrospective introduction of crucial plot developments, and its sudden and inconclusive ending. Even James himself, in his preface to the New York edition of *The Tragic Muse*, addresses the novel with the "special tenderness of charity" a parent feels for "the maimed or slighted, the disfigured or defeated the unlucky or unlikely child" (SM 1:vi). All too often, the novel is remembered in merely biographical terms, as the third commercial failure of the Middle Years, the prelude to James's even more disastrous career as a playwright.

Recently, however, scholars have begun to reconsider the interest and intricacy of *The Tragic Muse*. Peggy McCormack has shown the book to be quite carefully structured, its plot paral-

lels and doubled characters constructing an iron cage of economic exchange. Michael Anesko and Jonathan Freedman have
considered the novel's depictions of artists, aestheticism, and
the demands of the marketplace. Pierre Walker and Edwin Fussell have reinserted *The Tragic Muse* into the context of French
culture and society. William Macnaughton has even argued for
the literary superiority of the revised New York edition of *The
Tragic Muse* in an effort to give the text "its best chance of
being appreciated and enjoyed" (19). In joining the critical re-
valuation of *The Tragic Muse*, I concentrate on how the novel
explores the pervasive and often invidious articulation of gender norms in late-Victorian society. I am especially interested
here in how James deploys gender difference in his depiction of
two contemporary social issues invoked in *The Tragic Muse*'s
first scenes: the coercive power of social expectations and the
contentious uncertainty about the role of the artist in modern
society.

   At first glance, *The Tragic Muse* appears most interesting as
an exploration of the latter topos as a full-length recapitulation
of what James termed "the conflict between art and 'the
world' " (SM 1:v). Indeed, James often turned to this theme in
his short stories of the 1880s and 1890s, and recent analyses of
his tales about artists and writers reveal much about James's
attitudes toward creativity and sexual desire. *The Tragic Muse*
holds particular interest and promise for a gendered analysis of
James's fiction because both its main characters are—or might
be—artists. Tracing the history by which these two individuals,
Miriam and Nick, come into their artistry affords a rare opportunity to evaluate James's depiction of sexual difference.

   In addition, *The Tragic Muse* allows us to view the connections James understood to exist between the "public" problem
of vocation and the "private" vicissitudes of heterosexual relations. The plot lines for both main characters involve a halting
romance between a strong-willed, single-minded woman and
her uncertain, even passive male suitor. Miriam is the object of
intermittent interest from Peter. Nick is in the course of the
novel affianced to Julia, a woman whose consuming passion is
to become the wife of an influential politician. Surrounding
these characters are those others introduced in the novel's
opening pages, the Dormer family and Nash, all of whom are
working at cross-purposes in the development of Nick and Miriam's careers. James's novel appears to argue for an ideal of having one's feelings and one's career coincide—so that to live

would be such an art—but this is an ideal never achieved by any of the novel's characters.

The characters in *The Tragic Muse* are meant both to be rounded individuals according to the conventions of realist fiction and to be representative or exemplary types. Given James's ambition to portray a panorama of London life, "a mighty pictorial fusion" (SM 1:iv), the relatively small cast of characters must bear a heavy mimetic burden. James in his preface describes the novel's three principal figures (in his accounting: Nick, Miriam and Peter) as "my three typical examples . . . three general aspects" (SM 1:x, xiv). Nick, then, must stand in for the worlds of politics and painting, Miriam for that of the theater, Peter for diplomacy and *le gratin*. I stress this need for the characters to be in some sense typical in part because the novel itself is so centrally concerned with representation; as a number of critics have pointed out, *The Tragic Muse* is "virtually an inventory of aesthetic and political modes of representation, and their entanglement" (Seltzer 155).

I also stress this dimension of the novel because it suggests how Nick Dormer and Miriam Rooth come to embody the larger dilemmas of gender identity in late-nineteenth-century British culture. While their narratives of artistic self-discovery may appear to be quite particular, idiosyncratic, or even marginal instances, James's characters describe the contested terrain of late-Victorian gender ideology by their very efforts to negotiate it. That is, in their pursuit of art—"art, that is, as a human complication and a social stumbling block" (SM 1:v)—Miriam and Nick enact especially histrionic versions of contemporary gender troubles.

James is, in this regard, as often (unwittingly?) implicated in such troubles as he is the omniscient explicator of them. We might take as indicative of James's implication in his fiction the striking tensions within and between the formal devices organizing *The Tragic Muse*. The novel's narrative structure is, as McCormack has noted, chiasmic. The two central narratives trace opposite trajectories, with Miriam's rise to public acclaim intersecting Nick's steady withdrawal from public life at the text's midpoint (McCormack 35). The book's structure, then, can be cast as inverting the normative relation between the domestic and public spheres, disrupting gender ideology by banishing Nick to the "private" space of the atelier while thrusting Miriam more and more prominently into the world. At the same time, however, James's construction of the novel's narrative voice and point of view casts the meaning of this structural inversion into doubt. In a well-known passage from the preface, the writer describes how, in order to achieve "as near an approach to the dramatic as the novel may permit itself," he permitted his narrator access to Nick's and Peter's "consciousness" but none to Miriam's:

> [W]e have no direct exhibition of hers whatever . . . we get it all inferentially and inductively, seeing it only through a more or less bewildered interpretation of it by others. The emphasis is all on an absolutely objective Miriam. (SM 1:xv)

The result is that the reader knows of Miriam only what she says and does, only what others think of her speech and action. I will return to the implications of this "absolutely objective" depiction of Miriam, but here I would note only that it strips her of an inferiority comparable to that of the other characters. To invoke again Nash's distinctions, Miriam has a career but no feelings, doings but no apparent being. In other words, if the novel ends with Miriam having found her place before the public, the narration may be granting her possession only of an empty and debased realm, one valued much less highly than the introspective space of male ideation. *The Tragic Muse,* then, allows for no simple inscription or disruption of gender difference. Instead, James's text demonstrates how risky, mutable, and contingent the performance of gender may prove.

While *The Tragic Muse* is named for Miriam Rooth, the narrative begins and ends with—and is dominated by—the situation of Nick Dormer. Nick might easily be identified as what Kelly Cannon has termed the typical Jamesian hero, a "man at the margins." Cannon argues that James, writing out of his own sense of social marginalization, created a gallery of male characters who are "engaged in a war of fictions between society and self" (Cannon 41). These "displaced" male characters find themselves at odds with the dominant mode of masculinity for their class, one that emphasizes worldly success, social and physical aggression, and active heterosexuality. Nick, while corresponding to certain aspects of Cannon's general model, creates problems for it. Crucially, Nick spends much of *The Tragic Muse* not displaced from but occupying several central spaces of masculine authority as a politician, a fiancé, and a de facto patriarch. As Lady Agnes declares, Nick's career has been in many ways a model of masculine accomplishment:

> "No young man ever had a finer training, and he gave, from the first, repeated proof of having the highest sort of ability, the highest sort of ambition. Look how he got in everywhere." (HM 462)

Nick's ambivalence about his role as a public figure and as the head of his family eventually leads to a voluntary withdrawal to a more marginal position but never to a renunciation of male privilege. James so extensively dramatizes Nick's relation to the demands of masculinity—in Paris the young man realizes that "he had at last come to a crisis" (HM 21)—that it takes the form of a crisis in masculinity itself.

The novel establishes this sense of crisis in masculinity through a number of related means. First, the characters regularly quibble about whether male characters are or could be considered to be "gentlemen." In addition to Nick's own problematic status, the novel subjects to scrutiny Gabriel Nash (HM 22, 26, 80), Basil Dashwood, an actor from a respectable family (HM 131, 254), and even Peter Sherringham (HM 157, 254, 322, 478). Such attention to the putative status of the "gentleman" may at first appear to be an anachronism, a fusty peculiarity of James's own background, or the lingering remnant of what Robin Gilmour has identified as a central theme of mid-Victorian fiction. However, this constant reference to the "gentleman" points through sheer repetition to the hollowness or blankness of the term itself, as well as to its lack of currency and referent. In the social milieu depicted in the novel, where social and cultural capital are rarely aligned, Nick seems particularly sensitive to the archaic injunction to be a gentleman: while he has social status and social obligations, he lacks the financial wherewithal, not to mention the desire, to play the role fully.

The novel itself contains no male figures who might unambiguously serve Nick (or the reader) as the model for what a gentleman should be. The elder generation of men is strikingly absent. Peter and Julia are, seemingly, without parents. Nick's father, Lord Nicholas, is deceased, his memory carefully tended and strategically invoked by Lady Agnes. Nick's principal benefactor is the elderly bachelor Charles Carteret, a friend and confidant of Lord Nicholas. Nick feels a duty and some affection towards Carteret but is struck by his antiquated vocabulary of "old-fashioned political phrases"; he wonders how Carteret's lifetime of experiences "had never provoked him to any general reflection" (HM 231). Nick feels he must nonetheless attend to Carteret—even as the older man makes his financial support dependent on Nick's marrying Julia and following his political aspirations. When faced with Nick's artistic ambitions, Carteret declares, " 'The pencil—the brush? They're not the weapons of a gentleman' " (HM 418). For Nick, such advice is as relevant as Carteret's "production of anecdote in regard to the formation of early ministries" (HM 228).

In Nick's own generation, he has few examples to which to turn. As heir, his elder brother, Percy, should be shouldering the family responsibilities but has instead left Lady Agnes and his sisters in Nick's care. Percy indulges in hunting, "roaming about the world taking shots" (HM 69), an activity treated by the narrator and the Dormers less as the marker of traditional masculine valor than as a childish diversion. Certainly Gabriel Nash, the artist who works "in life," can only be seen as an inversion of traditional gentlemanly virtues. His own characterization of his life marks it as irregular: " 'I drift, I float . . . my feelings direct me—if such a life as mine may be said to have a direction' " (HM 26). Nash's valuation of being over doing and his theatrical effeminacy—he is variously described as "odd," a "solitary blossom" and a "strange creature"—are seen by the other characters as drawing Nick away from his "manly" duties. The only other figure against whom Nick might measure himself is Peter, with whom Nick has a sort of sibling rivalry. Close as children, over the years "[s]eparation and diversity had made them strange enough to each other to give a taste to what they shared; they were friends without being particular friends" (HM 73). Over the course of the novel, Nick has many opportunities to observe how Peter, though the elder in years, is the more constrained by and blind to his own situation. Nick's characterization of the diplomatic mind when teasing Peter— " 'Dry, narrow, barren, poor . . . wanting in imagination, in generosity, in the finest perceptions and the highest courage' " (HM 73)—is shown by the novel's close to be much too accurate a portrait. In particular, Peter's pursuit of Miriam reveals to Nick how unconnected Peter's professional life is from either his intellectual interests or his desires.

The lack of viable models does not, though, signal a lack of expectation of "masculine" behavior. Indeed, the admonish-

ment to appropriate masculine behavior comes most often in
The Tragic Muse from women. Nick's mother is one of the
principal articulators of Nick's duty, which consists of public
service, marriage, and care for his immediate family: " 'Everything's dreary but what you can do for us' " (HM 197). In taking
up this duty, Nick would be following the example of his father,
fulfilling a promise made to the patriarch on his deathbed. This
last meeting of father and son Lady Agnes imagines to have
been "a solemn communication of ideas on the highest national
questions" (HM 72), and she frames any deviation from such a
destiny as a breech of the social and moral order:

> "Together [with Julia Dallow] there is nothing you couldn't do. You
> can have the first house in England—yes, the first! . . . That's the
> crime—to throw away such an instrument of power, such a blessed
> instrument of good." (HM 195)

Julia urges Nick along the same path, both as a way of assuring his political inheritance and as a means to fulfilling her own
aspirations. As the narrator notes:

> The cause of her interest in him was partly the vision of his helping
> her to the particular emotion she did desire—the emotion of great
> affairs and public action. To have such ambitions for him appeared
> to her the greatest honor she could do him. (HM 119)

The marriage of Julia and Nick promises to combine their fortunes, in both senses of the word. Marriage, though, would
place Nick in a position of unwanted dependence on Julia. He
bristles when, after Julia has financed and insured his electoral
victory in the aptly named borough of Harsh, his mother suggests he is "Julia's" member (HM 191). The action of *The Tragic
Muse* suggests that the responsibilities attendant upon masculinity are largely insisted upon, shored up, and regulated by
women. Traditional upper-class institutions no longer comprise
a realm of self-definition and self-assertion for men but their
very opposite. As Nick explains to Julia, " 'Innumerable vows
and pledges repose upon my head. I'm inextricably committed
and dedicated' " (HM 346). Thus, it is not a surprise that in discussing his dissatisfactions Nick invokes with great frequency
the constraints placed on his "freedom" by his position in the
world (HM 194). The response of Percy Dormer and Gabriel
Nash to the constraints of such responsibilities has been to

evade them entirely by escaping into an "ungracefully selfish" (HM 70) refusal of both productivity and domesticity.

In a turn of the plot meant less to be ironic than fitting, then, Nick realizes he can no longer enact this sanctioned form of masculinity at the very moment of his greatest worldly success: when he has been elected to Parliament and Julia has agreed to their engagement. Both "achievements," though the political more strongly than the affectionate, represent for Nick less a demonstration of his mastery than of his being mastered: "[I]t appeared to him that he had done something worse than not choose—he had let others choose for him" (HM 206). At the root of Nick's distress is the "secret" he confided to Nash in Paris and to his mother at his moment of political triumph, his "double nature":

> "The difficulty is that I'm two men; it's the strangest thing that ever was. . . . I'm two quite distinct human beings, who have scarcely a thing in common; not even the memory, on the part of one, of the achievement or the adventures of the other." (HM 192)

The feeling of leading a double life is accentuated rather than ameliorated by his recent successes: " 'One man wins the seat—but it's the other fellow who sits in it' " (HM 192). Nick's image of himself as two men is seconded by the narrator, who explains Nick's facility at campaigning—"He rose to it as he had risen to matches at school"—as rising from his belief that his activity "was not really action at all, but only a pusillanimous imitation of it" (HM 205). This sense of traditional masculinity as a performance that Nick can no longer bring off becomes even more prominent as he tries to explain his sentiments to Julia:

> "I've imperilled my mortal soul, or at least I've bemuddled my intelligence, by all the things I don't care for that I've tried to be, and all the things I never can be that I've tried to look as if I were—all the appearances and imitations, the pretenses and hypocrisies in which I've steeped myself to the eyes; and at the end of it (it serves me right!) my reward is simply to learn that I'm still not half humbug enough!" (HM 296)

With Nick's increasingly hysterical confessions of his double nature, James introduces a crucial and immediately recognizable thematic of the fin de siècle crisis of masculinity, the double life. Though not as lurid a characterization of the double life as those found in Robert Louis Stevenson's *Dr. Jekyll and Mr. Hyde* or Oscar Wilde's *The Picture of Dorian Gray* (only two texts in a longer genealogy to which *The Tragic Muse* belongs), James's text does depict Nick's divided nature as posing a danger. Unlike Peter's "passion" for the theater (HM 66), Nick's other life cannot be contained or subordinated. Nick cannot bring himself to regard painting as what both Lady Agnes and Julia suggest it might be: merely a respectable recreation, "a little distraction" (HM 19). The threat of Nick's desires to disrupt orderly social relations is personified (both to the other characters and to Nick himself) by his "funny friend," Nash (HM 65), who is seen to draw Nick deeper into an irregular bachelorhood. I have described elsewhere how Nash's encouragement of Nick's painterly ambitions takes the form of a shared sexual secret (M. L. J. Wilson 262). Here I would rather stress how Nash represents the specter of Nick's abdication of traditional masculine behavior, how he functions as a counterweight to the burden of expectation Nick feels himself to bear: "[Nash] was to have dragged him in the opposite sense from Mrs. Dallow . . . he was to have saved him" (HM 304).

Indeed, Nash to some extent stages the pivotal moment in Nick's internal conflict by arranging for Nick to paint Miriam's portrait. When Julia arrives unexpectedly at Nick's studio during one of the sittings, she feels she must flee from the scene and its revelation of Nick's true nature: " 'That's your innermost preference, that's your secret passion' " (HM 342). Though Nick maintains that their differences are not insurmountable, Julia insists that her knowledge of "the only thing you want" creates a fundamental breach in their relationship:

"I hate art, as you call it. I thought I did, I knew I did; but till this morning I didn't know how much. . . . You're an artist: you are, you are! . . . Oh, I've suspected you! I had my ideas. It's all right for you, but it won't do for me: I'm different altogether." (HM 343–44)

Julia refuses to enter into a marriage of such extreme incompatibility, one in which " 'there are sacrifices for both of us, and I can't make them either. . . . Why should it always be put on me . . .' " (HM 344). Julia's recognition of "the ugly truth" forces Nick finally to face "the infinite possibilities of disappointment and distress" (HM 347) he might cause, and he renounces the social roles that have heretofore prescribed his actions. His engagement broken, he resigns his seat in Parliament. Then, in an uncanny repetition of his deathbed conversation with his father, Nick informs Mr. Carteret of both decisions, thereby losing his bequest.

The first half of *The Tragic Muse* reflects Nick's point of view by casting his struggle to define his vocation in melodramatic terms. Describing to Nash the " 'fight I shall have to make' " in order to become a painter, Nick lists the forces arrayed against him:

> "[E]verything, every one that belongs to me, that touches me, near or far: my family, my blood, my heredity, my traditions, my promises, my circumstances, my prejudices; my little past, such as it is; my great future, such as it has been supposed it may be." (HM 144)

In this account, Nick must take on his own conscience, his family, and the disapprobation of society in order to realize his private ambitions. We may recall Lady Agnes's evocation of Nick's potential for "crime" and his self-characterization as " 'a freak of nature and a sport of the mocking gods' " (HM 144). However, once Nick has made his decision to devote himself to art—once he has undertaken what Peter terms "the exercise of a virile freedom"— the meaning and consequence of this act become much less clear. Visiting his cousins, Peter discovers that their response "was not quite what Nick . . . had represented it." The view expressed most forcefully by Mr. Carteret, that an artist is not a gentleman, is regarded as "old-fashioned" (HM 461). Peter does find Lady Agnes, who Nick feared would be killed by his aesthetic ambitions (HM 146), visibly aged. Her distress, though, seems focused less on Nick's new career than on the loss of the possibilities promised by the old one:

> It was not what he had taken up but what he had put down that made the sorry difference, and the tragedy would have been equally great if he had become a wine-merchant or a horse-dealer. (HM 461)

Nick seems, then, to have abandoned not masculinity per se but certain perquisites of men of his class that were of benefit to his female relations. Indeed, the response of Lady Agnes and Grace to these changed circumstances is to focus on securing their own futures by marrying Biddy off to Peter:

> What that appeal would have been had it been uttered was: "Oh Peter, take little Biddy; oh, my dear young friend, understand your interests at the same time you understand mine; be kind and rea-

sonable and clever; save me all further anxiety and tribulation and accept my lovely, faultless child from my hands." (HM 466)

The aftermath of Nick's "apostasy" (HM 146) reveals that he needn't have feared social condemnation, since his position as a member of his class remains unchanged. Nor should he have feared neglecting his personal obligations, for it turns out that Julia need not marry him and his family need not depend on him for their support. Instead, the novel suggests that the masculinity Nick felt pressured to "take up" is an imposture, the product of "innumerable private calculations" (HM 460) by women of their self-interest. *The Tragic Muse,* then, appears to reinscribe a formulation central to James's narratives about artists and writers, a belief in the necessary, irreconcilable opposition between the needs of creative men and those of demanding, draining women.

But if in the course of the novel the ideals of traditional masculinity that Nick has inherited are revealed to be a "humbug," one he is heroic to reject, James remains fundamentally unclear about what more genuine form of masculine identity should take their place. As James admits in his preface, Nick's "repudiation" appears in retrospect "to resemble a surrender for absolutely nothing" (SM 1:viii). Making Nick's recognition of his vocation not the book's denouement but its midpoint undermines any easy opposition of "art" and "the world." Prior to his decision, Nick could cast his secret aspiration as a higher calling than electoral politics:

> The cleanness and quietness of it, the independent effort to do something, to leave something which shall give joy to man long after the howling [of politics] has died away to the last ghost of an echo. (HM 311–12)

In the latter half of *The Tragic Muse,* though, Nick must make good on these vague promises. He must discover what he might make of his talent, and this plot line admits of much less social drama than his initial struggle. The narrator is at pains to acknowledge the sensation of anticlimax accompanying so internalized a conflict, even for Nick himself:

> [T]here was an inevitable strong emotion in renouncing, in the face of considerable opposition, one sort of responsibility for another sort. That made life not perhaps necessarily joyous, but decidedly thrilling, for the hour; and it was all very well till the thrill abated.

When this occurred, as it inevitably would, the romance and the poetry of the thing would be exchanged for the flatness and the prose. (HM 486)

In the novel's second half, then, James explores the "disappointments and distress" of male freedom. Nick, his fight with "the world" won, now plays out the conflict between "art" and "the artist," attempting to realize ideals of artistic practice that may themselves elude representation.

That Nick has talent is taken as established fact; his abilities are repeatedly attested to by Nash, Biddy, Peter, even Julia and Lady Agnes. Only Grace demurs (HM 425, 462). Nick, though, recognizes his skillfulness as a limitation: "[N]ature had cursed him with an odious facility. . . . He had a talent for appearance, and that was the fatal thing" (HM 564). The ability to dissimulate and mislead by means of representation, which had been so central to his impersonation of a rising young politician, Nick now locates in his painting. He feels he must struggle to renounce its presence here, too:

He stood ready now to wring the neck of the irrepressible vice which certainly would like nothing better than to get him further into trouble. His only real justification would be to turn patience (his own, of course) inside out; yet if there should be a way to misread that recipe his humbugging genius could be trusted infallibly to discover it. (HM 564)

Nick's awareness of his "dual nature" reappears here as the knowledge that, without vigilance, his talent will be undone by his skill. Only by continual self-scrutiny, turning his own patience "inside out," can genuine achievement be won. Nick's doubts are thus recast as the recognizably masculine virtue of self-discipline. Unwilling to govern either the state or his family, Nick is shown to engage in an agonistic devotion to aesthetic ideals.

Nick's vision of the life of the artist is most clear before he takes it up. Nick proclaims, when announcing his decision to pursue art to Mr. Carteret, " 'I think the noble life is doing one's work well' " (HM 419). The standards by which such noble achievement might be judged, though, Nick finds difficult to articulate fully. The art of the past is not a trustworthy guide. During one visit to the National Gallery, Nick "recoil[s]" from the Old Masters on view, "so inadequately" do they represent "the idea that won the race" (HM 488). On a later visit, however,

"the perfection of their survival struck him as the supreme eloquence, the reason that included all others, thanks to the language of art, the richest and most universal" (HM 581). Even if
the achievement of the past could be agreed upon, Nick is set
"on working in the modern," to which this artistic patrimony
cannot speak (HM 580). Similarly, the aesthetic judgments of
contemporaries do not weight heavily; in this as in other matters he would "cultivate independence" (HM 430). His work,
Nick declares, " 'has hitherto been horrible rot' " (HM 496), and
he grows angry with those who find his portraits "clever" (HM
563). In his "own battle," in his "lonely" studio, he discerns
what others cannot, the inadequacy of his efforts:

> His late beginning was there, and his wasted youth, the mistakes
> that would still bring forth children after their image, the sedentary
> solitude, the clumsy obscurity, the poor explanations, the foolish-
> ness that he foresaw in having to ask people to wait, and wait
> longer, and wait again, for a fruition which, to their sense at least
> would be an anti-climax. (HM 580)

Confronted by his own distance from "the idea," and by how
little others can discern that distance, Nick must ground his
identity in the practice of painting itself. He tells Peter, " 'I
must just peg away here and not mind' " (HM 497) and confesses to Miriam, " 'I see before me an eternity of grinding' "
(HM 582). In the absence of external rewards—status, power,
money, approbation—Nick is now sustained by "a passion of
work fairly humming in his ears" (HM 574), by "the sense that
it was to the thing in itself he was attached" (HM 580).

As a consequence, Nick's process of masculine self-creation
takes place increasingly in isolation from the other characters.
He finds himself "shut up in his little temple with his altar and
his divinity . . . blissfully alone" (HM 514). Even Nash, the
"queer comrade" (HM 49) whose earlier role as confidant might
be expected to continue if not grow, now seems to Nick unnec-
essary:

> He had felt a good deal, before, as if he were in Nash's hands; but
> now that he had made his final choice he seemed to himself to be
> altogether in his own. Gabriel was wonderful, but no Gabriel could
> assist him much henceforth. (HM 432)

Nash does agree to sit for his portrait; but this causes a dis-
comforting shift in relations between the two friends and, be-

fore the painting has been completed, Nash vanishes " 'without a trace,' like a personage in a fairy-tale or a melodrama" (HM 597). Nick's sociability thereafter is largely confined to Paris, where he has "three or four professional friends (he had more of these there than in London)" (HM 600).

Nick thus comes to enact what James Eli Adams has called "virtuoso asceticism," a self-conscious renunciation of social status in favor of aesthetic ideals, of social obligation in favor of autonomy, of social bonds in favor of self-regulation. Adams has shown how, for a wide range of male Victorian writers, such "an elaborately articulated program of self-discipline" served to affirm and valorize the masculinity of intellectual labor (Adams 2). James in *The Tragic Muse* joins in this larger effort to reinvest the intellectual and creative professions with "manly" power and consequence, but he is unable to imagine this refashioned masculinity as without its own limitations and flaws. By the book's close, Nick's "ascetic regimen" has produced only equivocal results. The narrative of the painter's self-discovery is figured in later chapters of the novel less as a triumph than an impasse. Nick's artistic career cannot be termed a success, either in terms of public recognition or his own elusive criteria. The bonds with his family have been loosened but not broken, and his marriage to Julia remains a possibility. The welter of emotions and impulses animating Nick's behavior in the first half of the book has been, if not evacuated, then at least displaced: it is, after all, Nick's portrait of Julia that has attracted "general attention" in a recent exhibition (HM 618). Nick has had to confront his feelings in order to choose the "right" career for himself, but his vocation requires that his strongest attachments be to an inchoate ideal.

The complex relations between gender and vocation in *The Tragic Muse* can be put into sharper relief if we compare James's "political case" with his "theatric case," Miriam Rooth. The tale of Miriam's pursuit of a career on the stage is narrated in counterpoint to Nick's abandonment of politics for painting, but James's employment of the two stories forestalls any simple accounting. Nick and Miriam are never precisely each other's double, nor are they each other's opposite; their situations are never entirely commensurate. James seem to suggest by this that the fine arts are themselves as different as men and women; simultaneously, he suggests that art binds all those who practice it into a separate and distinct "tribe" (HM 163). Any comparison of these two artists must begin with the observation that both Nick and Miriam pursue vocations that require at once a renunciation of gender norms and an emphatic reinscription of gender identity. This seemingly paradoxical project, though, takes quite different forms. As *The Tragic Muse* shows, Nick's path of virtuoso asceticism is simply not open to "the artist who happened to have been born a woman" (HM 184). James's text outlines how gender constrains artistic aspirations in the most fundamental way: Nick must disavow his expected career to discover his vocation while Miriam's struggle throughout the novel is simply to be able to enter a profession.

Miriam herself offers a clear if lighthearted accounting of her position in the social world depicted by *The Tragic Muse*: " 'Oh, I'm an inferior creature, of an inferior sex, and I have to earn my bread as I can' " (HM 451). Her need to support herself economically in a society convinced of her "inferiority" makes Miriam emblematic of the larger nineteenth-century movement of women into the professions and into public life more generally. That is, if Nick can be seen to exemplify the late-Victorian crisis of masculinity, Miriam serves to represent one of the many sources of that crisis, the growing demand of (mostly privileged) women for autonomy and equality. In her situation as an intelligent woman confronting the strictures of a patriarchal society, Miriam is also typical of James's heroines. James often posed the "Woman Question" through his female characters, most commonly by depicting "a young woman struggling tenaciously to avoid entrapment by a marriage market economy" (McCormack 31). Miriam affords James an occasion for a more contentious portrait of the social position of women, for he couples Miriam's attempts to realize her artistic ambitions with the more conventional dramatic conflict between career and marriage.

Miriam is the only female character in *The Tragic Muse* to face this choice between matrimony and vocation. Her mother, Mrs. Rooth, had turned to a brief, "precarious traffic" in old pottery only when widowed and pursued it "to indifferent account" (HM 53). She wishes her daughter to be either a "great actress or a great lady" (HM 480). Lady Agnes is a more formidable figure: a "high, executive woman, the mother of children, the daughter of earls, the consort of an official, the dispenser of hospitality" (HM 34–35). As this description suggests, though "made for public life" (HM 195), Lady Agnes has used her skills in support of the political ambitions of her husband and later her son. Her aspiration for her daughters consists of their making "good" marriages, and she becomes engrossed in "the fidgety effort to work them off" (HM 574). In the absence of such suitable alliances, she can imagine their future only as disastrous and disreputable: "three dismal women in a filthy house" (HM 197).

The women of Miriam's generation are even more ambitious while still conceiving their futures in relation to marriage. Biddy Dormer studies sculpture and despairs that " 'men want women not to be anything' " (HM 509). Nick sees her pursuit of art as leading "in the direction of enlightened spinsterhood" (HM 601), but Biddy has already confessed to Peter that she would give up her career "in a moment" for "a good man" (HM 371). The most striking limitations on public ambitions are those seen to affect Julia Dallow. Her brother, Peter, fails to recognize that Julia has any "interests and consolations" in the larger world; he regards her political aspirations "as scarcely more a personal part of her than the livery of her servants or the jewels George Dallow's money had bought" (HM 350–51). Nick forms a more accurate impression of Julia's interests and capabilities. He reflects that "[s]he *was*, indeed, active politics" (HM 206) and he insists to her, " 'You're a prime minister yourself' " (HM 346). Still, Nick can only imagine that Julia's highest calling is "to be at the head of a political salon" (HM 88). Julia herself desires a future as the wife of a prominent politician. She is aware that her alliance with Nick appeals to her because it allows her to have ambitions for him (HM 119), and she breaks off the relationship when it threatens to recapitulate the disappointments of her first marriage: "her late husband's flat, inglorious taste for pretty things, his indifference to every chance to play a public part" (HM 344). Through these supporting characters, James reveals the pervasive restrictions gender norms and social expectations impose upon women of varying ambitions and temperaments. Moreover, he captures how these expectations—especially belief in marriage as the principal vehicle for female aspiration—are internalized and maintained by women.

If Miriam is allowed to contest the "marriage market economy," it is in large part because of her obscure social origins. Not only does she lack the social status of the Dormers and Sherringhams, but insofar as her standing can be determined, it is transgressive of the boundaries of class and nationality. Miriam is the product of a "mixed" marriage. Her deceased father was a German Jewish stockbroker and "dealer in curiosities" (HM 54). Her mother was Miss Neville-Nugent, purportedly of Castle Nugent, "a domain of immeasurable extent and almost inconceivable splendor, but . . . [not] to be found in any prosaic earthly geography" (HM 54). After the death of her father, Miriam and Mrs. Rooth wandered the continent, "scraping and starving" (HM 323), living in genteel poverty. As a result, Miriam knows four languages, but her English is full of "little queerness and impurities" (HM 161). Her lack of stable identity can be seen in the multiple stage names she has given herself: Maud Vavasour, Edith Temple, Gladys Vane (HM 50). Even Miriam's dramatic training has been polyglot; she studies with Mrs. Delamere, Signor Ruggieri, and then Madame Carré. Miriam's hybridity is evoked as well by the title Peter gives to her, "The Tragic Muse," an appellation earlier bestowed on the acclaimed actresses Rachel Félix and Sarah Siddons. The social distance between Miriam and the other female characters is much remarked upon and is not successfully bridged by Mrs. Rooth's continued assertion the she and her daughter are "very, very respectable" (HM 99). There could be no "normal" social intercourse between Miriam and the Misses Dormer or Julia Dallow—even were she not an actress. Yet Miriam's indeterminate status affords her the freedom of action Nick so desired because there is for her so little at stake socially. Arrayed against her theatrical ambitions is not the organized opposition of those closest to her but the more diffuse and impersonal resistance of economic forces and societal indifference.

Miriam is also afforded greater latitude than the other female characters because she has chosen to enter the theater, a decision that amplifies her "queerness." When, shortly after seeing her perform for the first time, Peter tells Miriam she is a "strange girl," she immediately responds,

> "Je crois bien! Doesn't one have to be, to want to go and exhibit one's self to a loathsome crowd, on a platform, with trumpets and a big drum, for money—to parade one's body and one's soul?" (HM 130)

This passage reminds us that, as a recognizable female profession, performing became a privileged symbol in Victorian debates over the place of women in public. In particular,

nineteenth-century writers were taken by the figure of the actress and saw in her a symbol of the Woman Question, because
of her paradoxical relation to prevailing gender norms:

> [W]hile embodying the ideals of feminine beauty and setting the
> standards for female fashion, they were "defeminized" by the very
> act of taking up a public career in the theatre. The same women
> who impersonated Dianas and Vestias also claimed a place in the
> competitive co-sexual world of work, spent their evening away from
> home, and exhibited themselves before the public gaze. (Davis 105)

This is particularly true in the final decades of the century, a
period of growth and recognition for the theatrical industry as
a whole but also an epoch in which, as Tracy C. Davis has shown,
the participation of women, particularly middle- and upper-
class women, expanded significantly. Moreover, the Victorian
public had a seemingly "voracious appetite" for information
about actresses, which was fed by a proliferation of journalistic
accounts, biographies and autobiographies, and novels about actresses' lives (Davis 71–78). James was quite well aware of bur-
geoning interest in and discourse about women in the theater.
He makes passing reference in his preface to Robert Louis Stevenson's view of the "histrionic temperament" as a low and vulgar topic (HM 1:xvi); but, as Gregory Pfitzer has illustrated,
these remarks serve to mask how James in writing *The Tragic
Muse* had been influenced by his acquaintance both with prominent actresses and with women writers, such as Mary Ward,
who had already treated the topic in their novels. Indeed, much
of the drama and interest of Miriam's story arises from the
manner in which James plays out a quite familiar theme: "The
private history of the public woman" (Letters 59).

The most prominent device James employs to complicate his
"theatric case" is his refusal to "go behind" Miriam (SM 1:xvi).
The effect is to cast Miriam as a spectacle, the object of the
other characters' (as well as the reader's) gazes and specula-
tions. Miriam is, in the early chapters of the novel, a puzzle that
those who observe her try to answer: Biddy, seeing her at the
Salon, wonders about her identity; Nick, Peter and Nash,
brought together to witness her audition with an older actress,
Madame Carré, wonder about Miriam's social origins and, more
crucially, whether she has talent. The latter question proves the
most unanswerable to the male spectators and becomes,
through James's withholding of Miriam's consciousness, the

motor for the theatrical plot line in much of *The Tragic Muse*.
Miriam's first two performances—the audition for Madame
Carré and a recital under Peter's aegis at an embassy tea—
testify to her ability to evoke responses in her audience but in
no way clarify whether she has a vocation.

Nash has arranged for Miriam's appearance before the distinguished French actress in order to discourage the "[d]eluded,
misguided, infatuated" Rooths (HM 45) from their theatrical
ambitions for Miriam. Mrs. Rooth makes clear to the assembled
spectators that "[s]o much depends" on Miriam's success, that
a career on the stage is necessary for Miriam to "escape" becoming a governess (HM 93, 96). Miriam is at first reduced to
tears by her anxiety and then, prompted by her mother, delivers
an inadequate performance. All assembled agree that she is
handsome, has *un beau* regard, and a strong voice—that she
looks the part—but differ in their responses to her acting. The
recitation works "violently . . . on the nerves of Mr. Gabriel
Nash" (HM 105), and Madame Carré decides that Miriam has
"[n]othing that I can see" (HM 107). Nick, though, is moved to
imagine her as the subject of a portrait, while Peter's response
is equivocal:

At the same time that Sherringham pronounced privately that the
manner in which Miss Rooth had acquitted herself offered no element of interest, he remained conscious that something sur-
mounted and survived her failure, something that would perhaps
be worth taking hold of. (HM 105)

Her performance the following afternoon, before a largely female audience, only intensifies these initial reactions. Biddy
and "the company in general thought her very clever and successful," but Peter imagines that Madame Carré "would have
deemed the exhibition, with its badness, its assurance, the absence of criticism, almost indecent" (HM 115, 114). In response,
though, to Julia's declaration that Miriam is " 'like a cow who
has kicked over the milking pail,' " Peter avers, " 'She's interesting. . . . And she's awful!' " (HM 117). The indeterminacy of
Miriam's character is, in fact, the source for Peter of her attraction:

Her mixture, as it spread itself before one, was a quickening spectacle: she was intelligent and clumsy—she was unbred and fine. (HM
128)

Miriam exhibits, then, a particular sort of femininity, at once characterized by lack (of restraint, decorum, judgment) and by excess (of emotion, physicality, confidence). Her early self-displays are manifestations of her vulgar and suspect origins, but they may also, Peter suspects, be "a sign that she really possessed the celebrated artistic temperament" (HM 129). Miriam herself is indifferent to such evaluations, revealing in these scenes only the fierceness of her ambition: " 'I will succeed—I will be great' " (HM 127).

Peter agrees to sponsor Miriam's theatrical training, to make her "his young pupil" (HM 148), in part because it would allow him to "take hold" of her, since "she was the instrument . . . that had come to his hand" (HM 180). The importance of Peter to Miriam's pursuit of an artistic career indicates only the first of several ways in which her mastery of her vocation differs from Nick's; rather than an assertion of independence, Miriam's artistic practice requires her dependence on others. She must also acquire precisely what Nick feels he must lose in his efforts to achieve success, a facility for appearances. Miriam's education will demand the same strenuous and persistent effort as Nick's; Madame Carré admonishes her that she must " 'Work—work—work!' " (HM 108). However, that effort will be undertaken largely in public, not in the solitude of the studio, and is best judged by the responses of a discerning audience, not Miriam herself. Moreover, her medium is her own body, "showing one's self" (HM 126). Miriam's aesthetic struggles thus appear to be more immediately physical and practical rather than psychological and social. All these comparisons suggest that James portrays acting as closely related to conventional female gender norms. Indeed, Peter tells Biddy,

"It's as the actress that the woman produces the most complete and satisfactory artistic results . . . [although] there's another art in which she's not bad . . . being charming and good and indispensable to man." (HM 509)

If beauty, charm and virtue are the ideals of femininity held by men of the higher social classes, Miriam's task is to learn to produce and reproduce these qualities convincingly on the stage. Peter, as Miriam's sponsor, puts the matter to her succinctly: " 'I would rather you acted like an Englishwoman, if an Englishwoman would only act' " (HM 162).

Hence the centrality to Miriam's training in imitation and increased control over bodily effects. The performance of Juliet she gives at the embassy tea, which "frightened . . . flushed and absorbed" the audience, was given "according the system of . . . Signor Ruggieri" (HM 115, 114). This system must give way to that of Madame Carré. The older actress herself was often a "religious imitation" of her own "rare predecessor" and her physiognomy is evidence of the effectiveness of somatic mastery: "a thing infinitely worn and used, drawn and stretched to excess, with its elasticity overdone and its springs relaxed, yet religiously preserved and kept in repair, like a valuable old time-piece" (HM 94). Madame Carré's tutelage consists of reciting while Miriam observes, " 'gaping at me with her big eyes' " (HM 149). Miriam then rehearses the same texts:

> What she mainly did was to reproduce with a crude fidelity, but with extraordinary memory, the intonations, the personal quavers and cadences of her model . . . with close, rude, audacious mimicry. (HM 153)

While she continues to enact this "gross parody of the lady's intentions" (HM 180), Miriam is also tutored by Peter in the canons of European high culture: he takes her to performances of the Comédie-Française, to visit the Louvre, and assigns her books to read (although she initially does not).

The advances in Miriam's skill occur, as it were, off-stage and are discerned by the other characters through the disappearance of the "low" and "vulgar" aspects of her earlier performances. For Peter, observing Miriam reciting after a long absence, "she seemed now like the finished statue lifted from the ground to its pedestal" (HM 261). Later in London, Nick finds Miriam "exempt from the curious clumsiness" of their previous meetings: "Miriam Rooth was light and bright and straight today—straight without being stiff and bright without being garish" (HM 316). Onstage the transformation is even greater. Nick views her performance as the embodiment of the highest aesthetic principles: "She was beauty, she was music, she was truth" (HM 531).

Peter is more aware of Miriam's ability to produce a dazzling effect in her spectators:

> He saw things as a shining confusion, and yet somehow something monstrously definite kept surging out of them. Miriam was a beautiful, actual, fictive, impossible young woman, of a past age and

undiscoverable country who spoke in blank verse and overflowed with metaphor, who was exalted and heroic beyond all human convenience, and who yet was irresistibly real and related to one's own affairs. (HM 534)

All these responses invoke Miriam's transcendence of her social identity, her crafting of a display of femininity beyond that which she could "naturally" claim. By the close of *The Tragic Muse*, Miriam can make of herself an "exquisite image" powerful enough to mark "an era in contemporary art" (HM 610).

Miriam's triumph is clearly figured as a female masquerade, the assumption of a culturally sanctioned femininity to conceal an originary lack. James's decision not to render Miriam's consciousness directly concentrates the reader's attention on the other characters' apprehension of Miriam's laboriously acquired surface luster. Miriam as the Tragic Muse is, in both senses, acting like a woman—at once exceptional in her ability to stage the appearance of feminine ideals and typical in her presentation of an image that men desire to see. Thus, Miriam's female masquerade invokes the long Western tradition whereby "the woman features as synonymous with artifice, inauthenticity and duplicity" (Tseelon 34–37). This sense of the essential falseness of public displays of femininity is explicitly thematized throughout the novel. For example, Peter observes that the French star, Mlle. Voisin "was almost as natural off the stage as on" (HM 278). Miriam, in turn, expresses admiration for Voisin, because both onstage and offstage, " 'She showed us nothing—nothing of her real self!' " (HM 288). Such an implacable surface is displayed again when Miriam visits Nick's studio for the last time:

Miriam entered the place with her charming familiar grandeur, as she might have appeared, as she appeared every night, early in her first act, at the back of the stage, by the immemorial central door, presenting herself to the house, taking easy possession, repeating old movements, looking from one to the other of the actors before the foot lights. (HM 606)

More importantly, however, the theme of female duplicity is expressed in Peter's constant uncertainty about when or if Miriam is acting. He first notes after her performance at the embassy that "she was very various," her behavior a "succession of phases" (HM 128, 129). This variety quickly provokes his suspicion:

It came over him suddenly that so far from there being any question of her having the histrionic nature, she simply had it in such perfection that she was always acting; that her existence was a series of parts assumed for the moment, each changed for the next, before the perpetual mirror of some curiosity or admiration or wonder. (HM 150)

Peter is struck that Miriam could be "a woman whose only being was to 'make believe,' " and that "such a woman was a kind of monster" because she has no genuine self:

[S]he positively had no countenance of her own, but only the countenance of the occasion, a sequence, a variety (capable possibly of becoming immense), of representative moment.... The expression that came nearest to belonging to her, as it were, was the one that came nearest to being a blank. (HM 151)

In his role as a "formative influence," Peter reprimands Miriam for having "no nature of your own":

"You're always playing something; there are no intervals.... You're an embroidery without a canvas.... Your feigning may be honest, in the sense that your only feeling is your feigned one." (HM 167–68)

Peter does seem to fear this form of monstrous femininity as an affront to the social and moral order. Much as Lady Agnes warned Nick about his potential for "crime," Peter chastises Miriam for her lack of character:

"Because you must destroy and torment and consume—that's your nature. But you can't help your type, can you? ... It's bad, perverse, dangerous. It's essentially insolent.... It's unscrupulous, nervous, capricious, wanton." (HM 279)

This charge, though, becomes part of their flirtation and seems to have a similar role in Miriam's relationship with Basil Dashwood, the gentleman turned actor (HM 267). While Peter never entirely loses his suspicion that Miriam is "always playing," her growing skill shifts its affective valence:

The same impression, the old impression was with him again; the sense that if she was sincere it was sincerity of execution, if she was genuine it was the genuineness of doing it well. She did it so well now that this very fact became charming and touching. (HM 478)

The confusion is also at the heart of his vision of Miriam on stage as "a beautiful, actual, fictive, impossible young woman." The text repeatedly counterpoises Peter's fascination with and horror of Miriam's wanton blankness, her overflow of artifice, to his desire to control the inscription of that void, his desire to discover "if she could be corrupted into respectability" (HM 248).

Peter's view of Miriam and her career, the primary lens through which she is presented, recapitulates a narrative commonplace in late-Victorian literature, "a certain patronizing and ironic domestication of one . . . whose cultural wildness is a source of superiority and amusement" (Russo 147). *The Tragic Muse*, however, keeps its distance from such a master narrative. The text makes clear that Miriam takes up her masquerade in the manner recent feminist critics have explored: as a way of disrupting "the claustrophobic closeness of the woman in relation to her own body . . . a way of appropriating this necessary distance or gap . . . deploying it for women" (Doane 37). Miriam undertakes her painstaking rehearsal of femininity deliberately and self-consciously to carve out a space for herself economically and socially. James gives Miriam several speeches in which she mocks the narcissism of her profession while defending the seriousness of her craft:

> "An actress has to talk about herself; what else can she talk about, poor vain thing? . . . If one really wants to do anything one must worry it out; of course everything doesn't come the first day. . . . If there's anything to be got from trying, from showing one's self, how can it come unless one hears the simple truth, the truth that turns one inside out? It's all for that—to know what one is, if one's a stick!" (HM 125–26)

Miriam's pronouncements have a comic tone early in the novel, when she has yet to exhibit any real skill, but they take on more substance as her abilities do. Since he will not "go behind" Miriam, James can demonstrate the intelligence animating Miriam's "posing" only in her dialogue with the other characters. While sitting for her portrait, Miriam offers Nick an extended and lucid analysis of her relationship with Peter:

> "The principal difficulty is that he doesn't know what he wants. The next is that I don't either—or what I want myself. I only know what I don't want. . . . I don't want a person who takes things even less simply than I do myself. . . . He expects others—me, for instance,

to make all the sacrifices. Merci, much as I esteem him and much as I owe him." (HM 523–24)

Nick's response stands for the reader's: " 'I like to hear you talk—it makes you live, brings you out' " (HM 526). Miriam is brought out most clearly and forcefully in the discussions she has with Peter each of the three times he proposes. Each time Peter insists more determinedly on the seamlessness of Miriam's female masquerade, on the interchangeability of her public and private performances. He does so, though, because Miriam's ability to represent femininity is "precisely what Peter wishes to put on the stage of his private career, rather than see displayed on a public stage" (McCormack 43).

Their final argument comes after the triumphant performance that left Peter in "shining confusion." Peter praises Miriam as "the perfection of perfections" and promises to marry her if she will renounce the stage. Miriam points out the illogic of his proposal:

"I please you because you see; because you know; and because I please you, you must adapt me to your convenience, you must take me over, as they say. You admire me as an artist and therefore you wish to put me into a box in which the artist will breathe her last." (HM 542)

Peter can only insist that the stage he offers "is a bigger theater than any of those places in the Strand" and that the artist in Miriam will find her greatest expression in "the deepest domesticity of private life" (HM 543, 546). Miriam's rejoinder is pointed: " 'Stay on my stage; come off your own' " (HM 545). Peter is reduced by this suggestion to reiterating the imbricated norms of gender and class against which Miriam has struggled throughout the novel:

"The cases are not equal. You would make of me the husband of an actress. I should make of you the wife of an ambassador." (HM 546)

Responding to Peter's entreaties, Miriam offers her lengthiest and most articulate defense of the theatrical profession and her place within it:

"Yes we show it for money, those of us who have anything to show, and some no doubt who haven't, which is the real scandal. What will you have? It's only the envelope of the idea, it's only our machinery, which ought to be conceded to us; and in proportion as the idea takes hold of us do we become unconscious of the clumsy body. . . . Of course I'm a contortionist and of course there's a hateful side; but don't you see how that very fact puts a price on every compensation, on the help of those who are ready to insist on the other side, the grand one . . . the way we simply stir people's souls." (HM 553–54)

Like Nick, Miriam ties her artistic practice, her display of her "clumsy body," to a transcendent idea that both redeems and eludes the base machinery of representation. She insists that her dramatic exhibitions are of her own making; they are not a form of duplicity or fraud—" 'I represent, but I represent truly' " (HM 528)—nor are they a stratagem for social mobility through marriage. Peter's own preference for "the representation of life" over "the real thing" notwithstanding (HM 66), he is no more able to recognize the value, integrity, and autonomy of Miriam's aesthetic labors than Julia is able to recognize those of Nick. When Peter returns to London to see Miriam's "magnificent" performance as Juliet, he learns that she has wed Dashwood, who is now her manager.

The marriages that conclude *The Tragic Muse* comment on the comedic genre's conventional endings. Matrimony remains the goal of most of the novel's characters, male and female, though it is not a goal that necessarily brings happiness. Miriam's choice of Dashwood marks a descent from her "tremendously high ideal . . . [of] a closeness of union" to a mere economic "identity of interests" (HM 555). Her private compromise appears to be compensated for by her tremendous public acclaim. Peter's marriage to Nick's sister, Biddy, like his "superior appointment" (HM 618), similarly represents the defeat of feeling by career. Between these two uneven matches, Nick and Julia's alliance hangs precariously suspended. Nash predicts that Nick will reconcile with Julia, who would make of him her dependent, but his concerns "have not up to this time been justified" (HM 619). In all three of James's cases, then, a marriage between equals is deemed impossible; as Miriam tells Peter, " 'the gratification of [passion] would interfere fatally, with the ambition of each of us. Our ambitions are odious, but we are tied fast to them' " (HM 482).

Some ambitions are less odious than others, however, and James (here as elsewhere) portrays the artist's vocation as the most noble of those available in a debased society. Artists are those who aspire to "the idea," those who "stir people's souls." As many critics have noted, James, while insisting in the novel that "all art is one," cannot help establishing a hierarchy of artistic professions. Twice in the latter pages of *The Tragic Muse* he suggests the inferiority of the theater to painting. First Nash composes for Nick a portrait of Miriam's future theatrical triumphs, an image of the "vulgarity" and "publicity" required for dramatic success:

> Gabriel brushed in a large bright picture of her progress through the time and around the world, round it and round it again, from continent to continent and clime to clime; with populations and deputations, reporters and photographers, placards and interviews and banquets, steamers, railways, dollars, diamonds, speeches and artistic ruin all jumbled into her train. (HM 437)

Nash's vision ends with Miriam "young and insatiate, but already coarse, hard and raddled . . . curious and magnificent and grotesque," an ending much like her beginning (HM 438). One might easily attribute this caricature of the actress's career to the anti-theatrical character James has given Nash were it not for Miriam's own reiteration of these themes. During her final visit to Nick's studio, Miriam compares her vocation to his, stressing the ephemerality of her theatrical effects and the superficiality of her discipline:

> "You're the real thing and the rare bird. I haven't lived with you this way without seeing that: you're the sincere artist so much more than I. You'll do things that will hand on your name when my screeching is happily over. . . . I haven't before me a period of the same sort of unsociable pegging away that you have. For want of it I shall never really be good. However, if you don't tell people I've said so, they'll never know. Your conditions are far better than mine and far more respectable: you can do as many things as you like, in patient obscurity, while I'm pitchforked into the mêlée, and into the most improbable fame, upon the back of a solitary cheval de bataille, a poor broken-winded screw." (HM 583, 585)

The price of Nick's achievement, it seems to her, is that he strikes her " 'as kind of lonely, as the Americans say—rather cut off and isolated in your grandeur.' " Contradicting her admiration of his "patient obscurity," underlining the distinction between her practice and his, she suggests he needs "fellow-artists and people of that sort,' " the world Miriam feels is too much with her (HM 583). In her final textual appearance in "private life," then, Miriam takes on a knowledge of her own inferiority that can only be termed perverse:

> "I'm too clever—I'm a humbug."
> "That's the way I used to be," said Nick.
> She rested her wonderful eyes on him. . . . "Become great in the proper way and don't expose me." (HM 586)

In this moment, James reveals his stake in the articulation of gender and vocation all too clearly: despite his sympathy for all those aspirants whose lives are constrained by patriarchal society, the artist "who happened to be born a woman" cannot escape either marriage or the marketplace and thus must always defer to the solitary male genius.

"His little heart, dispossessed": Ritual Sexorcism in *The Turn of the Screw*

ERIC HARALSON

"There are depths, depths! The more I go over it, the more I
see in it. . . . . I don't know what I don't see."

"MR. JAMES IS IN A QUEER MOOD," BEGINS AN ENGLISH REVIEW OF
The Turn of the Screw (1898), or else why would he be trying to
make his reader—as the story's famous governess would say—
"a receptacle of lurid things" (*TS* 348)? James's most offensive
piece of "putrescence," it seems, emanated from what the reviewer saw as a fundamental "misunderstanding of child nature": "Even in colder moments, if we admit the fact of infant
depravity, . . . we must deny . . . the extent of the corruption as
suggested here. . . . We have never read a more sickening . . .
tale."[1] Other British journals chimed in, agreeing that the
work's "morbid psychology" and the "weird knowledge" attributed to young Miles and his sister Flora would "outrage many
minds far from prudish" with the implication of evil "nestling
in the fairest of all fair places," the consciousness—if not, indeed, the physical experience—of childhood. Taking a different
tack, discomfited American reviewers hastened to reassure
themselves that the children were only "dimly conscious" of
any doings of Peter Quint and Miss Jessel, former servants of
the remote estate at Bly who stalked the grounds as predatory
ghosts, if we are to believe the governess (*CR* 303, 308, 305).

Yet more cosmopolitan readers, in both England and the
United States, excused any affront to the moral sensibilities
and gave in to the gothic frisson—to James's artistic efficacy in
presenting a picture of two exquisite children "holding unholy
communion" with two sinister spirits. According to one de-
lighted Boston reviewer, the "subtle crowning horror" of the
tale lay not in how Quint and Jessel "pervert in ways inexpressible" the two young souls in question but rather in how the chil-

dren themselves solicit such contact with "a joy so depraved" (*CR* 308, 307). Members of the guild applauded also, with Oscar Wilde pronouncing the work "most wonderful" because of its "poisonous" insinuation, and even the more sedate Joseph Conrad lauding James's skill in "extract[ing] an intellectual thrill out of the subject."[2]

But what *was* this subject whose power of suggestion "makes the blood bound through the veins," whether in pleasure or in disgust (*CR* 312)? Notably, neither those who relished nor those who reviled the story were able or willing to say. Conrad had to concede that the subject "evades one but leaves a kind of phosphorescent trail in one's mind" (*Letters* 2:122). Wilde was satisfied to leave its delectable toxicity as vague as those "poisonous influences" that coursed through the life of his ill-fated Dorian Gray.[3] And while all reviewers judged that some serious transgression was "darkly, potently hinted at" in *The Turn of the Screw,* its substance and operation remained "inexpressible" except by terms, such as "depravity," that fell short of concretizing. One hears, for instance, that both Quint and Jessel "died in strange ways—[but] how, no one knows"; and although the governess purportedly learns "what it is from which the boy [Miles] suffers," this finding does not get reported to the public (*CR* 304, 309–10).

Only a few alert reviewers discerned that dark hinting was an integral part of James's method—that in avoiding "unnecessarily ample details," he was "by elimination creating an effect of . . . unimaginable horrors" (*CR* 303, 306). Of course, we now know (if ever we doubted) the degree of self-consciousness with which James stimulated in readers the same "dreadful liability to impressions" to which the governess confesses, compelling them (like her) to "restlessly read into the facts . . . almost all the meaning they were to receive," then leaving them to marvel at the uncanny way in which "knowledge gathered" into a coherent account, until at last "there was no ambiguity in anything" (*TS* 321, 325, 327). "I evoked the worst I could," James put it in one letter,[4] and his mode of evocation—as he justifiably gloats in the preface—was by means of artful "*adumbration*": the reader's sense of "portentous evil" would be spoiled if the narrative named any "imputed vice" outright, causing it to "shrink to the compass" of a "particular infamy." Since ugliness is in the eye of the beholder, thereby ensuring that "no eligible *absolute* of the wrong" could ever be isolated, the gambit was to make the individual reader "*think* the evil . . . for himself" and thus supply its constituent features.[5] If, for example, "everything" had passed between Quint and Jessel, as the housekeeper Mrs. Grose ominously recounts, then nothing could be disqualified from the roster of their sins (*TS* 331).

In short, since the tale designedly contained "not an inch of expatiation" on James's part, but rather a sequence of gestures that were "positively all blanks," those readers appalled by its "monstrous" content had only the motions of their own prurient minds to blame (*LC* 1188). They should have accepted that Miles's school infraction was a "mystification without end," even when the governess herself cannot (*TS* 340). By an added sophistication of technique, readers were seduced into replicating not only the governess's compulsive cerebration but also her *resistance* to playing this game of fill-in-the-blank, their keenness for explanatory details being continually blunted by a sense of (as she says) "directions in which I must not . . . let myself go" (even as she proceeds to do so). Thus the governess's record of her progress from suspicion to detection to conviction—and I use these terms of criminological connotation advisedly—at once patterned and promoted the ambivalence of readers and reviewers, who confronted (as she does) an influx of information that "suited exactly the . . . deadly view" of events that they were "in the very act of forbidding [themselves] to entertain" (*TS* 337).

In all of this, the most that James would admit about his own vision of the vile extremity portrayed in the tale (again, in correspondence) was that its victims were children "as *exposed* as we can humanly conceive children to be" and that some depradation of "the helpless plasticity of childhood" was involved; yet these remarks clearly served to aggravate rather than to answer curiosity. Nimbly sidestepping all invitations to specify the nature of this "most infernal imaginable evil," the author of *The Turn of the Screw* was content to have conferred "the beauty of the pathetic" upon the wreckage left in its wake (*L* 4:84, 88).

Today's reader, being well-schooled in the grammars of preterition and unspeakability employed in late-Victorian fictions of sexuality, feels warranted in suspecting James's commentary of disingenuousness—or at a minimum, of some good old-fashioned self-blinkering. Virginia Woolf suggested as much as early as 1921, if only in her own suggestive diction, which implied a collusion of sorts between audience *and* author in assigning a (homo)sexualized burden to the text: fearing Quint, she held, readers were actually "afraid of something unnamed . . . in ourselves," which nonetheless reveled in James's representation of "beauty and obscenity twined together worm[ing] their way to the depths." That this unnamed something was not just anything, for Woolf at least, shows in both her imagery of coupling and her recycling of that hoary catchphrase for same-sex passion, "unutterable obscenity."[6]

More pointedly, though less publicly, E. M. Forster named "homosex" as the disavowed subtext of *The Turn of the Screw*: the "fluster" that James so effectively communicates was none other than his own, as he went on steadily "declining to think about" what he was all the while thinking about.[7] On this view, James unwittingly inscribed his own psychology (if also, by a happy coincidence, the reader's) in the governess's giddy struggle to maintain *her* narrative balance through self-censorship: "[M]y equilibrium depended on . . . my rigid will . . . to shut my eyes as tight as possible to the truth that what I had to deal with was, revoltingly, against nature" (*TS* 392). This interpretation, it will be noted, posits an author who could retail yet another period euphemism for homosexual love—"a union against nature," as James's own criticism refers to it, or "something peculiarly against nature," in the words of one review—without noticing or acknowledging that he was doing so (*LC* 772, *CR* 308). If this were the case, which does not seem beyond James's constitutional complexity, his claim not to have "expatiated" would be technically true, and perhaps we are the beneficiaries (once again) of his willingness to write out "the truth . . . at the back of my head" without subjecting it to extensive and potentially disabling analysis (*L* 4:84). Yet as both Forster and Woolf attest, the resulting work "adumbrates" not some nebulous gestalt but a known political obsession of its place and season of provenance: that of codifying, regulating, and punishing forms of sexuality *contra naturam*, with special attention to (homo)-sexual acts that traversed boundaries of age and/or social class.

To cite only the most obvious examples, it cannot be innocuous (as James would have it) that the same "hunger, fierceness, and encroaching desperation—inescapably sexual in origin" that Terry Castle ascribes to Olive Chancellor's feeling for Verena Tarrant (*The Bostonians*, 1886) resurfaces whenever the governess swoons to Flora's charms, "closing my eyes . . . yieldingly . . . as before the excess of something beautiful that shone out of the blue of her own" (*TS* 343).[8] Nor does it seem casual that the organ of vigilant surveillance closes here in order to open as a window to desire, as if epitomizing the ambivalence that pervades—if it does not animate—the cultural policing of sexuality. "Restless" being a standard Jamesian tag for sexual energy or sublimated forms thereof—think of Maria Gostrey's "distinctly restless" reaction to Lambert Strether or of James himself as a "restless analyst" of American life[9]—the "restlessness" occasioned by this "beatific" girl whom the governess "should have . . . as a matter of course at night" symptomatizes the disturbing aura of what James R. Kincaid calls "the erotic child" of Victorian culture (*TS* 300).[10] Equally problematic—and symptomatic—is the governess's mixed response to Miles's "occasional excess of the restless," which seems alternately a "defect" to be remedied and an irresistible call to her own stifled passions. Should she rechannel his agitation into book reading (as she does her own) and risk effeminizing him, or should she let herself be "carried away by the little gentleman" and fill in the blanks of *his* text (" 'Oh, *you* know what a boy wants!' ")—a desire eventuating in her much-cited "whims[y]" that she and Miles are newlyweds preparing for a night at the inn (*TS* 326, 301, 371, 394)?

In the same vein, far from being a garden-variety bogey in a generic "bogey-tale" (as James sometimes dismissed the work), Quint is felt as a palpable form of "living, detestable, dangerous presence" in late-Victorian society, one whose "secret disorders" manifest themselves in distinctly corporeal and polymorphous license (*L* 4:84; *TS* 342, 325). Although "too free with everyone" (which person, of which age or gender or class, does this not include?) and doing "what he wished with them all," Quint is most concertedly associated with Miles, the two having been "perpetually together" on rambles beyond the confines—and oversight—of the household regime at Bly. Although James would like (us) to believe that Quint amounts to a tabula rasa, awaiting any reader's act of any reading-in, this "hound" of a man, this "visitor most concerned with my boy," as the governess jealously styles him, was a pre-scribed figure for contemporaries, whether consciously named or not, and the reader's capacity to "think the evil for himself" was more preconditioned than James recognized (*TS* 346).

Indeed the profile of Quint—and to a lesser degree that of Miss Jessel, the governess's predecessor cum alter ego—corresponds with the construct of sexual "deviant," and particularly of "pedophile," generated by the schizophrenic Victorian imagination of the bourgeois child, "that horrible and lovely product" of social engineering, in Kincaid's terms (4). What

James called the "rosy candid English children" were still, superficially, "the most completely satisfactory thing the country
produce[d]"; but the "stream . . . of clear infancy"—as figured
by Bronson Alcott, for example, speaking for an earlier paradigm of child development—looked increasingly polluted as
psychologists traced adult sexuality back to its source.[11] The
ideological reflex evidenced in reviews of *The Turn of the
Screw*—that edgy insistence on the innocence of "child nature"
as proof against "something against nature"—shows the child
functioning in culture much as James's "blank" functioned in
narrative, enticing observers to project their illicit desires, and
hardly diffuse ones at that. Protesting too much the child's
erotic emptiness "created a subversive echo," writes Kincaid,
making "absolutely essential" a screen upon which to cathect
these troubling impulses of normal, decent citizens (4–5).
James's tale furnishes a textbook case as the governess's hyperbolic confidence in the children's moral fiber—Flora is one of
"Raphael's holy infants," while Miles emits a "positive fragrance of purity"—seems to activate a hermeneutics of suspicion from which the lineaments of their respective despoilers
emerge (*TS* 300, 307). As reviewers gushed, reassimilating this
process to commonsense standards of practice for the model
"devoted governess," her "love . . . probes beneath their
beauty"—that is, their pretense of innocence—to discover a
"sink of corruption" (*CR* 306, 308). Or, more succinctly: every
Miles must have his Quint, every Flora her Miss Jessel.

These are large claims, I realize, which fly in the face of Shoshana Felman's wise counsel for readers eager to pin down the
meaning of James's story—counsel that nevertheless glosses
this meaning well, if generally: "[S]exuality is precisely what
rules out simplicity as such," being "essentially the violence of
its own non-simplicity."[12] But I wish to go one (reckless) step
further and argue that the alarming significations of Quint's
predilection for Miles and Miss Jessel's for Flora—which the
governess's muddled yearnings for both children mimic and
compete with—reached Victorian readers independently of
genre and that subsequent critical disputes on the terrain of
verisimilitude or "reliability"—engaging sport though they be—
miss the point. The cultural work performed by James's piece
had little to do with the epistemological soundness or narrative
authority of the governess's "portentous clearness" (or hysteria, as the case may be), for the tale is an allegory of sexual
panic—a very real allegory of the fin de siècle, if you will (*TS*

322). And although it is tempting to construe the gothic as a mode meant to dodge, displace, or minimize fear of queer specters in Victorian life (as in James's own labels of "bogey-tale" or "shameless pot-boiler"), period science and "psychical research" impede such an interpretive move: even as ghosts, as we shall see, Quint and Jessel would have been substantial enough to be realized as threats to the developing child—especially the male child as heritor of class and state power—and thus quite literally to haunt the adult reader's mind (*L* 4:86).

The Turn of the Screw can best be seen as a fable of masculine becoming (Flora's fate is always secondary and subsidiary) in which the governess acts as a ruthless enforcer of heteronormative investment—a "govern-er" whose "fierce rigor," however, is fueled by a self-division and an experiential impoverishment that reveal her, ultimately, as the mere (murderous) handmaiden of patriarchy. The hidden hand of patriarchy reaches out not only from Harley Street in London, where the master of Bly resides, but from the governess's deep past: the unspecified "eccentric nature" of her puritanical father, the "slavish idolat[ry]" exacted by her older brothers (*TS* 342, 355, 340).[13] Her "dispossession" of Miles's little heart—that word that so nicely conjoins economic, lineal, and spiritual disfranchisements—indexes the heavy sacrifice that British society stood ready to incur to prevent "little gentlemen" like him from straying into the "wrong path altogether" taken by redheaded corrupters like Quint (better dead than red?) (*TS* 325). Understanding that Jamesian allegory resembles dreamwork more than Bunyan, the allusiveness of this implied relation between "pedophile" and "child victim" went even further, taking in the two major sex scandals of the previous decade, the Cleveland Street brothel affair of 1889–90 and the Wilde trials of 1895 (the latter coincident with the tale's germination). In these key defining episodes of homosexual regulation, the lever of public opprobrium rested on the fulcrum of not only age disparities but social distinctions between the well-heeled defendants and the working-class adolescents who sometimes served their "unnatural lust"—"our boys," in the parlance of the tabloids. In the Cleveland Street incident, Ed Cohen observes, "the nature of the sexual crimes seem[ed] only of interest insofar as it underscore[d] the inequities of class privilege"; yet the proletarian "boys" also aroused resentment in some quarters, as Richard Dellamora has shown, for their profiteering in the sex trade made them forget (to adapt the governess) "the place of a servant in the scale" (*TS* 331).[14]

In the parallel universe of *The Turn of the Screw*, where considerations of proper hierarchy inflect all personal agency and interpersonal commerce, the most loaded—partly because it is the least explicit—site of negotiation is sexuality, that famously "dense transfer point for relations of power."[15] It is bad enough when Miss Jessel—"a lady," in the eyes of the housekeeper—undergoes "abasement" by yielding herself to a valet like Quint, so "dreadfully below" her for all his pretensions to wear the pants (or waistcoat) of the master. But any like traffic between Miles and Quint—"a base menial," besides being an adult male, as the governess reminds the boy—would violate an even stronger taboo, constituting the extreme case of combined age, sexual, and status "incongruity," in the governess's discreet term (*TS* 335). No surprise, then, that the tale begins with a character named Douglas (as in Lord Alfred) and culminates in a tribunal and humiliation ritual à la Oscar Wilde's, with the governess simulating a prosecutorial force whose "infatuation" with disclosure ("I should get *all*") renders her "blind with victory" and Miles "a gentleman" whose "supreme surrender of the name" of his partner in crime actuates his "fall in the world," while the ghost of Quint stalks about like "a sentinel before a prison" (*TS* 398–403). "But the *fall*—" James had written to Edmund Gosse after Wilde's sentencing, "from nearly twenty years of a really unique . . . conspicuity . . . to that sordid prison-cell[!]" Refracting this chapter of "hideous human history," as James then called it, *The Turn of the Screw* (re)presented a melodrama of perceived sexual danger and retaliative disgrace that was—now in the governess's words—"hideous just because it *was* human," the gothic infused with the all too real (*L* 4:10).

As his own formulations suggest, James's fascination with scandalous downfall was mainly dramaturgical, the agon of the Wildean "spectacle" making the largest claim on his interest. By the same token, the impact of Miles's demise is meant to be measured on the nerve endings and heartstrings and not necessarily to inform the moral or social consciousness. Yet may we not also glimpse a latent queer politics in the pathos that, by James's stated aim, suffuses the tragedy for culture wrought by this instance of fanatical "absolutism"—this "playing out of the rights of those over [Miles], a ghastly game . . . between obsessions that destroy the field in contest" (Kincaid 81)? The staging of the boy's death, with its profound emotional appeal, coaxes the audience toward a more careful reckoning of the costs of such a rescue operation, such an expensive "liberation," as that conducted by the governess. Her typically unstable phrasing permits one to read "the loss I was so proud of"—in *her* meaning, the divestiture of Quint's influence—as "the loss that Miles dies of," the throttling of some life source. Likewise, when she excuses the "sternness" of her intervention as "all for his judge, his executioner"—in her meaning, all for the schoolmaster behind Miles's dismissal—the confessional mode is patent, to us if assuredly not to her. Taking our cue from Forster and Woolf, then, we may plausibly hear in that "faint and far . . . cry of a child"—the keynote of the landscape lying beyond the bright facade of Bly—an accent of what Eve Kosofsky Sedgwick has called the "melancholia—the denied mourning—caused by . . . originary foreclosures of . . . homosexual possibility" (*TS* 402, 403, 300).[16]

Here it might be countered that the perceptions of modern novelists and postmodern theorists are dubious guides, inasmuch as they look back on Victorianism from the vantage of a century in which sex "has become . . . more important almost than our life" (Foucault 156). Leon Edel, for one, declined to participate in the governess's hunt for the cause of Miles's expulsion, stating that it "little matters" what the nature of his transgressive utterance had been.[17] E. A. Sheppard extends this line, arguing that a variety of politico-allegorical gestures (e.g., "Miles as a boy . . . anarchist, Flora as infantile 'new woman' ") would have been traumatic for James's readers, while flatly ruling out the idea that homosexuality was among them: "Quint is not a paederast, nor Miss Jessel a lesbian, so . . . their physical abuse of the children can hardly be . . . the author's intention." Even assuming Miles *had* regaled his schoolmates with "details of a vulgar debauch" between a valet and a governess, Sheppard adds, such "smut" would not have sent him packing under a cloud—so that (sexualized) hypothesis fails, too.[18] This last contention draws support from the London *Times* reviewer of James's tale, whose regret for the primitiveness of boy culture was tempered by a weary tolerance: "Alas, little boys need no Quint to make them talk in a style that would disgust an Apache" (*CR* 311). On the face of it, then, there need be no sex whatsoever—let alone "homosex"—lurking in the background of *The Turn of the Screw.*

Yet two of James's contemporary correspondents suggest otherwise. It is material—given the rise of medico-psychological authority in Victorian sexual politics—that both were men of science: an American physician with prominent public health credentials, Dr. Louis Waldstein, and a cofounder of the British Society for Psychical Research, F. W. H. Myers. Just which "conscious intentions" Waldstein imputed to *The Turn of the Screw*, we do not know, but James's reply establishes their common solicitude for the "hideous . . . exposure" of the children (*L* 4:84). Waldstein's treatise, *The Subconsious Self and Its Relation to Education and Health* (1897), issued a year before the tale, enables us to infer at least the general ground of his probe for James's meaning or message. Anglo-American culture, the doctor there prescribes, should strive "to create numberless impressions of beauty and harmony upon the child, and to exclude everything that is ugly and squalid." As if with a premonition of a certain valet of unbridled appetites, and of an eagle-eyed governess watching for "the outbreak . . . of the little natural [i.e., carnal] man" in her precious charge, Waldstein stressed the causative and predictive value of early attention to nurture and environment, urging that "persons habitually in [the child's] company . . . should be chosen with care," their "carriage and behavior" distinguished by "true . . . refinement" (*TS* 337). That he had a Peter Quint in mind, rather than a Miss Jessel, becomes clear when it turns out (predictably) that "the child" in question is male, and the apprehension, that he will "grow to the man who . . . surprise[s] his friends by acts . . . out of harmony." Admittedly such decorous talk leaves vague and plural the discordant masculinities to be avoided, but Waldstein's final word on the subject narrows the range of reference considerably: "[S]trange vagaries of affection and passion, which affect the whole existence . . . can be traced to . . . small beginnings."[19]

A more salient commentator, however, was F. W. H. Myers, an acquaintance of both William and Henry James since the early 1880s. We lack his letter of late 1898 about *The Turn of the Screw,* and James takes refuge in lamenting the plight of unprotected childhood, downplaying his horror show as "a very mechanical matter" (*L* 4:88). But again, the angle of Myers's query can perhaps be read from another letter he simultaneously sent to Oliver Lodge, a Liverpool physics professor also involved in psychical research. There Myers asserts, matter-of-factly, that Flora feels "lesbian love" for Miss Jessel ("a harlot-governess," no less) and Miles "pederastic passion for the partially-materialized ghost" of Quint, who may have died at the hands of another "male victim of his lust."[20] If indeed Myers dispatched such a reading to Lamb House for the author's imprimatur—not improbable, when one remembers his longstanding intimacy with the Jameses—Henry's claim not even to *understand the principal question*" posed to him invites comparison with Walt Whitman's famous repudiation of "morbid inferences" drawn from his work by John Addington Symonds.

Speculation aside, though, the menace to society that mainstream Victorians associated with a Quint or a Jessel—or, in generic terms, the interpenetration of gothicism and naturalism—cannot be gauged without recalling the empirical earnestness of psychologists such as Myers and the prestige accorded their labors, even by the often skeptical James. William James, following the English example, had helped to found the American Society for Psychical Research in 1884 (see "The Confidences of a 'Psychical Researcher' " [1909]); and Henry had dipped into *Phantasms of the Living* (1886), coauthored by Myers, before writing *The Turn of the Screw*. Moreover, the London *Times* faulted James's homework, finding Quint and Jessel "not in conformity with the results of science" as chronicled in "the vast collections of phantasms brought together by the S.P.R." (*CR* 311). Thus when Myers, the veritable voice of "the S.P.R.," not only takes James's phantasms seriously but classifies them as "partially-materialized," his clinical term speaks for a sizable constituency that would *not* have discounted the worries of the "good and virtuous" governess as medieval superstition or deemed her aggressive tactics groundless. Paradoxically, if James's realist fictions transported audiences to "a land where the vices have no bodies" (as F. M. Colby complained in a much-quoted remark), his supernatural tale embodied those vices (even "partially" would seem to have been enough) and thus linked their theater of operations at Bly with a familiar and, for many readers, fearful social world.[21]

Still, it remains to ask how James, in annexing parapsychology to retell (mutatis mutandis) recent convulsions of London sexual politics, arrived at just these conceptions of Quint and Miles. Why must the putative "pederast" be déclassé yet with such "straight, good features" and such a "tall, active, erect" bearing that he might pass for the master of Bly (*TS* 320)? Why must the child in jeopardy, the nephew of that master and presumable heir of the estate, be repeatedly invoked as a "little gentleman" in the making? Not unlike Robert Louis Stevenson's *The Strange Case of Dr. Jekyll and Mr. Hyde* (1886), *The*

Turn of the Screw conjures up a schematics of bourgeois masculine performance in which "gentlemanliness" hovers always on
the verge of the abyss—in which a man, to quote Henry Jekyll's
well-suited confession, could "plod in the public eye with a load
of genial respectability, and in a moment, like a schoolboy, strip
off these lendings and spring headlong into the sea of liberty,"
sinking rapidly from "undignified" to "monstrous" means of
self-gratification.[22] " 'But if he isn't a gentleman—' " begins
Mrs. Grose, musing initially on Quint's identity, and the governess completes her thought: " 'He's a horror,' " a horror (Conrad's *Heart of Darkness* is another obvious intertext) whose
moral contours and antisocial practices are not merely unspeakable but inadmissible to consciousness. " 'God help me if
I know *what* he is.' " What is more significant here is not the
commonplace that Victorian "gentlemen" guarded against for-
feiting that good name as a factor of public standing—against
"carry[ing] a bad name," as the governess frets that Miles will
do (*TS* 295). Rather, it is the way in which this anxious self-fashioning betrayed "gentleman" and "horror" to be not mutually
exclusive but miscible categories without a reliable boundary
between them (*TS* 295, 319, 307). When Gerard Manley Hopkins
esteems "gentleman" a more valuable pedigree than "Christian," when William Dean Howells cites the restraining power
of *ungentlemanly* ("that word, which from a woman's tongue always strikes a man like a blow in the face"), when Gosse teases
Howells that "a quantity of cads have sworn to behave like
gentlemen" after reading his tutelary novels, these overdeter-
mined testimonials signal a radical insecurity in gentlemanliness itself.[23] The point is amply made not only in Mrs. Grose's
weird question regarding the unknown man on the tower—
" 'Was he [i.e., Quint] a gentleman?' "—but in her weirder relief
upon learning that apparently he was not (*TS* 318). Wouldn't the
sole fact that he had "taken a liberty rather gross" with the
sanctity of Bly brand him as not a gentleman? Alternatively,
what can it mean that plain, simple Mrs. Grose, who keeps to
her station in life, should conceive that a gentleman—say, the
master/uncle supposedly in London—might prowl the grounds
covertly?

These fissures in "gentlemanliness," as a matter of both
social and self-epistemology, greatly intensify the problem of
Miles's maturational "outbreak"—that is, the behavioral and
sexual-object choices he will make—by placing him in the bind
of the (so to speak) "quint-essential" Victorian boy. The double

standard of a patriarchal gender system, which, as the governess primly observes, relegates girls to "the inferior age, sex, and intelligence," evidently privileges Miles over Flora (their respective martial and horticultural names are noted by Sheppard [29]). Yet Miles's "freedom" also carries a tax, for the relative latitude of boys, which can imperil "harmony" through "vagaries of affection" (Waldstein), requires a strong regulatory frame within which their advent into adult masculinity will occur (or, in this instance, not occur). As the governess chips away at her early asseverations of Miles's beatitude—his "only fault" is too much "gentleness," but then his "only defect" is that "excess of the restless"—the contradiction indicates the difficult, if not impossible, balance he must strike to meet ambivalent cultural expectations. Her deduction that Miles had been simply "too fine and fair for the little horrid, unclean school world" provides only fleeting relief; for although it assures his exemplary gentility—he is a future pillar of state, society, and empire, after all—it also raises concern that such finesse "made Miles a muff." Without "the spirit to be naughty," the governess and Mrs. Grose concur, a boy is not much of a boy, but a creature drifting toward effeminacy—passive, sentimental, detached from worldly endeavor; though yet again, in this endless vacillation, his naughtiness must never be of a kind or of a degree to "contaminate" other boys (*TS* 392, 340, 322, 326, 305).

Cases illustrative of these tensions within masculine "education for the world," and of homosexuality as a prime source of normative anxiety, are not hard to find in the annals of English private schooling (*TS* 308). Another delicate boy who drew the epithet "muff" was Charles Dodgson, also known as Lewis Carroll, whose "arrested sexual development" (in the judgment of a recent biographer) originated in what Dodgson called "annoyance[s] at night" while at Rugby in the 1840s.[24] Symonds's more candid memoirs describe Harrow in the 1850s as a place of "animal lust" in which "every boy of good looks had a female name . . . as some bigger fellow's 'bitch' " and "acts of onanism, mutual masturbation, the sports of naked boys in bed together" were widespread. These portraits of life in the long dormitory provide a likely context for the fears surrounding the "incredibly beautiful" Miles, as do items of sexological discourse—at once lexical and conceptual—that crop up in James's tale. For example, the governess's "big word" for the contagiousness of one particular excess ("contaminate") is arguably glossed in Sy-

monds's report of the "repulsive" yet shaping effect of those
schoolboy "sports": he "remained free in fact and act from this
contamination," yet the exposure exerted a "powerful influence" on his evolution as a man-desiring man. Likewise, Symonds's view that boys who did indulge "permanently injured
[their] constitution"—a platitude of both child-rearing manuals
and sexual "science"—may well inform what "the gentlemen"
at Miles's school perceived as his egregious and unspeakable of-
fense: he had been "an injury to the others."[25] Readers such as
Edel and Sheppard, in taking James at his (overt) word, over-
looked how his narrative absorbed both a vocabulary and an implicit etiology of male homosexuality, connecting the plot with
a specific institutional history of Victorian England. The injuri-
ous contamination, let us recall, consisted in Miles's having
"said things" to "only a few [boys] I liked," who "must have *repeated* them. To those *they* liked"—a daisy chain of endear-
ments that may not have "only one meaning," as the governess
mentality would think, but that clearly favors one meaning over
all others (*TS* 304, 400–401, emphasis mine).

Finally, we miss something vital to James's political allegory
if we fail to note how Miles, in his thwarted bid for the gentlemanly property that comes with proper manliness, has been
threatened with "dispossession" all along—and not simply by
the machinery of sexual regulation. The drama of his short life,
as well as the part of sexuality in determining that drama, is
located squarely within imperial culture: in "the huge, hot, horrible century of English pioneership, the wheel that ground the
dust for a million early graves," including those containing the
bodies of Miles's (and Flora's) parents; in the law of primogeniture, which had forced Miles's father—his uncle's younger "military brother"—to India in the first place; and in social
attenuation caused, at the center of the empire, by a homosocial elite uninterested in the rising generation (*TS* 296). That
uncle—"a bachelor in the prime of life," "a lone man without
the right sort of experience or a grain of patience" for children—keeps literally miles away from Miles (*TS* 296).[26] For all
his upper-crust trappings, then, the boy's claim on genteel patriarchal entitlement is impaired from the start. The governess—or rather, the regulatory apparatus that lays to rest the
ghost of homosexuality—only finishes the job, eliminating in
the process a prospective bearer of civilization. "If he *were* innocent," the governess ponders, just moments before the circumstances of Miles's death appear to prove otherwise, "what

then on earth was *I?*" (*TS* 401). This is a timely and potentially productive doubt, for what if Miles's nominal crime—incipient same-sex desire—were grasped as purely a cultural fabrication, rather than a theological "evil" or a pathological "deviance"? How on earth would one then judge "his executioner"?

Notes

Henry James, *The Turn of the Screw and Other Short Novels* (New York: New American Library, 1962), 329–30; hereafter cited as *TS*.

1. Kevin J. Hayes, ed., *Henry James: The Contemporary Reviews* (Cambridge and New York: Cambridge University Press, 1996), 304; hereafter cited as *CR*.

2. Wilde quoted in Philip Sicker, *Love and the Quest for Identity in the Fiction of Henry James* (Princeton: Princeton University Press 1980), 8; *The Collected Letters of Joseph Conrad: Volume 2: 1898–1902*, ed. Frederick R. Karl and Laurence Davies (Cambridge: Cambridge University Press 1986), 111; hereafter cited as *Letters*.

3. Oscar Wilde, *The Picture of Dorian Gray* (Harmondsworth, England: Penguin, 1985), 149.

4. Henry James, *Letters, Volume IV*, ed. Leon Edel (Cambridge: Harvard University Press, Belknap Press 1984), 88; hereafter cited as *L*.

5. Henry James, *Literary Criticism: French Writers, Other European Writers, the Prefaces to the New York Edition*, ed. Leon Edel (New York: Library of America, 1984), 1187–88; hereafter cited as *LC*.

6. Virginia Woolf, "The Ghost Stories," in *Henry James: A Collection of Critical Essays*, ed. Leon Edel (Englewood Cliffs, N. J.: Prentice-Hall, 1962), 53–54. See also Linda Dowling, *Hellenism and Homosexuality in Victorian Oxford* (Ithaca: Cornell University Press, 1994).

7. E. M. Forster, *Commonplace Book*, ed. Philip Gardner (London: Scolar Press, 1985), 17–18. See also my " 'Thinking about Homosex' in Forster and James," in *Queer Forster*, ed. Robert K. Martin and George Piggford (Chicago: University of Chicago Press, 1997), 59–73.

8. Terry Castle, *The Apparitional Lesbian: Female Homosexuality and Modern Culture* (New York: Columbia University Press, 1993), 155.

9. Henry James, *The Ambassadors*, ed. S. P. Rosenbaum (New York: W. W. Norton and Co., 1964), 341; *The American Scene*, ed. W. H. Auden (New York, London: Charles Scribner's Sons, 1946), 7.

10. James R. Kincaid, *Child-Loving: The Erotic Child and Victorian Culture* (New York and London: Routledge, 1992), 4–5.

11. Henry James, *Letters*, vol. 3, ed. Leon Edel (Cambridge: Harvard University Press, Belknap Press 1980), 212; *American Poetry: The Nineteenth Century*, vol. 1, ed. John Hollander (New York: Library of America, 1993), 226.

12. Shoshana Felman, "Turning the Screw of Interpretation," in *Literature and Psychoanalysis: The Question of Reading: Otherwise* (Baltimore and London: Johns Hopkins University Press, 1982), 109–11.

13. John Carlos Rowe, *The Theoretical Dimensions of Henry James* (Madison: University of Wisconsin Press, 1984), 127–146.

14. Ed Cohen, *Talk on the Wilde Side: Toward a Genealogy of a Discourse on*

Male Sexualities (New York and London: Routledge, 1993), 123; Richard Dellamora, *Masculine Desire: The Sexual Politics of Victorian Aestheticism* (Chapel Hill: University of North Carolina Press, 1990), 207.

15. Michel Foucault, *The History of Sexuality, Volume 1,* Translated by Robert Hurley (New York: Random House, 1978), 103.

16. Eve Kosofsky Sedgwick, *Tendencies* (Durham, N.C.: Duke University Press, 1993), 80.

17. Leon Edel, *Henry James: The Treacherous Years: 1895–1901* (Philadelphia: Lippincott, 1969, 198; quoted in Sheppard, 99.

18. E. A. Sheppard, *Henry James and "The Turn of the Screw"* (Auckland: Auckland University Press, 1974), 99–100.

19. Louis Waldstein, M.D., *The Subconsious Self and Its Relation to Education and Health* (New York: Charles Scribner's Sons, 1897), 46–47.

20. Peter G. Beidler, "The Governess and the Ghosts," *PMLA* 100, no. 1 (1985): 96–97.

21. Roger Gard, ed., *Henry James: The Critical Heritage* (London: Routledge and Kegan Paul; New York: Barnes and Noble, 1968), 337.

22. Robert Louis Stevenson, *The Strange Case of Dr. Jekyll and Mr. Hyde* (New York: Bantam, 1985), 86.

23. Hopkins quoted in David Kalstone, *Becoming a Poet: Elizabeth Bishop with Marianne Moore and Robert Lowell,* ed. Robert Hemenway (New York: Farrar, Straus and Giroux, 1989), 241; William Dean Howells, *April Hopes,* in *Novels, 1886–1888,* ed. Don L. Cook (New York: Library of America, 1989), 427; Gosse, in Evan Charteris, ed., *The Life and Letters of Sir Edmund Gosse* (London: Heinemann, 1931), 155.

24. Michael Bakewell, *Lewis Carroll: A Biography* (London: Heinemann, 1996), 28–29. See also Kincaid 196–97.

25. *The Memoirs of John Addington Symonds,* ed. Phyllis Grosskurth (London: Hutchinson, 1984), 94–95.

26. Henry James, *Literary Criticism: Essays on Literature, American Writers, English Writers,* ed. Leon Edel (New York: Library of America, 1984), 1395, 1397.

Jamesian Sadomasochism:
The Invisible (Third) Hand of Manhood in
The Golden Bowl

LELAND S. PERSON

THE "LIKENESS" OF CHARLOTTE STANT'S "CONNEXION" TO ADAM Verver, James comments, "wouldn't have been wrongly figured if he had been thought of as holding in one of his pocketed hands the end of a long silken halter looped round her beautiful neck" (24:287). The "shriek of a soul in pain" (24:292) that Charlotte utters in response to such bondage constitutes not the only example of violent imagery in *The Golden Bowl*.[1]Fanny Assingham describes Prince Amerigo as a "domesticated lamb tied up with pink ribbon" (23:161), for instance; Maggie Verver later thinks of him as "straitened and tied" (24:192) and, like Charlotte, "writhing in his pain" (24:193). Reversing the lines of power, Maggie herself fantasizes that Amerigo might "some day get drunk and beat her" (23:165), and then later, as she contemplates his sexual power, she recognizes that even his "single touch" would "hand her over to him bound hand and foot" (24:142). Although Charlotte distinguishes Amerigo from men who are "brutes," because he can "check himself before acting on the impulse" (23:290), these examples of brutality in *The Golden Bowl* suggest that the psychic economy James represents and dissects might usefully be explored for its potential sadomasochism—more precisely, as exemplifying and finally challenging a masochistic paradigm. In particular, Amerigo and the vexed subject position he inhabits suggest James's experimentation with male masochism.

Although she has not explicitly applied the idea to James, Kaja Silverman explains male masochism in *Male Subjectivity at the Margins* in terms that can be helpful in understanding *The Golden Bowl* and particularly Amerigo's position—subject position, in her terms—within the novel's larger psychic econ-

149

omy. Although I think that James ultimately deviates significantly from the model of male masochism that Silverman derives from Sigmund Freud, Theodor Reik, Gilles Deleuze, and others, the Prince, as he appears in "abject" relation to Maggie at the end of *The Golden Bowl* (24:193), can be usefully understood as a "feminine yet heterosexual male subject" (Silverman 212)—that is, as an example of "feminine masochism," which as Silverman points out, is a "specifically *male* pathology, so named because it positions its sufferer as a woman" (189).

Silverman argues that "feminine masochism" is an "accepted—indeed a requisite—element of 'normal' female subjectivity, providing a crucial mechanism for eroticizing lack and subordination," but the male subject "cannot avow feminine masochism without calling into question his identification with the masculine position" (189–90). In Amerigo's case James explores the paradox that Silverman's distinction suggests: the case of a "feminine" male masochist who remains identified—strategically identified—with the "masculine position." The passages I quoted at the beginning of this essay, moreover, alternately represent *both* Amerigo and Maggie as bound and tied. Despite this seeming paradox—two objects occupying the same subject position, so to speak—the paradox is more apparent than real. Put simply, male sadism represents the form that Amerigo's feminine masochism is allowed to take; in turn, Maggie's female masochism masks the masculine sadism she executes with her father's authority. In its paradoxical representation of a radically unstable masculinity, *The Golden Bowl* represents one of James's most complex efforts to experiment with a multivalent manhood that does not rest easily in any traditional subject position.[2]

Like Peggy McCormack, who sees the "triumph of passionate marital love" in *The Golden Bowl* (70), Mark Seltzer claims that, through Maggie's regulatory agency, the novel works toward the characters' conformity to a normative vision of marriage (65). This normative vision, however, does not inhibit exploration of a more fluid gendered economy or nonnormative gender identifications.[3] Positioning his male characters within quadrangular relationships, James destabilizes even as he valorizes their phallocentric authority. While McCormack emphasizes how both Adam and Amerigo view "human relations as a sexual and economic exchange system" (71), the two men occupy very different subject positions within James's sexual economy, especially in relation to each other. James transposes his characters, making them subjects *and* objects of diversified desires—dividing male desire, for example, among two men and a woman and dividing male subjectivity between Amerigo and Adam, making each man the codependent of the other. James unsettles male subjectivity even further, feminizing it in the process, when he delegates authority to Maggie in the second half of the novel. Put another way, James divides the "hard" labor within his sadomasochistic economy between Adam and Amerigo along traditional capitalistic lines. Amerigo's potent manhood works for Adam to reinforce patriarchal authority, leaving Amerigo to constitute his male subjectivity on his own time. Phallically and seminally empowered through the female subject position delegated by the patriarchal capitalist to his daughter, Amerigo becomes the invisible third hand of the Ververs' capitalist economy, laboring to remain more a complex male subject than a passive, feminized male victim.

James anatomizes Adam Verver, on the other hand, in traditionally gendered terms within the context of Maggie's marriage to Amerigo, Adam's own marriage to Charlotte, and his zeal for looting European museums in behalf of his own art collection. Adam values everything for its collectibility, and economic principles of exchange govern his psychology and his relationships with the other characters. Seltzer notes "a distribution or dispersion of the political into economic, linguistic, and sexual relations" (67). In James's terms, Adam "put into his one little glass everything he raised to his lips, and it was as if he had always carried in his pocket, like a tool of his trade, this receptacle, a little glass cut with a fineness of which the art had long since been lost, and kept in an old morocco case stamped in uneffaceable gilt with the arms of a deposed dynasty" (23:196). Arguably phallogocentric, this "pocket" image cuts several ways, suggesting Adam's specular and ethical rigidity on one hand, his attenuated, miniaturized phallic authority on another, and the feminization of his manhood (the phallus transfigured as receptacle) on a third. Indeed, James complicates Adam's manhood even further by suggesting its covert, even closeted, potential—something illicit that he must keep under wraps. He had "learnt the lesson of the senses, to the end of his own little book," James concludes, "without having for a day raised the smallest scandal in his economy at large; being in this particular not unlike those fortunate bachelors or other gentlemen of pleasure who so manage their entertainment of compromising company that even the austerest housekeeper, occupied and competent below-stairs, never feels obliged to give warning" (23:197). Seltzer notes that Adam "represents power" by "appearing powerless" (68). In fact, Adam *husbands* his power, as he does his sexual energy—husbands it in the act of "husbanding" in a classic illustration of spermatic economy. He husbands his sexual energy by spending it at secondhand—by employing another man to make love to his daughter and his wife.

"Nothing might affect us as queerer," observes the narrator, describing Adam's collecting project, "than this application of the same measure of value to such different pieces of property as old Persian carpets, say, and new human acquisitions" (23:196). As James positions him relationally, however, Adam strategically deploys power by delegating it to a hired hand. Adam figures less as the "stage-manager or the author of the play," James observes, than as the "financial 'backer,' watching his interests from the wing" (23:170). Adam represents one of James's most extensive investigations of phallocentric power— what Seltzer calls the "continuity between love and power" (94)—but neither his possession nor use of phallocentric privilege proceeds without complication. Indeed, reflecting the paradoxical desire to have his power and use it, too, Adam represents the lure of husbanded and secondhand power that is essentially narcissistic—ideally, that is, reserved to a self-enclosed and self-perpetuating psychic economy.

Adam's lips "somehow were closed—and by a spring connected moreover with the action of his eyes themselves," James observes. "The latter showed him what he *had* done, showed him where he had come out; quite at the top of his hill of difficulty, the tall sharp spiral round which he had begun to wind his ascent at the age of twenty, and the apex of which was a platform looking down, if one would, on the kingdoms of the earth and with standing-room for but half a dozen others" (23:131). Specular, as well as phallic, Adam's "grandiose fantasy of being master of a created world," as Beth Sharon Ash calls it (59), seems firmly embodied, part of a well-regulated organic system in which sight and speech coordinate to produce pleasure. Phallocentric pleasure involves not immediate but indirect involvement with others—a sublimation of sexuality in collection and observation that requires, it turns out, some "other" agency. Adam devotes himself to the "creation of 'interests' that were the extinction of other interests" (23:144), because his "real friend, in all the business, was to have been his own mind, with which nobody had put him in relation" (23:149).[4] He fears marriage—even fears the "supreme effort" of saying "no" to remarriage—because he conceives of marriage masochistically as a form of "bondage" and "contempt" (23:133). One of Charlotte's services is keeping off the "ravening women" who would otherwise "beset" him—"without being one herself" in the "vulgar way of the others" (23:389). In other words, by not being a "ravening woman," Charlotte will enable Adam not to be a ravenous man who provokes "vulgar" desires that threaten to bind him in a contemptible form of manhood. In that respect, Charlotte will cover his "other interests."

Fanny realizes that Adam chooses Charlotte because she is the only woman Maggie would accept (23:389), but Charlotte "works," as it were, more directly for Adam himself. Adam equates his manhood with his money—with the "huge lump" he has "thrust" under Charlotte's "nose" (23:217)—but unlike Amerigo, he does not equate masculinity with sexual expenditure. While Adam feels the responsibility to propose marriage to Charlotte after so displaying his "huge lump," he has externalized himself and his manhood in the act—representing himself at "secondhand" and, like any good capitalist, letting his money work for him. Like Gilbert Osmond, who appreciates Isabel's marital value because she spurns Lord Warburton, Adam takes a secondhand pleasure in watching other men watch Charlotte—"quite merged in the elated circle formed by the girl's free response to the collective caress of all the shining eyes" (23:216).

Although Maggie believes at the end of the novel that Adam offers himself "as a sacrifice" (24:269), he returns to America with his male power confirmed and, apparently, endlessly confirmable through Charlotte's ready sacrifice of individuality. Indeed, in the sadomasochistic economy with which James flirts in The Golden Bowl, Adam maintains the aggressive, arguably sadistic power conferred by his wealth and position—that power made manifest in the "silken noose" by which, through the "trick of his hands in his pockets" (24:330–31), he keeps Charlotte tethered. Adam's sadism only masquerades as masochism—or "sacrifice." His power and male identity may depend upon female construction and confirmation—Maggie and Charlotte's coincidentally cooperative efforts—but in his dependency he retains the capitalist's privileged position of seeing others work in his behalf. When Maggie appraises him at the end of the novel, she only seems to discount his patriarchal status by considering him the "perfect little father" as she valorizes his patriarchal position in a veritable object lesson in hagiography: "The 'successful' beneficent person, the beautiful bountiful original dauntlessly willful great citizen, the consummate collector and infallible high authority" (24:273). Adam's traditional manhood may be constructed, but it does not seem thereby subject to significant destabilization.[5] For as Maggie continues to appraise him, she continues to appreciate, or inflate, his masculine value. He "seemed to loom larger than life for her," she thinks, and she sees him in a "light of recognition" that had "never been so intense and so almost admonitory" (24:273). James's language, carefully and insistently registered in a woman's subjectivity, offers a virtual blueprint for patriarchal manhood—the Law of the Father incarnate but delegated to his daughter.

As they appear at the end of *The Golden Bowl*, in fact, Adam, Maggie, and Amerigo suggest the masochistic tableau that Deleuze discusses in *Masochism*. As Silverman explains, Deleuze "argues that masochism is entirely an affair between son and mother, or, to be more precise, between the male masochist and a cold, maternal, and severe woman whom he designates the 'oral mother.' Through the dispassionate and highly ritualized transaction that takes place between these two figures, the former is stripped of all virility, and reborn as a 'new, sexless man,' and the latter is invested with the phallus" (*Male Subjectivity* 210–11). Deleuze's paradigm helps to explain Adam's banishment to America and the installation of Maggie and Amerigo as a new first couple. "A contract is established between the hero and the woman," Deleuze argues, "whereby at a precise point in time and for a determinate period she is given every right over him. By this means the masochist tries to exorcise the danger of the father and to ensure that the temporal order of reality and experience will be in conformity with the symbolic order, in which the father has been abolished for all time" (quoted in Silverman 211). In this "utopian" rereading of masochism, as Silverman terms it, Deleuze "celebrates" a "pact between mother and son to write the father out of his dominant position within both culture and masochism, and to install the mother in his place" (211). In the capitalistic variation on this masochistic scenario that James establishes in *The Golden Bowl*, Adam may be banished, but he retains full patriarchal prerogatives in his mastery of the "haltered" Charlotte, while Maggie's power over Amerigo derives from Adam's still massive fortune and, most importantly, seems dedicated to Amerigo's phallic empowerment. Rather than abolish the father's power, James incorporates it. Amerigo retains the "use-value," in Lynda Zwinger's term, of his phallic manhood, while Adam and Maggie retain the "exchange-value."

Amerigo's half of the novel may be "decidedly masculine" (McCormack 71), and he himself may be struck from a classic masculine mold, but James complicates his manhood from the beginning by quadrangulating it relationally. Quentin Anderson considers him "the lordly male, whose sense of himself depends on his ability to subordinate women to himself" (282), and the Prince prides himself in his lovemaking, confident that his "recompense to women" was "more or less to make love to them" (23:21–22). As if representing a natural manhood, an essential, heterosexual male principle—a "basic passional force," in R. B. J. Wilson's phrase (74)—Amerigo seems more "lady-killer" than "ladies' man," but any "straight" deployment of his desire or identification of himself as a love maker to women proves difficult as he orients himself in relation to Maggie and Adam.

The novel opens, of course, as the Prince engages himself to Maggie, whom he "had been pursuing for six months as never in his life before," but that pursuit has "unsteadied" rather than settled him in an instrumental masculine role (23:4). Oscar Cargill views Amerigo as an amoral "hollow man" who has inadequate inner resources for handling the Ververs (390–91), and Dale M. Bauer calls him "empty or bankrupt" because he is inscribed by so many different cultural discourses (53). Indeed, commitment to Maggie has made Amerigo vulnerable—"sealed" his "fate"—and even threatened to emasculate him, like a "crunched key in the strongest lock that could be made" (23:5). Adam possesses that "strongest lock," the lock to his "museum of museums" (23:145), and in engaging himself to Maggie, the Prince does indeed risk being collected, locked away, and "crunched" by her father. Amerigo is "part of his collection," Maggie explains, "an object of beauty, an object of price" (49). Elizabeth Allen argues that Adam marries Amerigo through their exchange of women and thus "attempts to render the Prince feminine, the woman in their marriage," by controlling him as a sign (178), but Amerigo's emasculation or feminization coincides with his "immasculation"—with his triangulation and deployment as Adam's "secondhand" lover.

Amerigo may descend from the "godfather, or name-father,"

of the new continent (23:78), but in marrying Maggie he subjects himself to Adam's colonization.[6] He may have a "beautiful
personal presence, that of a prince in very truth, a ruler, war-
rior, patron," as Fanny believes (23:42), but within the patriarchal capitalist economy that Adam superintends, Amerigo hires
himself out. As Cheryl Torsney puts it, Adam and Amerigo not
only exchange women, they "commodify each other. The man
with the past wants the man with the cash, and vice-versa"
(142). Marrying Maggie is as much a business decision as a romantic one, a homosocial exchange "between men," in Eve Kosofsky Sedgwick's term, and the Prince negotiates the match
using his own "man of business, poor Calderoni" (23:5). Adam's
economic superiority, however, positions the Prince more in
the role of hired hand than in the role of coinvestor. Acknowledging that Adam's larger capital and "easy way with his mil-
lions" taxes his own capacity to reciprocate in this homosocial
exchange and thereby become an equal rather than minority
shareholder (23:5), the Prince examines himself in the mirror
that Adam's presence provides. He objectifies and commodifies
himself in Adam's gaze. He considers Adam "simply the best
man" he has ever seen in his life (23:6), and motivated by a desire to "*make* something different" of himself and thus "contra-
dict" or write over his "old" history (23:16), the Prince seeks to
incorporate Adam. Comparing himself to a chicken that has
been " 'chopped up and smothered in sauce; cooked down as a
creme de volaille, with half the parts left out,' " he admires
Adam as the "natural fowl" still running free. " 'I'm eating your
father alive," he tells Maggie, "which is the only way to taste
him' " (23:8). Covering Adam's incestuous desire for Maggie on
the one hand, Amerigo covers the homosocial and homoerotic
desire that his marital transaction with Adam entails. James's
imagery—of fragmentation, castration, and fellatio—destabilizes Amerigo's gendered self. Like Adam, he becomes a "false
subject," in Torsney's term, because he functions as an object
for the "other's desire" (142). To like and want to be like Adam
represents a writing over of homoerotic desire with narcissistic
longing—redirecting homoerotic desire into emulation. To
"eat" Adam, primitively speaking, means to destroy him in the
act of incorporating him and his power.[7] But in the capitalistic
terms that pervade the novel, eating Adam means incorporating him in another sense—forming a corporation, or single
body, with him through an arguably "friendly" takeover.
    From Adam's point of view, furthermore, to "collect" Amer-

igo as Maggie's husband-lover also suggests a sublimation of homoerotic desire. He enjoys characterizing Amerigo as a "variously and inexhaustibly round" man who offers no impediments to his hand "for rubbing against" (23:138)—a very different man from the sort of "rough trade" that George Chauncey has discovered in late nineteenth-century culture. Indeed, it is fair to ask which of the partners Adam actually uses. Does he employ Amerigo to make love to Maggie, or does he use Maggie to "rub against" Amerigo?[8] Most tangibly, of course, Adam uses Amerigo as a surrogate father—a sperm bank from which to sire the son he himself cannot father. Mimi Kairschner notes that Adam's apparent impotence, which Charlotte confirms (23:307), requires him to make a deal with the Prince to ensure perpetuation of the Verver empire (191). Adam's motives are not simply mercenary, however, for he also covets the second-hand pleasure of displacing Amerigo in the triangle the Principio forms with Maggie. Converting the "precious creature into a link between a mamma and a grandpa," Adam renders the Principio a "hapless half-orphan, with the place of immediate male parent swept bare and open to the next nearest sympathy" (23:156). Adam finds the capitalist-manager's ideal way of playing father—hiring out the "dirty work," as Zwinger terms it (80), to another man, who becomes an invisible *third* hand in the process.[9]

James seems especially fascinated by the tension this cooperative arrangement creates for Amerigo. One of the most attractive and phallically empowered male characters James ever imagined, Amerigo also faces one of the most severe challenges to his manly power. Bauer argues that Amerigo resists Adam's "finalizing" definition of his role, playing out that resistance in his affair with Charlotte (59). Zwinger claims, in contrast, that even though Amerigo possesses both of Adam's "daughter-wives," he "usurps use-value only." Exchange-value, the "cornerstone of capitalist economy," remains in Adam's hands (80). Even within his roles as husband and father, Amerigo gets the better of his deal with Adam—both fathering a child and endowing that child with another man's money. He beats Adam at his own capitalist game—out-fathering his father-in-law.

Looked at another way, however, *The Golden Bowl* shows James getting the sexually potent male character under control—if not exactly taming the masculine, at least harnessing and deploying it. Whatever he may have been as a man before his marriage, Amerigo performs masculinity for pay as a married man. Charlotte feels amazed at the "disproportionate intensity" with which he affects her sight, but that intensity proves more constructed than natural. In the relational economy in which Amerigo finds himself embedded, a woman's desire constructs its own ideal male object—at least to the woman's perception. "What did he do when he was away from her," Charlotte wonders, "that made him always come back only looking, as she would have called it, 'more so'?" (23:248). James emphasizes Amerigo's ability to perform himself—to perform a desirable manhood—by comparing him to an "actor who, between his moments on the stage, revisits his dressing-room, and, before the glass, pressed by his need of effect, retouches his make-up" (23:248). In the process, James subverts Amerigo's male self, rendering his manhood something that exists only in performance and depends even at that upon a female audience to give it vitality. Fanny realizes, for example, that Amerigo understands perfectly well the role that Adam and Maggie have hired him to perform: "[H]e after all visibly had on his conscience some sort of return for services rendered" (23:268). Even though he represents a "huge expense," he "had carried out his idea, carried it out by continuing to lead the life, to breathe the air, very nearly to think the thoughts, that best suited his wife and her father" (23:268–69). Amerigo's ready cooperation in producing a masculine performance on demand effectively reduces him, in the extended financial metaphor that James prosecutes throughout the novel, to a kind of bank—a sperm bank—of masculinity. Adam himself may be impotent and may figure as a "little boy" and "infant king" (23:324) to Amerigo's perception, but he has found the way to manage Amerigo and the fund of masculine power he possesses. As Amerigo himself recognizes, sitting under Adam's powerful gaze:

> This directed regard rested at its ease, but it neither lingered nor penetrated, and was, to the Prince's fancy, much of the same order as any glance directed, for due attention, from the same quarter, to the figure of a cheque received in the course of business and about to be enclosed to a banker. It made sure of the amount—and just so, from time to time, the amount of the Prince was certified. He was being thus, in renewed instalments, perpetually paid in; he already reposed in the bank as a value, but subject, in this comfortable way, to repeated, to infinite endorsement. The net result of all of which moreover was that the young man had no wish to see his value diminish. He himself decidedly hadn't fixed it—the "figure" was a conception all of Mr. Verver's own. (23:324–25)

Impotent on his own account, Adam can fulfill a capitalist and patriarchal fantasy—a form of spermatic alchemy—through the infinitely endorsable Amerigo.

This is not to say that reducing Amerigo to a value—even an infinitely endorsable one—or to a masculine performance enhances Adam's own manhood at Amerigo's expense. In the long passage quoted above, the Prince can take an ironic view of himself as a possession, but he effectively remains Adam's accomplice in producing his own "value" by working not to "diminish" it. As Bauer notes, Amerigo's perception of himself under Adam's gaze is "double-voiced." His "sideward glances at Adam's language conflict with Amerigo's own attempt to reaffirm his self, not as representative object, but as sexual subject" (61). The two characters remain interdependently connected—as labor and management—sharing what James calls a "community of interest" (23:293). Indeed, Amerigo savors the "particular 'treat,' at his father-in-law's expense, that he more and more struck himself as enjoying," even as he realizes that Adam relieves him of all "anxiety about his married life in the same manner in which he relieved him on the score of his bank-account" (23:292). In fact, to Fanny's perception, the Prince's "pay," so to speak, is Charlotte. That is, Fanny believes that she has procured two women (Maggie and Charlotte) for the Prince—that marrying Charlotte to Adam has prevented her taking some husband with whom Amerigo "wouldn't be able to open, to keep open, so large an account as with his father-in-law" (24:129). If Fanny is correct, then in effect she implicates Adam himself as an accomplice in his own cuckolding—this form of masochism being the price he has paid for the procreative (and recreative) services Amerigo provides.[10]

Is there, in fact, an independent Amerigo and in turn an independent manhood? Does Amerigo the man exist apart from his performance of a masculine part, his role as a "smoothly-working man" in the great social machinery (23:352)? At Matcham, he realizes that his "body" was "engaged at the front—in shooting, in riding, in golfing, in walking"; it also "bore the brunt of bridge-playing, of breakfasting, lunching, tea-drinking, dining, and of the nightly climax over *bottigliera,* as he called it, of the bristling tray; it met, finally, to the extent of the limited tax on lip, gesture, on wit, most of the current demands of conversation and expression" (23:327–28). But the Prince also realizes that "something of him" was "left out." The Prince thinks that "it was much more when he was alone or when he was with his own people—or when he was, say, with Mrs. Verver and nobody else—that he moved, that he talked, that he listened, that he felt, as a congruous whole" (3:328). Bringing Charlotte into the equation suggests that the Prince seeks to define himself as a "sexual subject," in Bauer's term (61), but James complicates that concept of sexual, or gendered, subjectivity—splitting, objectifying, and attenuating Amerigo's masculinity:

> "English society," as he would have said, cut him accordingly in two, and he reminded himself often, in his relations with it, of a man possessed of a shining star, a decoration, an order of some sort, something so ornamental as to make his identity not complete, ideally, without it, yet who, finding no other such object generally worn, should be perpetually and the least bit ruefully unpinning it from his breast to transfer it to his pocket. The Prince's shining star may, no doubt, have been nothing more precious than his private subtlety; but whatever the object he just now fingered it a good deal out of sight—amounting as it mainly did for him to a restless play of memory and a fine embroidery of thought. (23:328)

In this startling passage, James objectifies Amerigo's individuality, the most important part of him, as an ornament that signifies nothing but without which his identity is not complete. At the same time, James marginalizes the object that presumably makes him a "congruous whole," shuffling it into his pocket where, phallicized as it is, he can finger it "a good deal." To be a "congruous whole," in these terms, means at best playing with oneself. Amerigo's manhood has been rendered an attenuated, narcissistic "trace" or residue. In addition, Amerigo finds himself remanded to a woman's position—marginalized as a "kept man" valued chiefly for his appearance and forced to content himself, like a reincarnated Hester Prynne, with the "fine embroidery of thought."

Within the space of two paragraphs in Book Second (chapter 3), James compares Amerigo to a "domesticated lamb tied up with pink ribbon" and observes that he was "saving up" all the "wisdom, all the answers to his questions, all the impressions and generalisations he gathered; putting them away and packing them down because he wanted his great gun to be loaded to the brim on the day he should decide to fire it off" (23:163). The Prince seems to understand the doubleness that these two extravagant figures describe. " 'There are two parts of me,' " he tells Maggie in another context. " 'One is made up of the history' "—things that are " 'written,' " " 'literally in rows of volumes, in libraries' "—but " 'there's another part, very much smaller doubtless, which, such as it is, represents my single self, the unknown, unimportant—unimportant save to *you*— personal quantity' " (23:9). Amerigo struggles throughout the novel to liberate himself from the cultural and familial inscriptions that fix identity instrumentally in terms of role, but in allying himself with the house of Verver he risks a secondary, or secondhand, inscription. He feels himself to be some "old embossed coin, of a purity of gold no longer used, stamped with glorious arms, medieval, wonderful, of which the 'worth' in mere modern change, sovereigns and half-crowns, would be great enough, but as to which, since there were finer ways of using it, such taking to pieces was superfluous" (23:23). Coming to terms with his own value in a marital exchange market, he recognizes that he is "invested with attributes" and that if Adam and Maggie don't "change" him, "they really wouldn't know—he wouldn't know himself—how many pounds, shillings and pence he had to give" (23:23). Risking the inscription of a new male identity, Amerigo fears the loss of his "single self," which would be subject to "change" in the exchange economy the Ververs control. Amerigo's challenge involves marketing his manhood without marginalizing it—deploying it without rendering it deplorable (or "contemptible," in Adam's term).

The "personal quantity" in which Amerigo holds such stake resides largely in his sexual subjectivity, and he predicates that subjectivity on relationships with women who afford him opportunities for exercising sexual power. Although Amerigo thus seems to perform a conventional masculine role, he differs significantly from the more aggressive Christopher Newman and Caspar Goodwood. Possessing a more "gentlemanly" manhood, he resembles Gilbert Osmond at the end of *The Portrait of a Lady*, as he waits to see what Isabel will do. Like Osmond, the Prince waits passively—spiderlike—for women to put themselves in his power. As a "man conscious of having known many women, he could assist, as he would have called it, at the recurrent, the predestined phenomenon, the thing always as certain as sunrise or the coming round of saints' days, the doing by the woman of the thing that gave her away" (23:49). Invoking a kind of gender determinism, James archly notes that it was a woman's "nature, it was her life, and the man could always expect it without lifting a finger." "This was *his*, the man's, any man's, position and strength—that he had necessarily the advantage, that he only had to wait with a decent patience to be placed, in

spite of himself, it might really be said, in the right" (23:49–50).
Much as Adam represents power, in Seltzer's view, "by appearing powerless," James disguises Amerigo's brand of power as a
strategic passivity or patience. The Prince's manhood, his re-
curring subject position as a man, will be constructed reflex-
ively—and sadistically—at the site of women's weakness.
Weakness "produced for the man that extraordinary mixture of
pity and profit in which his relation with her, when he was not
a mere brute, mainly consisted," James explains, "and gave him
in fact his most pertinent ground of being always nice to her,
nice about her, nice *for* her. She always dressed her act up, of
course, she muffled and disguised and arranged it, showing in
fact in these dissimulations a cleverness equal to but one thing
in the world, equal to her abjection" (23:50). I can think of no
other passage in James's fiction—not even in *The Portrait of a
Lady* or *The Bostonians*—in which he so succinctly anatomizes
the internal experience of psychological brutality or the psychic
economy of sado-masochistic male-female relations. Male and
female subjects cooperate in a carnival of gendered dominance
and subordination in which weakness and abjection masquerade as strength. Male brutality, furthermore, exists most bla-
tantly in its calculated absence—as a power held in reserve
whose disguised presence in effect coerces women into laboring, or "acting," in a man's behalf. Later, in fact, as Amerigo reviews the "books" of his relations with women, he thinks that
"he had after all gained more from women than he had ever
lost by them; there appeared so, more and more, on those mystic books that are kept, in connexion with such commerce, even
by men of the loosest business habits, a balance in his favour
that he could pretty well as a rule take for granted" (23:350–51).
This male psychology, so clearly rooted in a heterosexual economy—indeed, upon a compulsive heterosexuality—compen-
sates the Prince for the abjection he feels in Adam's clutches
without canceling the "debt," as it were, in Amerigo's homosocially constructed manhood.
    Amerigo's power over women appears all the more striking in
view of his progressive disempowerment over the course of the
novel. Moving him from this naturally empowered male position, denaturalizing his manhood and manly privilege by subjecting him to the Ververs' reconstruction, James suspends him
between heterosexual and homosocial economies, as well as between sadistic and masochistic desires and identifications.
Clearly subordinate when identified homosocially and masoch-

istically, the Prince feels empowered when he is identified het-erosexually and sadistically, even as that sense of power disguises his own feminized abjection. All men are "brutes," Charlotte believes, "but the Prince's distinction was in being one of the few who could check himself before acting on the impulse. This, obviously, was what counted in a man as deli-cacy" (23:290). Charlotte attributes willpower to Amerigo that he may possess in relation to her, but in relation to Maggie and Adam his sense of empowerment—to be "brutal" or "delicate," as he may choose—seems more delusory than real, because James subjects Amerigo's manhood to a cooperative male and female gaze that brackets his power and converts it to use.

The "boundless happy margin" that Amerigo enjoys in his marriage has been carefully furnished by his father-in-law and maintained by his wife. When Maggie speculates that he might "some day get drunk and beat her," she feels imaginatively compensated by the projected masochistic thought that he can reduce other women to the "same passive pulp." Indeed, the "spectacle" of Amerigo with "hated rivals would, after no mat-ter what extremity, always, for the sovereign charm of it, charm of it in itself and as the exhibition of him that most deeply moved her, suffice to bring her round" (23:165). Ash comments that Maggie "occupies a place of passive, staring victimage, but at the same time surmounts this by scripting Amerigo's role of abuser and, more generally, by enacting this role herself as the scene's stage-director" (70). Exhibited to Maggie's gaze in a kind of carnival for one, Amerigo finds his masculinity trans-formed more into a pose than into a self-liberating and trans-gressive force. Hugh Stevens argues that Maggie's "economic power displaces the strength of the Prince's masculinity," prov-ing that money "can act as a (metaphorical) phallus" (66), but I think the Prince's phallic masculinity is not so much displaced as deployed. He performs the masculine, as it were, and so re-tains—indeed, must retain—the phallus, but Maggie's leverage and her willingness to play the battered wife appropriate his power in the act of theatricalizing it.

Later in the novel, for example, as Maggie contemplates Am-erigo's "dazzling person" at the very moment she takes charge of managing the four relationships, she thinks that she had "never felt so absorbingly married, so abjectly conscious of a master of her fate. He could do what he would with her" (24:21). Subjecting herself to Amerigo's desire only apparently empow-ers him as a sexually dominant subject, however. Indeed, somewhat like Babo in Herman Melville's "Benito Cereno," who parodies the master-slave relationship in the shaving scene he stages for Captain Delano, Maggie stages her own abjection and in turn the Prince's "mastery." Priscilla L. Walton reads this passage straightforwardly, as evidence of an abjection to masculine ideology from which Maggie then begins to liberate herself (152), but I think James stages this master-slave symbiosis ironically. By carnivalizing their gender identities as roles or poses, Maggie inscribes them with the reifying power of convention, stiffening both of them into stereotypical figures and neutralizing if not neutering Amerigo's manhood.[11] In Silverman's Freudian terms, Amerigo occupies a male subject position under the "sign of femininity" rather than masculinity (203). Amerigo must remain manly—empowered in a sadistic, masculine pose—because only then does he remain useful. Thus, when Maggie silently announces her "idea" to rearrange the four characters' relations, Amerigo responds by embracing her—a demonstration, "better than any words," designed to "dispose of" her idea for reconfiguring relations and restore their relationship at least to a traditional male-dominant, female-submissive form. Even though he thereby puts her "in his power," as she gives up and lets herself go, tasting the masochistic "terror" of her own weakness (24:28–29), she remains ultimately in control—enjoying the performance of weakness without jeopardizing her possession of strength.

James luxuriates in *The Golden Bowl*, as he does in no other novel, in the exercise of masculine and phallocentric power. Why does he go to such lengths to stress Amerigo's phallocentric potency when in fact that power is consistently contained and harnessed—employed by Adam as a hired (third) hand in a sexual "man-u-factory" and domesticated by Maggie's "labour" within a "steel hoop of an intimacy compared with which artless passion would have been but a beating of the air" (24:141)? The attraction for James arguably cuts both ways by producing pleasure from both subject positions. He can write an exaggeratedly masculine subject into being and simultaneously become the object, masked as the desiring female subject, of masculine desire.

Such confusion of sexual subjectivity intrigued James as he represented his own authorial subjectivity as writer, reader, and reviser of *The Golden Bowl*. Adam's secondhand fatherhood, for example, mirrors James's as he defines it in his preface. Initially, he observes that the figures he creates amount to

"nought from the moment they fail to become more or less visible appearances," but when they do so the result is "charming"
for their creator because he can see "such power as he may possess approved and registered by the springing of such fruit from
his seed" (23:x). In this progenitive view of literary creativity,
James names himself the father of his characters—out-Adam-
ing Adam. But James also dismisses himself from the scene of
creation, much as he does Adam—surrendering power over the
"fruit of his seed" by attributing it to others. "His own garden,"
he says, "remains one thing, and the garden he has prompted
the cultivation of at other hands becomes quite another" (23:x).
Literary paternity, he suggests, is often secondhand.

Much as he divides male subjectivity between Adam and Amerigo, furthermore, James's sense of his own authorial second-
handedness takes the form of gender doubling and inversion—a
splitting of an androgynous authorial self into separate personae. As re-reader and reviser of his earlier work, James takes
his reader's place, transposing himself as it were into *self* and
other and playing both roles. He thereby closes the writerly cir-
cuit, collapsing "difference" through a self-authorizing act of
auto-aesthetic intercourse. The "march" of his "present attention" coincides sufficiently with the "march" of his "original expression," he says with some satisfaction:

> As the historian of the matter sees and speaks, so my intelligence
> of it, as a reader, meets him halfway, passive, receptive, apprecia-
> tive, often even grateful; unconscious, quite blissfully, of any bar to
> intercourse, any disparity of sense between us. Into his very foot-
> prints the responsive, the imaginative steps of the docile reader
> that I consentingly become for him all comfortably sink; his vision,
> superimposed on my own as an image in cut paper is applied to a
> sharp shadow on a wall, matches, at every point, without excess or
> deficiency. This truth throws into relief for me the very different
> dance that the taking in hand of my earlier productions was to lead
> me. (23:xiii)

Characterizing the arguably erotic pleasure that reading offers,
James reconfigures that pleasure autoerotically by doubly gendering himself—masculinizing his original writerly self (the
sower of "seed," the historian) and feminizing (and homoeroti-
cizing) his readerly self (the "docile" and "passive" receptor,
the one who takes "in hand").

James goes on, in fact, to elaborate his own feminization as
reviser, characterizing himself as a nursemaid or governess—

another form of secondhand parent. Not least among the "creeping superstitions" he experienced, as he kept his finished work "well behind" him, "rioted doubtless the fond fear that any tidying-up of the uncanny brood, any removal of accumulated dust, any washing of wizened faces, or straightening of grizzled locks, or twitching, to a better effect, of superannuated garments, might let one in, as the phrase is, for expensive renovations" (23:xiv). Playing governess to someone else's literary progeny, even when that someone else is oneself, can prove dangerous because of the threatened loss of control—the demands for attention and revision—and the potential destabilization of the author's male self. The "moment a stitch should be taken or a hair-brush applied," he recognizes, "the *principle* of my making my brood more presentable under the nobler illumination would be accepted and established, and it was there complications might await me" (23:xv). What interests me about this imagery is the traditional gendering in which James indulges. In positioning himself as the rereader and reviser of his texts, he removes himself from the procreative moment, which he figures androcentrically as an autogenetically primal scene. Rereading and revising, on the other hand, James feminizes as woman's work. Analogously, he thus identifies himself with Maggie in the novel itself; for Maggie revises the Verver "brood" in the process of normalizing relations and making them all more "presentable." But in consenting to become a kind of "docile" reader and then reviser of the relational text, Maggie masks her power in order to leave Amerigo's masked manhood intact. So too, it can be argued, does James play the female—nursing his "brood" through the revising process while he valorizes the creative, procreatively masculine self that authored them in the first place.

As Maggie contemplates Amerigo's "sovereign personal power" in the context of her own plot to revise proper relationships, she recognizes that she has opened herself to the possibility of attack—has subjected herself, in Silverman's terms, to "feminine masochism." "Attack, real attack from him as he would conduct it," she thinks, "was what she above all dreaded; she was so far from sure that under that experience she mightn't drop into some depth of weakness, mightn't show him some shortest way with her that he would know how to use again" (24:139–40). In her martial view of marriage, Maggie translates fear and desire into defensive and offensive strategies, but James goes on in this extended passage to probe at her "dread" of weakness, explicitly if indirectly balancing female weakness with male power at the site of his own authorial desire. The weaker Maggie feels, the stronger and more potent the Prince appears. "She loved him too helplessly still to dare to open the door by an inch to his treating her as if either of them had wronged the other," James observes, submerging morality in the politics of desire. The "result of the direct appeal of *any* beauty in him would be her helpless submission to his terms" (24:140). Indeed, a "single touch from him—oh she should know it in case of its coming!—any brush of his hand, of his lips, of his voice, inspired by recognition of her probable interest as distinct from pity for her virtual gloom, would hand her over to him bound hand and foot" (24:142). Anatomizing Amerigo in a manner usually reserved for female characters in male-authored texts, James emphasizes his masculine instrumentality—the eroticized, desiring actions of his body—and his power to fulfill an arguably feminocentric sadomasochistic fantasy. Sadism is simply the form that Amerigo's masochism is allowed to take. The more powerful he can be made, the bigger his "gun," the more enjoyable his domestication as a "lamb." Phallically empowered in a masterful position within a femininely constructed economy, Amerigo can be heterosexualized through the secondhand power of the female gaze and female desire, even as he becomes homosexualized—at third hand—by Adamic and authorial desire. Playing "rough trade" to Maggie's performance of submissive wife, Amerigo effectively reverses positions and roles off the stage—in the closet that compulsively heterosexual relationships hide from view.

Whereas Amerigo had predicated his male subjectivity on being able to wait patiently and passively for women to "place" him "in the right," the tables seem turned in his relationship with Maggie. In effect, she occupies what James called "the man's, any man's, position and strength," while Amerigo's only choice, like Charlotte's, involves "arranging appearances"— that is, showing in *his* "dissimulations" of male strength a cleverness equal to his "abjection." Immediately after Fanny smashes the golden bowl, for example, leaving the stunned Amerigo at Maggie's mercy, Maggie feels almost embarrassed by the power she suddenly wields, and she feels a "strong, sharp wish not to see his face again till he should have had a minute to arrange it" (24:181). In dreading her own advantage, Maggie reveals her stake in controlling but not emasculating her husband—in allowing him a margin in which to reconstruct his

manhood not just for his own sake but for hers. Take all the
time you need, she wants to say to him; "arrange yourself so as
to suffer least, or to be at any rate least distorted and disfigured" (24:184). Amerigo's manhood has been cast suddenly, violently into a state of suspense. In the metaphorically sadomasochistic dance he performs with Maggie, instead of exercising the power to bind her "hand and foot" with a "single touch"
or simple "brush" of his lips, he himself is subject to disfig-
urement. As I noted, however, Maggie has reason to exercise
her power in Amerigo's behalf—at least to the extent of enabling him to recover the appearance or pose of manhood.
"Above all," she continues to fantasize, "don't show me, till
you've got it well under, the dreadful blur, the ravage of suspense and embarrassment produced, and produced by my
doing, in your personal serenity, your incomparable superiority" (24:184).

Amerigo's protean willingness to perform different parts and
occupy different gender positions becomes clear as Maggie's
plan unfolds. Part of that plan involves reaffirming her ties with
Charlotte and in turn repositioning both Adam and Amerigo in
homosocial relation to each other. Just as Maggie's marriage
upset the delicately balanced relational economy between herself and her father, restoration of the new married economy requires careful rebalancing. If Maggie spends more time with
Charlotte, someone must fill the void Charlotte leaves with
Adam. Maggie requires that Amerigo, acting on the "cue" he
takes from simply observing "the shade of change in *her* behaviour," take Charlotte's place—sitting with Adam while Maggie
goes out with Charlotte or making some display that "would
represent the equivalent of her excursions" (24:39–40). So thoroughly inscribed and inscribable is Amerigo that Maggie can
safely rely on his ability to play "sublimely a gentleman," using
his "instinct for relations" and fulfilling the mission she has
tacitly marked out for him (24:40). He allows himself to be positioned—indeed, readily positions himself—in Charlotte's place
with Adam, feigning desire for Adam's company, letting it seem
to Adam that he "suits" him (24:59), because any desire generated by such dangerous repositioning will be carefully covered
through Maggie's mediation. " 'If I didn't love you, you know,
for yourself,' " she tells him, " 'I should still love you for *him*' "
(24:40). Mediating Maggie's love for her father, Amerigo occupies a doubly feminized position, but James screens out of the
text the full homosexual implications of his relation to Adam,

emphasizing Amerigo's *performance* of this role under Maggie's direction and thus covering homoerotic with filial heterosexual desire.

Here, as elsewhere, Maggie works to ensure Amerigo's retention of masculine prerogatives and power even as she employs his gentled manhood for her own purposes. Ironically, in fact, Maggie empowers herself within a heterosexual, marital economy precisely to the extent that she apparently cedes sexual power to Amerigo. When she feels herself "in his exerted grasp," she lies at the same time "in the grasp of her conceived responsibility," and "of the two intensities the second was presently to become the sharper" (24:56). Amerigo can be "so munificent a lover," she recognizes, at the same time that his munificence "was precisely a part of the character she had never ceased to regard in him as princely" (24:56–57). She calculates her own role and pose, trusting to Amerigo's quick apprehension of the complementary role and pose—the complementary manhood—her desire constructs for him. "She should have but to lay her head back on his shoulder with a certain movement," she understands, "to make it definite for him that she didn't resist" (24:57). In fact, however, for one of the few times in the novel, Amerigo resists the role that Maggie inscribes, refusing to speak the lines she tacitly prompts. Although "touch by touch she thus dropped into her husband's silence the truth about his good nature and his good manners," he does not speak the "five words" (an invitation to be together, just the two of them) that "would break her utterly down" (24:59–60).

In resisting his part as aggressively heterosexual male, Amerigo preserves a certain integrity even as he jeopardizes it by opening himself to the implications of Maggie's alternative plan. For in refusing to utter the words that would "break" her down and thereby empower himself in a conventionally aggressive or brutal male role, Amerigo leaves himself little choice but to substitute for Charlotte with Adam. If he won't go off with Maggie, he will have to go off with Adam—indeed, according to Maggie's project, escape with Adam from their domestic confinement "like a shot." As Maggie says, "[F]or the question of going off somewhere, he'd go readily, quite delightedly, with you" (24:61). While this projected realignment of the couples along same-sex lines exemplifies the carnivalesque spirit of the novel—the swapping of positions with which James has such fun experimenting within his strict relational economy—the planned excursion, as well as the female-to-female relationship it would leave behind, seems to founder because both Maggie and Adam need to keep up the pretense that they and their spouses "perfectly rub on together" (24:89). In this case, then, the normalizing pressure of heterosexual marriage, in Seltzer's term, seems to operate effectively to prevent "other," deviant sexualities or subjectivities from emerging. In fact, heterosexual marriage effectively covers "other" relationships, enabling Amerigo to "rub on" with Adam without jeopardizing his subject position within a heterosexual matrix of desires.

Amerigo's male subjectivity, of course, is sufficiently threatened with instability within that heterosexual matrix. In his analysis of late-nineteenth- and early-twentieth-century New York culture, George Chauncey notes that the "relationship between men and 'fairies' was represented symbolically as a male-female relationship" because "gender behavior rather than homosexual behavior per se was the primary determinant of a man's classification as a fairy" (66). More specifically, Chauncey points out, as long as a man "maintained a masculine demeanor and played (or claimed to play) only the 'masculine,' or insertive role in the sexual encounter—so long, that is, as they eschewed the style of the fairy and did not allow their bodies to be sexually penetrated—neither they, the fairies, nor the working-class public considered *them* to be queer" (66).

While *The Golden Bowl* seems to work toward Adam's masculine reempowerment, at least at second or third hand, it seems to work toward Amerigo's emasculation—or immasculation under the sign of the feminine. In his case, as in Adam's, James seems to close off possibilities for plural masculine performances. Both male characters, furthermore, occupy their final positions largely through a woman's agency. If they are not exactly positioned *in* the feminine, they are positioned *by* the feminine. Adam may figure as the capitalist patriarch, in Kairschner's term, but Maggie plays the role of "fore-woman," whose job is to train and get the work out of Amerigo. As I noted earlier, James describes Amerigo as "straitened and tied" under the spotlight of Maggie's insistent gaze. His "discomfort" yearns at Maggie "out of his eyes," and so deeply does he feel the suspense into which his manhood has been cast that he seems to move back from his felt condition "as from an open chasm" (24:192). James represents him as "writhing in his pain," the pain, among other things, of gender inversion—of being, "like his wife, an abjectly simple person" (24:193).

Although Joseph Allen Boone claims that James leaves Maggie's marriage to Amerigo "suspended, open to question, at text's end" (189), it seems difficult to argue convincingly that the two characters' gender identities end in a state of suspense. Boone posits a second story parallel to Maggie's in which Amerigo and his perspective "refuse assimilation into one univocal pattern" (194), but that second story—presumably a manly male narrative of prolific and transgressive lovemaking—seems more theoretical than real. At the end of the penultimate chapter, for example, Maggie confronts the Prince's "irresistible, overcharged" presence (24:351), but she finally gets herself "off" from the threat (24:353). The scene certainly tests the proposition that Amerigo retains his power to write his own role and story by writing over the character and plot Maggie has inscribed. Approaching her as she prepares to leave, with her hand on the door knob, Amerigo seems reempowered in the masculine role of "lady-killer" he had played at the beginning of the novel, and he seems to override Maggie's own intentions, leaving her only the "endless power of surrender"—suggestively, the power to yield "inch by inch." Maggie "couldn't for her life with the other hand have pushed him away," James notes. Registering phallogocentrism through an ostensible female subject position, James displays Amerigo enforcing his authority with his body, which he converts into a kind of weapon. "He was so near now that she could touch him, taste him, smell him, kiss him, hold him," James notes; "he almost pressed upon her, and the warmth of his face—frowning, smiling, she mightn't know which; only beautiful and strange—was bent upon her with the largeness with which objects loom in dreams" (24:352). Maggie does finally resist Amerigo's power, as well as her own desire; she puts out her hand, which he holds, and like a policewoman instructs him to "wait" (24:352). Perhaps Maggie only temporizes, postponing the real confrontation over sexual mastery, but she effectively wins this battle with herself and with her husband in the terms I have already suggested—simultaneously appreciating and controlling his powerful masculine performance and, by leaving him his "reserve," enforcing a spermatic economy. Amerigo's hand may be over her "cast" of the dice in the final scene of the novel, but it seems to me that Maggie remains the one who hires and "commissions" that hand to work.[12] With his hands on her shoulders, his "whole act enclosing her," he plays the part she has written for him—seeing only her, dedicating his complete manhood to her alone, specularly causing feelings of "pity and dread," and therefore enabling her safely to bury her face in his breast (24:369). She can have her "dread" and eat it, too.

At best, it seems to me, James has established a state of uneasy tension in Amerigo's case between being and performance. By that I mean that the Prince reemerges as a "congruous whole"—a complete man—but largely because his performance of that part fulfills the job description under which he was hired in the beginning. The challenge James has set himself involves finding a place within a masculine discourse in which Amerigo can remain a male subject—a way to leave Amerigo's masculinity intact, to leave him not one inch less a man while simultaneously harnessing and directing his masculine power.

Although Maggie wonders if Amerigo has "recovered himself" and retains "any thought of wounding her" in order to "reestablish a violated order" (24:220), the Prince appears to have settled himself into the role she has written for him—a male masochist under the aegis of female authority rather than the arguably sadistic "lady-killer" of his earlier incarnation. He received the crisis from her, James notes, "as he might have received a bunch of keys or a list of commissions—attentive to her instructions about them, but only putting them for the time very carefully and safely into his pocket" (24:219). Earlier, James had represented Adam's acquisitiveness as a glass "receptacle" that he "always carried in his pocket"; he had represented Amerigo's male identity as a "shining star" he could transfer to his pocket and "finger" a good deal "out of sight." In returning to such a "pocket" metaphor at the end of the novel, James emphasizes the change that has occurred in Amerigo's sense of himself—the extent to which he now experiences his manhood at secondhand, as a performance that Maggie "commissions." The phallic woman in effect gives or lends the phallus to her husband, enabling him to reconstruct himself according to her "instructions"—to police himself, in Seltzer's terms (61), by dedicating his manhood to her. Indeed, as she penetrates the depths of Amerigo's eyes, Maggie discovers, or perhaps only projects, the "tacitly-offered sketch of a working arrangement." "Leave me my reserve; don't question it—it's all I have just now," she imagines Amerigo pleading; "if you'll make me the concession of letting me alone with it for as long a time as I require I promise you something or other, grown under cover of it, even though I don't yet quite make out what, as a return for your patience" (24:221). Like a debtor pleading for more time to the loan shark's collector, Amerigo effectively begs for his manhood—for the chance, under Maggie's supervisory eye, to "grow" a little "something or other" under the protective "cover" she and their marriage provide. There was "but one way," James writes, "in which a proud man reduced to abjection could hold himself" (24:228), and to underwrite that "one way," to "make sure of the beauty shining out of the humility and of the humility lurking in all the pride of his presence," Maggie "would have gone the length of paying more yet, paying with difficulties and anxieties compared to which those actually before her might have been as superficial as headaches on rainy days" (24:228–29). If Charlotte ends up with a silken halter around her neck, Amerigo ends up, to Maggie's perception, "caged" and even more under her control than Charlotte is under Adam's—the difference being that Amerigo appears caged "by his own act and his own choice" (24:338). In assuming such a position within the sadomasochistic sexual economy James has established, Amerigo has put the whip and the chair—as well as the third hand of his invisible, or "pocketed," manhood—in Maggie's hand.

Notes

Editor's note: Person's citations to The Golden Bowl *are to the Scribner's New York edition.*

1. As Joseph Allen Boone comments, this "image of male mastery" simply "underlines the role of sexual differentiation in upholding the power structure of matrimony and patriarchal society" (193).

2. David McWhirter notes that James's characterization of his infamous "obscure hurt" "points to a strong masochistic element in James's psychological dynamic" (166) and provides him with a "cornerstone" for his lifelong myth of himself as a "powerless victim of a pre-determined fate" (167). McWhirter goes on to argue, however, that "it is this disturbing, ultimately masochistic aesthetic fatalism, and its concomitant failure of artistic responsibility, that James emphatically rejects in *The Golden Bowl*—largely through Maggie's exercise of freedom and full embrace of love.

3. Beth Sharon Ash, in fact, cogently argues that Maggie's reconstitution of relationships "is not a restoration of relations according to the conventional marital norm, but rather a concealment of psychic regression in a manifest devotion to the marital norm" (80).

4. Ash reads Adam as essentially narcissistic and motivated by a desire for the "assertion of narcissistic mastery" (59). Using James Clifford's paradigm of the "Eurocentric collector," Ash concludes that Adam "does not so much

use the gathering of objects to make a place for the self in the world as deploy his accumulation to fashion the world as a reflection of self" (60).

5. Ash argues, in fact, that Maggie "devotes herself to maintaining the childhood fantasy of paternal perfection" and thus consigns herself to a regressive, "narcissistic 'folie a deux' " with her father (61).

6. Seltzer observes Maggie's "domestic colonialism" by way of arguing that the "ability to put oneself in the other's skin underwrites the infiltration and displacement of the other fellow" (72). "The very ability Maggie displays—her ability to stand in two places at once—indicates the instability of her own position" (73). Amerigo's desire to occupy Adam's place, not only maritally but also socially and economically, similarly destabilizes his gendered subject position.

7. Deriving the terms from Max Scheler, Silverman distinguishes between "idiopathic" and "heteropathic" identification in terms that seem useful for understanding Amerigo's relation to Adam. Idiopathic identification "conforms to an incorporative model," she points out, "constituting the self at the expense of the other who is in effect 'swallowed' " (205). Amerigo's eating Adam "alive" seems designed to constitute a male self through such an act of incorporation. Heteropathic identification, on the other hand, "subscribes to an exteriorizing logic, and locates the self at the site of the other." Vicariously, like Adam, one "lives, suffers, and experiences pleasure through the other" (205)—in Adam's case, through Amerigo and his marriage to Maggie.

8. In the famous "pagoda" passage that begins Book Second, Maggie herself reviews the simple relational economy that her marriage apparently established. She "had been able to marry without breaking, as she liked to put it, with her past," James notes. "She had surrendered herself to her husband without the shadow of a reserve or a condition and yet hadn't all the while given up her father by the least little inch." Indeed, marrying Amerigo has enabled an intimate male bond to emerge, as the "two men beautifully take to each other," and "nothing in her marriage" makes her happier than "this fact of its having practically given the elder, the lonelier, a new friend" (24:5).

9. Kairschner refers briefly to Adam Smith's theory of the "hidden hand" to characterize the "ideological distortion" in Adam's representation of his wealth. The "mere suggestion that his collection multiplies by itself [see GB 23:140] depends upon an ideological distortion—fundamental to finance capital—that material wealth is self-generated in some ethereal realm (guided, no doubt, by Adam Smith's 'hidden hand'), rather than in the realm of production, where it is created by human labor" (189).

10. My view of male cooperation is compatible with Seltzer's observation that "every exercise of power is inevitably doubly binding. To arrange and to control is to enter into a relation with one's 'adversary,' and the bond thus formed is reciprocally coercive" (70).

11. Bauer makes a very different claim about Maggie's "carnivalization of her relations." "Because carnival celebrates the joyful relativity of all relations in lieu of hierarchy," she argues, "Maggie is able to break Adam's economic and sexual power and assert her own" (78). But it seems to me that carnivalizing Amerigo's manhood fantasmatically, as Maggie does, exaggerates it and thereby subjects it to control.

12. Seltzer claims that Maggie normalizes relations by transferring power to the Prince. He takes literally and straightforwardly the "truth" that James attributes to Maggie's awareness—that the Prince's recovered "force" causes

her "pity and dread." Boone sees ambiguity in the final scene and in its gestures, noting that if the Prince decides to "spend" himself sexually, as his
holding out the money bag to Maggie might suggest and as her obvious desire
to consummate their remarriage would encourage, he will have implicated
her in an "essentially masculine 'plot' of desire whose linear trajectory must
inevitably curtail the 'loosening' and 'float[ing]' tide that figures her own
wished-for release" (199). Bauer sees ambiguity, too, although she sees Maggie triumphing over Adam, if not necessarily over Amerigo. "With no other
interpretive model, Maggie is left to invent for herself a discourse which does
not shut out Amerigo's," she argues, "but does not admit her father's selfish
monolithic discourse of money and sexuality back into the picture" (88). For
Ash, however, the ending represents only the appearance of mature love—
"the semblance of a psychic dissolution of the father-daughter bond" (66). In
her view, then, Amerigo ends up conscripted into the Ververs' mutual narcissistic fantasy—an "extension" of oedipal and preoedipal desire (75).

James and the Representation of Women: Some Lessons of the Master(')s

SARAH B. DAUGHERTY

MY ESSAY RESPONDS TO A CENTRAL QUESTION: WHY HAS THERE NOT been more gender-focused criticism of James? The interest of the case, as the novelist might have said, is heightened by his apparent emphasis of women's themes, as when he wrote of "how absolutely, how inordinately, the Isabel Archers, and even much smaller female fry, insist on mattering" (*Literary Criticism: French Writers* 1077). The rhetoric of the Prefaces, however, which celebrates women yet covertly belittles them, suggests one reason why James has puzzled would-be analysts and theorists. Should we commend him for his "feminist sympathies," as Peggy McCormack has done (31)? Or should we follow Alfred Habegger and stress his condescension toward little women, whose fictional houses had to be constructed by a master builder? Each perspective must be qualified by the other. In representing women, James improved on the art of most of his rival novelists, introducing thematic subtleties that merit feminist recognition. But like the "strong poets" described by Harold Bloom, he asserted his will to power over his competitors—male and female alike—and over the characters he created.

Those who regard James as a feminist author must contend, first of all, with his lack of interest in women's political movements: by his own admission, the gaps in *The Bostonians* resulted from his "knowing terribly little about the kind of life [he] had attempted to describe" (*Henry James Letters* 3:121). As Richard H. Brodhead has noted, James's fiction derives less from social and political history than from "the works of other writers. . . . His intercourse is first and foremost with other masters of his form; nonliterary influences act on him more remotely, through the mediation of literary relations" (116–17). Brodhead is likewise perceptive in focusing on James's inti-

176

macy with his male predecessors. As we shall see, the novelist minimized the importance of women writers, directing his most serious critical efforts toward the men he sought to displace.

Yet James cannot merely be dismissed as a Bloomian male chauvinist. His close relationship with his sister Alice and his sense of being besieged by more masculine contemporaries led him to sympathize with oppressed women; and his interest in these figures as literary subjects was enhanced by his reading of fiction, both by his acknowledged masters and by others whose influence he effaced. The female victim of a patriarchal culture, personified by a despotic father, suitor, or husband, is the most common protagonist of the novels James read and reviewed. She frequently appears in the works of the British Victorians, notably Anthony Trollope and George Eliot. One encounters her again in American fiction—the romances of Nathaniel Hawthorne and the women's novels of the 1860s and '70s. And she is a key figure in scores of European novels: the now forgotten works of Gustave Droz and Victor Cherbuliez as well as those of George Sand, Gustave Flaubert, Ivan Turgenev, and, of course, Honoré de Balzac. James could hardly have failed to perceive how much she mattered, particularly to an aspiring novelist and his audience of female readers. But as a subject, she also posed a challenge, for she had been dealt with so often that a young writer might have seen little chance for originality in his treatment of her. Fortunately for James, however, the majority of nineteenth-century novels—even those by writers we now regard as canonical—were diffuse, sentimental, amateurishly written, and thematically confused. In a word, they were bad: so bad that they invited revision and reinscription; so bad that scholars undertaking to read them may very well shrink from the task.

I would argue, then, that feminists should forgive James for his pomposity and his occasional chauvinism, because his novels are indeed superior to most of their prototypes. Nonetheless, we should be cautious about inferring that their superiority results from James's feminism, or from his having been more of a feminist than were his predecessors. Almost invariably, his critical judgments were aesthetic rather than political: he complained of novels that were dull or sentimental without commenting on the ideological reasons for their flaws, which often stemmed from the writers' belated efforts to defend the patriarchal system they had called into question. Further, James rejected some of the lessons of Eliot and Hawthorne, whose political and social concerns were greater than his own. From Turgenev, whose influence he accepted with fewer reservations, he learned to idealize women in a manner resistant to analytical criticism. And from Balzac, his chosen master, he learned that a conservative ideology, not a democratic or a radical one, best served the novelist's primary need—the need for dramatic material.

James's critiques of Trollope (the subject of four early reviews and a memorial essay) provide the best example of how the novelist's aesthetic interests could serve ends we would identify as feminist. James approved of Trollope's *Linda Tressel* and *Nina Balatka,* whose European heroines rebel against the marriages arranged for them by their elders. While Sir Walter Scott, said James, "travelled through romantic gorges and enchanted forests . . . Mr. Trollope trudges through crowded city streets and dusty highways and level garden paths. But the two roads converge and meet at the spot where a sweet young girl lies dying of a broken heart" (*Literary Criticism: Essays* 1330). In these remarks of 1868, one discerns the literary origins of Daisy Miller and Milly Theale, women who could redeem a reality James found commonplace and banal. But he was bored by Trollope's "prosaic" English novels, whose female protagonists had "no adventures" save the conventional one of finding an appropriate spouse (*Literary Criticism: Essays* 1313).

Can You Forgive Her? illustrates Trollope's virtues and his defects as James perceived them. The plot involving Alice Vavasor, who prefers her "wild" cousin George to the paternalistic John Grey, contains the germ of a feminist theme: that a woman needs to satisfy her passions as well as the demands of polite society. But as a believer in patriarchal order, Trollope reverses this theme by making George into a scoundrel whom Alice comes to loathe and by transforming Grey into a paragon of masculine virtue. ("She knew now that she must follow his guidance. She had found her master, as we sometimes say"[2:358].) James had little patience with such anxious moralizing ("What are we to forgive?") or with the dullness of the narrative, which might have been alleviated, he said, if George and Alice had actually been lovers. "Our desire . . . is simply founded on the fact that [a sexual affair] would have been so much more interesting" (*Literary Criticism: Essays* 1318, 1319). In James's view, the true heroine of the novel was not the dutiful Alice but her less conventional friend: "Lady Glencora, young and fascinating, torn from the man of her heart and married to a stranger, and pursued after marriage by her old lover, . . . touches at a hundred points almost upon the tragical" (*Literary Criticism: Essays* 1320). Once again, however, James was displeased with Trollope's conservative denouement, in which Glencora and her husband, the unimaginative Plantagenet Palliser, are reconciled following the birth of a son and heir. "[W]e have more respect for Lady Glencora's humanity than to suppose that [this] incident . . . is for her anything more than an interruption" (*Literary Criticism: Essays* 1321).

Thus, for reasons both humane and aesthetic, James sided with female characters against male writers who belatedly defended the status quo. Without venturing into political criticism, he deplored the dullness of predictable plots and the falseness of happy endings. But he quickly recognized an important fact—one that feminist critics should acknowledge as well. These flaws were even more pronounced in the fiction of female writers, who often portrayed women's oppression as necessary and even as desirable. Hence James, early in his career, could easily (perhaps too easily) assume the role of the experienced man of letters giving salutary correction to neophytes. If Bloom's major writers had to "wrestle with their strong precursors" (5), James had the luxury—and the potential disadvantage—of contending with those who were weaker than himself.

In *Henry James and the "Woman Business,"* Habegger takes the novelist to task for his "appropriation, masterly and distorting, of American women's fiction" (4). Nonetheless, as Habegger himself implies in his discussions of individual texts, James's critical barbs were usually well aimed. Prior to the Civil War, there had been a strong tradition of women's fiction, one that celebrated the heroine's ability to make her own way in the world. But as Nina Baym has shown, the tradition was weakened after 1865, when female writers became less assured in their ideology yet more didactic in their purpose (*Woman's Fiction* 13, 23, 50, 298). Thus, the women's novels James reviewed in the late 1860s were marked by the authors' ambivalence, their efforts to fit their subject—women's sexual and romantic desires—into an acceptable moral framework.

Consider, for example, Anne Moncure Crane Seemueller's *Emily Chester* (1864). The heroine makes the fatal error of marrying Max Crampton, a chauvinist whom she finds sexually repulsive. ("There is," says the narrator, "a certain degree of heart starvation which will kill any naturally constituted

woman" [132].) Emily's misjudgment results partly from her
Puritan background (13), partly from her vulnerability following
her father's death (94), and partly from the fact that Frederick
Hastings—the suitor to whom she is drawn "by a species of animal magnetism" (19)—is a dilettante who is not initially in love
with her. But the narrator's rhetoric transforms the novel into
a fable concerning "the use and office of pain" (7). Even as her
soul consumes her body, Emily recognizes that "pain and trial
are the means for [her] development" (137); and after a long
career as a domestic saint, she becomes an "angel before the
throne of God" (366). Hence, as in so many novels of the nineteenth century, the fact of women's suffering is transmuted
into the proposition that they ought to suffer. James's review of
this novel is slightly comical in its gravity. ("Beasts and idiots
act from their instincts; educated men and women . . . act from
their reason, however perverted, and their affections, however
misplaced" [*Literary Criticism: Essays* 592].) But one can hardly
quarrel with his judgment that the novel typifies an "age of con-
scientious poor books" (*Literary Criticism: Essays* 588). In a
continuation of this tradition of suffering heroines that im-
proves upon the tradition—as Habegger admits—we can admire James's decision to endow such victims as Isabel Archer
"with the steel of personal accountability" (123).

Louisa May Alcott's *Moods* (1865) furnishes yet another example of the kind of sentimentality James learned to avoid. As
in *Emily Chester,* the narrator argues against confounding
friendship with passion, calling Sylvia's marriage to the stolid
Geoffrey Moor "the fatal false step of her life" (147). Predictably, however, this heroine also remains faithful unto death, encouraged by a friend named Faith. But supreme virtue is
embodied in Sylvia's true love, Adam Warwick, whose "grand
lines" suggest those of "the perfect man" (284). He comforts
the unhappy Sylvia, assuring her that he "design[s] no French
sentiment nor sin" (215), and eventually sacrifices his life to
save Geoffrey from drowning ("a great and tender heart went
down into the sea" [281]). Wrote James, "There is a most dis-
couraging good-will in the manner in which lady novelists elaborate their impossible heroes" (*Literary Criticism: Essays* 190).

Another novel, Elizabeth Stoddard's *Two Men* (1865), illustrates the extent to which James's female contemporaries
sometimes pursued antifeminist themes. Jason Austen, Stoddard's Emersonian protagonist, is tormented by his frigid wife
and by the ward he secretly loves, a girl said to be "cold as a

glacier" until (following the wife's death) she returns his passion and discards her misguided interest in his son (270). (Stoddard's "whole point," according to Habegger, is that "it [takes] a man like Jason to wake Philippa up to her womanhood" [96].) In his unpublished review, James objected to the novel's "violent style" and to its reliance on stereotypes. "A silence like the stage imitation of thunder interrupted by remarks like the stage imitation of flashes of lightning: such to our perceptions are the chief attributes of Jason Austen" (*Literary Criticism: Essays* 616). Thus, James resisted the hero of women's fantasies, "ardent, resolute, overpowering" (Stoddard 268). Contrast his own unromantic portrayal of Caspar Goodwood. The young reviewer may or may not have seen that "[t]he cruelest aspect of the process of oppression is the logic by which it forces its objects to be oppressive in turn" (Douglas 11). But he did recognize, and condemn, the distortions of sentimental fiction.

For James, the supreme exemplar of the female imagination was Sand, whose novels provided a counterpoint to those of American women. Characteristically, he was ambivalent toward Sand's franker treatment of sexual themes: at times he lamented her failure to distinguish "between the pure and the impure," but he also praised her for representing "*passion*" as the timid Anglo-Saxons had not (*Literary Criticism: French Writers* 707, 724). Moreover, he commended her for being a better stylist than the amateur writers he was paid to review: "The narrative gushes along copious and translucent as a deep and crystalline stream . . . " (*Literary Criticism: French Writers* 698). Elise Miller has argued persuasively that James may have felt threatened by Sand's fluid, feminine style, which subverts rigid distinctions—including those of gender (31, 36). But the rhetoric of his remarks is mainly laudatory, suggesting his admiration of one who could write "as the bird sings" (*Literary Criticism: French Writers* 717).

He was unimpressed, however, by the content of Sand's romances, which celebrate the sacrifices women make in the name of love. From a masculine point of view, Sand's heroines could be treacherous, abandoning their lovers and lying to their husbands "from motives of highest morality" (*Literary Criticism: French Writers* 732). James's story "Eugene Pickering" (1874) is a satire on this femme fatale, who manipulates the poor young man until he comes to his senses and is rescued by a nice American girl (significantly named Isabel). Nonetheless, as in his reviews of American fiction, James acknowledged that the myth of romantic self-sacrifice was equally damaging to women. Sand, he remarked, used her "immense imagination . . . for the benefit, absolutely, of the so-called stronger sex, . . . to liberate her sisters up to the point at which men may most gain and least lose by the liberation" (*Literary Criticism: French Writers* 781).

As I have argued elsewhere ("Henry James, George Sand" 42–49), *The Bostonians* may be read as a fable on the vulnerability of these misguided sisters. Verena, who "speechifie[s] as a bird sings" and characterizes women as "the Heart of humanity" (*Bostonians* 232, 273), directly recalls Sand and her female protagonists. Basil Ransom is an amalgam of the forceful "woman's man" and the male analytical critic—James in Southern disguise. " 'I don't listen to your ideas; I listen to your voice,' " he tells Verena (341) as he dreams of appropriating her eloquence for himself. James was honest in portraying the brutality of the male ego, yet the novel also marks the limits of his ability to imagine a feminist counterforce. Basil's victory is a foregone conclusion, since Olive Chancellor is too intent on martyrdom to be a worthy antagonist.

Returning to James's essays on Sand, we can also observe his tendency to regard all women as sentimentalists. "Women, we are told," he wrote in 1877, "do not value the truth for its own sake, but only for some personal use they make of it. My present criticism involves an assent to this somewhat cynical dogma" (*Literary Criticism: French Writers* 712). James perpetuated this stereotype by making Sand the subject of three later essays, reprinted in *Notes on Novelists* (1914). Citing Balzac, the male hero of this critical volume, James noted that Sand "hangs together perfectly if judged as a man." But again citing Balzac, he argued that Sand lacked the attributes that he and his French master associated with masculine literary genius— "intensity of conception," "the constructive gift," and "the faculty of reaching the truth" (*Literary Criticism: French Writers* 772). James's conception of female weakness was shaped by literary history: if so many women's novels had not been flawed by sentimentality, he might have resisted sexist dogma. At the same time, he was responsible for fashioning a version of history that favored himself and Balzac, his literary father. So also, in his fiction, if he exposed the egotism of Ransom, the brilliance of the portrayal depended on his inside knowledge of that egotism.

At this point readers may ask whether any of James's competitors posed a genuine threat, one that could not be neutralized by satirical criticism. The answer is yes: he had serious rivals, especially notable for their depictions of female subjects. Among the women novelists, Eliot stood alone as a writer of formidable intellectual power. Reading *Middlemarch* prompted James to write his now familiar comment to his brother William, "We know all about the female heart; but apparently there is a female brain, too" (*Henry James Letters* 1:351). Among the men, Hawthorne is noteworthy for his challenges to the patriarchal system often taken for granted by his British and European counterparts. James mined the fiction of Eliot and Hawthorne for material he could use, but his very indebtedness caused him to distance himself from his sources. Further, as we shall see, his aesthetic interests were comparatively narrow: in trying to improve on the art of his rivals, he limited the development of political—and especially of feminist—themes.

Initially, James condescended to Eliot as a creator of "respectable" characters "indifferent to their duties as heroes" (*Literary Criticism: Essays* 915, 924). Eliot, he said in an early review, "is eventually a feminine—a delightfully feminine— writer. She has the microscopic observation, not a myriad of whose keen notations are worth a single one of those great synthetic guesses with which a real master attacks the truth . . . " (*Literary Criticism: Essays* 911). As Sandra Corse has noted, James viewed "the appropriating power of the imagination" as a masculine trait and "more passive" observation as a feminine ability (57), even though Trollope, on the one hand, and Sand, on the other, furnished obvious counterexamples. But it was Eliot herself who forced James to question the stereotypes he had accepted. Although he was bored by such stalwarts as Adam Bede and Felix Holt, he could not deny the imaginative power of Eliot's portrayals of women. His essays record his interest in these female protagonists: Maggie Tulliver *(The Mill on the Floss),* "worth a hundred of her positive brother . . . yet on the very threshold of her life . . . compelled to accept him as her master"; Dorothea Brooke *(Middlemarch),* "framed for a larger moral life than circumstance often affords, . . . and only wasting her ardor and soiling her wings against the meanness of opportunity"; and Gwendolen Harleth *(Daniel Deronda),* married to a man who epitomizes "English brutality" and acquiring a conscience as a result of her tragic choice (*Literary Criticism: Essays* 929, 959, 979, 989–90). From Eliot, then, more than from the lesser female writers, James learned to see the dramatic po-

184   SARAH B. DAUGHERTY

tential of women's themes. And significantly, as the majority of scholars recognize, *Middlemarch* and *Daniel Deronda* are the most important sources of *The Portrait of a Lady*.

Yet this indebtedness increased his own will to mastery. Again and again, James underscored the aesthetic limitations of Eliot's novels. They were diffuse and protracted, failing to "[gratify] the reader with a sense of design and construction"; they lacked "the great dramatic *chiaroscuro*"; they were marred by an "absence of spontaneity" and an "excess of reflection"; and their plot machinery creaked (*Literary Criticism: Essays* 958, 960, 930). (In his review of *Deronda*, James made fun of Eliot's penchant for drowning such inconvenient figures as Gwendolen's husband *Literary Criticism: Essays* 990.) As I have argued at length in another essay ("Henry James and George Eliot" 153–66), *The Portrait of a Lady* may be read as James's effort to improve on Eliot; but the improvements attenuate some of the themes of interest to feminist critics. Although the focus on Isabel makes for structural neatness, it de-emphasizes the comparisons (so often found in Eliot) between the protagonist's story and those of other, less-privileged women. Unlike Eliot's Gwendolen, Isabel is economically secure and hence not "vulgarly, pettily, drily selfish" (*Literary Criticism: Essays* 989). But readers may then wonder why she marries Gilbert Osmond, and the novel's emphasis on scenes of confrontation—"the great dramatic *chiaroscuro*"—leads to more obscurity than do Eliot's sometimes tedious expositions of her characters' motives. The largest problem of all is created by Isabel's presumed return to Osmond. James avoids the crudity of killing off his villain, but readers may not be fully persuaded by his attempt to make his ending "the logical consequence of [his protagonist's] final state of mind" (*Literary Criticism: Essays* 922). As Eliot wrote, "character is destiny" but "not the whole of our destiny" (*Mill on the Floss* 419), and skeptics may doubt the sufficiency of Isabel's newfound spiritual freedom. In short, James paid a price for his efforts to make the novel more subtle yet more dramatic. We cannot complain of Isabel, as he did of Dorothea, that "she plays a narrower part than the imagination of the reader demands" (*Literary Criticism: Essays* 960); but we can say that, in allowing his protagonist to be the "center," he narrowed his thematic focus, neglecting the web of social relationships that Eliot so thoroughly explores. And while he cited the novelist as an example "[t]o her own sex" (*Literary Criticism: Essays* 1010), he never ranked her with his masters, Turgenev and Balzac. Defining himself through his paternal heritage, James (like many other male writers) effaced his kinship with his literary mother.

The case of Hawthorne—another writer to whom he owed much but was often condescending—again illustrates the primacy of James's aesthetic concerns, as well as his relative indifference to political and social issues. Baym has written persuasively of Hawthorne's sympathy with "feminist ideas," notwithstanding his occasional ambivalence (*Shape* 199). In reading James's *Hawthorne* (1879), however, one notices how little the younger novelist cared for the ideas that engaged his predecessor. James's Hawthorne was not Baym's critic of patriarchal culture but a morbidly diffident writer with a "contemplative turn" and a preference for "old ideals": "We may be sure that in women his taste was conservative" (*Literary Criticism: Essays* 371, 379). American authors, Bloom observes, "tend to see [their] fathers as not having dared enough" (68). Yet James himself was more conservative than radical; and in writing of Hawthorne's fiction, he focused not on sexual politics but on the dramatic interest generated by the personal conflict between victims and their antagonists. Concerning *The Scarlet Letter*, he wrote that the narrative deals with Hester only to "a secondary degree": "The story goes on for the most part between the lover and the husband. . . . The attitude of Roger Chillingworth, and the means he takes to compensate himself—these are the highly original elements in the situation that Hawthorne so ingeniously treats" (*Literary Criticism: Essays* 403–4). Significantly, too, James compared the romance unfavorably with John G. Lockhart's *Adam Blair* (1822), whose heroine indeed possesses "roundness and relief" (*Literary Criticism: Essays* 406) but shares none of Hester's doubts regarding the justice of women's fate. Lockhart's Charlotte dies after nursing her former lover, praying for God's mercy, and reproaching herself for having troubled Adam's "calm" and "pure" spirit: "I will kneel to him. . . . I will rain tears upon his feet" (Lockhart 169, 170). Compared with Charlotte, James's heroines are self-respecting; yet they never dream, as Hester does, of the day when "the whole relation between men and women" might be established "on a surer ground of mutual happiness" (*Scarlet Letter* 245).

Also instructive is James's treatment of *The Blithedale Romance*, the novel in which Hawthorne, inspired by Margaret Fuller, most clearly raises feminist issues. As James applauded

the drama of Chillingworth and Dimmesdale, so he admired
that of Hollingsworth and his female victim: "The most touching element . . . is the grasp that this barbarous fanatic has laid
upon the fastidious and high-tempered Zenobia, who, disliking
him and shrinking from him at a hundred points, is drawn into
the gulf of his omnivorous egotism" (*Literary Criticism: Essays*
421). But James said nothing concerning the novel's challenge
to "the patriarchal system," nor did he comment on the specific
reason for Zenobia's defeat: the "fatal man-centeredness" that
undermines her pleas for women's freedom (Baym, *Shape* 198,
199). And for James, the novel as a whole was not the "gloomy
book" that has become the subject of feminist critique (Baym,
Shape 184) but rather a "charming" story told "from a point of
view comparatively humorous" (*Literary Criticism: Essays* 418,
419). One wonders how he might characterize *The Bostonians*.
Would he say that feminists, like the New Englanders, take
life—and literature—terribly hard? [Cf. *Bostonians* 11].

Most revealing of all, from a feminist perspective, are
James's comments on *The Marble Faun*. In this romance, Hawthorne resorted to stereotypes that can easily be criticized as
sexist. Miriam, the dark woman whose nature is "turbid with
grief or wrong" (64), is occasionally the object of the narrator's
sympathy; but ultimately she reenacts the role of Eve, assuming responsibility for the murder committed by Donatello. ("My
eyes bade him do it!" she exclaims [155].) Hilda, the light heroine, is arguably too inflexible as a moral judge, but the narrator
treats her with a cloying sentimentality: "Poor sufferer for another's sin! Poor wellspring of a virgin's heart, into which a
murdered corpse had casually fallen, . . . tainting its sweet atmosphere with the scent of crime and ugly death!" (239). Far from
objecting to this saccharine rhetoric, James was emphatic in his
praise:

> The character of Hilda has always struck me as an admirable inven-
> tion—one of those things that mark[s] the man of genius. It needed
> a man of genius and of Hawthorne's imaginative delicacy, to feel
> the propriety of such a figure as Hilda's and to perceive the relief
> it would both give and borrow. This pure and somewhat rigid New
> England girl, . . . unacquainted with evil and untouched by impurity,
> has been accidentally the witness, unknown and unsuspected, of
> the dark deed by which her friends, Miriam and Donatello, are knit
> together. This is *her* revelation of evil, her loss of perfect innocence.
> She has done no wrong, and yet wrongdoing has become a part of

her experience, and she carries the weight of her detested knowledge upon her heart. (*Literary Criticism: Essays* 446)

This passage sheds considerable light on James's own fiction—
especially on *The Wings of the Dove,* for which *The Marble Faun*
is a key source (Bewley 31–54). The portrayal of Kate Croy, who
reflects ruefully on "the way she might . . . pull things round
had she only been a man" (11), is, of course, far richer and more
complex than Hawthorne's voyeuristic presentation of Miriam.
Likewise Milly Theale, another victim of a system in which
women are commodities, is much more subtly represented than
Hilda. Politically, James had narrower interests than Hawthorne's, but thanks to the influence of the realists, he was also
more resistant to sentimental typology. Nonetheless, the resemblance of the two novels is significant. The dramatic tension
so valued by James depends on our seeing the light and dark
heroines not as sisters oppressed by the patriarchy but as antagonists in a plot of innocence versus evil: "the angular, pale princess, . . . mainly seated, mainly still, and . . . the upright,
restless, slow-circling lady of her court, who exchanges with her,
across the black water streaked with evening gleams, fitful
questions and answers" (*Wings of the Dove* 315). The power of
these images is undeniable. Of necessity, however, James limits
the analysis of a culture that victimizes both women, innocent
and fallen, and that holds the latter responsible for sexual
temptation and evil.

Turgenev, like Hawthorne, reinforced James's early associations between the art of the great man and the portrayal of female innocence. Turgenev was a master acknowledged more
gratefully by the ambitious writer: if Hawthorne embodied the
provincialism James sought to overcome, the Russian personified the cosmopolitan status to which he aspired. "Turgenieff is
my man," says James's persona as he discusses Eliot with two
opinionated women (*Literary Criticism: Essays* 982). And
James's essays on Turgenev are almost embarrassing in their
paeans to the novelist's "magnificent manhood" and his "de-
lightful, mild, masculine figure," "massive and towering" (*Literary Criticism: French Writers* 1015,1031). The motive for this
rhetoric was highly personal: as Leon Edel has written, Turgenev was a mentor during James's Parisian sojourn of 1876—a
confrere "old enough to be his father and young enough to be
his friend" whose "enchantment of talk . . . made Henry behave
like a young man in love" (182, 183).

Turgenev's role was all the more critical because the other members of the Parisian circle—Flaubert, Émile Zola, Alphonse Daudet, and the Goncourts—were much less congenial, as acquaintances and as artists. James was particularly disdainful of their depictions of female sexual depravity. As he complained in a review of Zola's *Nana*, "The figure of the brutal *fille*, without a conscience or a soul, with nothing but devouring appetites and impudences, has become the stalest of the stock properties of French fiction . . . " *(Literary Criticism: French Writers* 870). He relied on Turgenev, then, to support his claim that a real man—a man of genius—would represent the spirit, not the appetites, of his female characters. James's eagerness to prove this point was compounded by his fear that Turgenev, like the cruder "grandsons of Balzac," would regard his own fiction as effeminate. "I do not think my stories struck [Turgenev] as quite meat for men," James wrote. "The manner was more apparent than the matter; they . . . had on the surface too many little flowers and knots of ribbon" *(Literary Criticism: French Writers* 1012, 1011). James's anxiety may well have been unfounded (Edel 184), but it probably increased his desire to associate himself with his predecessor.

Even before meeting Turgenev, James was, as Dale E. Peterson says, virtually "seduced" by the novelist's heroines (28). A lengthy essay of 1874, reprinted in *French Poets and Novelists,* celebrates these women who represent "strength of will" with "all that heroic intensity which says so much more to M. Turgenieff's imagination than feline grace" *(Literary Criticism: French Writers* 982). Elena in *On the Eve,* for example, rejects two conventional suitors in order to marry a Bulgarian patriot. "To appreciate [her] oddity," James wrote, "you must read of the orthodoxy of the people who surround her" *(Literary Criticism: French Writers* 979). Compare his own strategy in portraying Isabel Archer. Another of James's favorites was Lisa, the heroine of *A House of Gentlefolk.* A deeply religious girl, she falls in love with a man whose unfaithful wife is presumed dead; but upon learning that the woman is alive, she urges him, with "deferential sweetness," to remain true to his marriage vows. "Her love for Lavretzky is a passion in its essence half renunciation. . . . Lisa is altogether a most remarkable portrait, and one that readers of the heroine's own sex ought to contemplate with some complacency" *(Literary Criticism: French Writers* 982–83).

Today's readers, however, are more likely to notice the conservative ideology responsible for these depictions of feminine virtue. Though Elena may be unorthodox in her thirst for "active well-doing," she is entirely conventional in her subordination of herself to her lover. ("It's true our tastes are alike. . . . But how much better he is than I!" [*On the Eve* 45, 137].) As for Lisa, she enters a convent after bidding Lavretzky to be reconciled with his wife. ("Happiness," she tells her aunt, "was not for me . . . " [*House of Gentlefolk* 295].) Clearly, Turgenev's aim was not social criticism—much less feminist criticism—but the creation of a lyric beauty based on conservative values. The following passage, describing Lavretzky's observation of Lisa as she attends church, is a fair illustration of the kind of scene James admired:

> She noticed [Lavretzky] though she did not turn round towards him. She prayed fervently, her eyes were full of a calm light, calmly she bowed her head and lifted it again. He felt that she was praying for him too, and his heart was filled with a marvellous tenderness. He was happy and a little ashamed. The people reverently standing, the homely faces, the harmonious singing, the scent of incense, the long slanting gleams of light from the windows, the very darkness of the walls and arched roofs, all went to his heart. . . . He glanced at Lisa. "You brought me here," he thought, "touch me, touch my soul." (190)

As Peterson has observed, Turgenev's purpose, like that of James, was to retrieve spiritual values from the banality of experience; and "[the magic behind this] transfigurative performance . . . was stylistic" (39). Once more, consider *The Wings of the Dove,* in which James uses a series of "reflectors" to create the tableaux for which the novel is justly famous: Milly on the mountain top, "looking down on the kingdoms of the earth" (94); Milly before the Bronzino, reflecting on the brevity of human life (158–59); Milly at the soiree in her "wonderful white dress" and her "long, priceless chain" of pearls (365, 368). Although we are moved by the heroine's spirituality and her capacity for love, the idealized presentation restricts her development as a complex subject and discourages us from posing awkward questions about her trust in her male admirers. To quote John P. O'Neill, "No one asks with any seriousness or persistence why it is that Milly loves and wishes to be loved by . . . Merton Densher" as a "particular individual" (108). If we "read against the grain," the magic disappears, and we are left with an ironic novel about a woman's unwarranted devotion to a chauvinistic weakling. Little wonder, then, that Jamesians have been slow to adopt the demythologizing strategies of feminist criticism.

James's favorite writer, Balzac, was a thoroughgoing antifeminist. As James himself conceded in an essay of 1875, the novelist's view of women would hardly "commend him to the 'female sympathizers' of the day." For Balzac, James continued, "Woman is the female of man and in all respects his subordinate. . . . The *métier de femme* includes a great many branches, but they may be all summed up in the art of titillating in one way or another the senses of man" (*Literary Criticism: French Writers* 61, 62). The tone of these comments is critical, for the youthful James was ambivalent, at best, toward authors who stressed "the sexual qualities" of their fictive women, disregarding the "moral ideal" (*Literary Criticism: French Writers* 62, 47). Ultimately, however, Balzac's robust masculinity made him an irresistible father figure. As a writer characterized by "the incomparable vividness of his imagination," he possessed the "power" James identified with male literary genius: his inventions (implicitly like those of the deity) assumed the aspect of reality itself (*Literary Criticism: French Writers* 36, 68). And as the grandfather of the French realists, he was also a progenitor James sought to claim as his own. Whereas Turgenev's masculinity, like that of James, was qualified by "a certain expansive softness" (*Literary Criticism: French Writers* 1009), Balzac's potency was beyond question.

Moreover, Balzac's scorn of "female sympathizers" made him a useful ally in James's battles against women rivals. In 1885, James cited Eliot's hostility toward *Le Père Goriot* as evidence of her lack of "free aesthetic life" (*Literary Criticism: Essays* 1003). And "The Lesson of Balzac" (1905), which hails the master as "the father of us all" (*Literary Criticism: French Writers* 120), conveys the message that female writers are inferior artists. The fiction of Sand, James said, "presents about as few pegs for analysis to hang upon as . . . a large, polished, gilded Easter egg"; Jane Austen "leaves us hardly more curious of her process, or of the experience in her that fed it, than the brown thrush who tells his story from the garden bough"; and the popular enthusiasm for the Brontes was "the highwater mark of sentimental judgment" (*Literary Criticism: French Writers* 117, 119). In a genre dominated by women, James relied on Balzac, as his Bloomian precursor, to reassert masculine control.

James's idealism, of course, remained at odds with Balzac's

cynicism. But without adopting the Frenchman's view of women, James shared his resistance to democratic reform. As James preferred Europe to America—for novelistic purposes, at least—so he sympathized with Balzac's defense of a conservative, patriarchal culture. "A hierarchy," James said, "is as much more picturesque than a 'congregational society' as a mountain is than a plain. Bishops, abbés, priests, Jesuits, are invaluable figures in fiction, and the morality of the Catholic Church allows of an infinite *chiaroscuro*" (*Literary Criticism: French Writers* 45). Further, James argued, Balzac appropriately subordinated his beliefs—political as well as religious—to the demands of his art:

> His sincere, personal beliefs may be reduced to a very compact formula; he believed that it was possible to write magnificent novels, and that he was the man to do it. He believed, otherwise stated, that human life was infinitely dramatic and picturesque, and that he possessed an incomparable analytic perception of the fact. His other convictions were all derived from this and humbly danced attendance upon it. (*Literary Criticism: French Writers* 45)

In thus describing Balzac, James revealed his own priorities. For the practicing novelist, aesthetic values—"le plaisir du texte," as Roland Barthes might say—almost always overshadowed the ideology that produced them. And to the extent that James endorsed America over Europe, he hoped the new culture would yield a new kind of magnificence.

James's allusions to Balzac's fiction confirm his taste for sheer brio, as distinct from the serious themes beloved of academic critics. He was fascinated, for instance, by Madame Marneffe, the courtesan in *La Cousine Bette* who aids the title character in destroying the Hulot family. Ostensibly, Balzac's novel has a conservative moral purpose: "This sketch," intones the narrator, "will enable guileless souls to understand what mischief Madame Marneffes may do . . . " (269). But as James pointed out (quoting Hipployte Taine), " 'Balzac aime sa Valerie' " (*Literary Criticism: French Writers* 131). She is lavishly described with similes and metaphors; she is the subject of the novel's best epigrams ("women, when they have made a sheep of a man, always tell him that he is a lion with a will of iron" [185]); and she stars in its most dramatic scenes, as when she entertains several lovers at once, informing each that he is the father of her child (247–53). Writing of the novel, James contrasted it favorably with *Vanity Fair:* Balzac, he said, gave his predaceous woman "all her value," whereas "Thackeray's attitude was the opposite one, a desire positively to expose and desecrate poor Becky" (*Literary Criticism: French Writers* 132). In a sense, Balzac's lesson had a feminist use: James learned that bad women (Kate Croy, Charlotte Stant) might be as interesting as good ones (Isabel Archer), especially if represented from "their [own] point of vision" (*Literary Criticism: French Writers* 132). But Balzac's chief role was to liberate James from moral seriousness, including that which some feminist critics are at times inclined to value.

These points are further illustrated by *The Two Young Brides* (Les deux jeunes mariées), to which James wrote a critical introduction (1902). The novel might be summarized as an epistolary bragging contest between Renee, who devotes herself to motherhood, and Louise, who lives for romantic love. Renee wins the argument when her friend dies of jealousy, but Louise has most of the good lines. (Describing her lover, she writes, "My eyes were drawn as by magic towards two shining orbs that blazed like two jewels out of a dark corner of the orchestra" [94].) Modern readers may bridle at 350 pages of frivolity, but James applauded Balzac's "splendid, . . . attaching swagger." He especially liked the portrayal of Louise: "[W]e swallow her bragging, against our better reason, or at any rate against our startled sense, under coercion of the total intensity" (*Literary Criticism: French Writers* 112, 114). "Intensity" was a key term in James's critical vocabulary. It signaled a writer's success in creating human drama, regardless of thematic complications or the absence thereof.

Reading these essays may help us better understand *The Golden Bowl,* a Balzacian novel whose "intensity" the narrator underscores on virtually every page. Significantly, James's preface pays homage to Balzac as the author of "our greatest exhibition of felt finalities, our richest and hugest inheritance of imaginative prose" (*Literary Criticism: French Writers* 1336). Likewise, the preface articulates the Balzacian pleasure principle: the "ideally handsome way" to repay a reader's interest is "to multiply in any given connexion all the possible sources of entertainment—or, more grossly expressing it again, to intensify his whole chance of pleasure" (*Literary Criticism: French Writers* 1338). The masculine pronoun here is more than conventional: James's ideal reader is a man able to share the master's "fun."

Nonetheless, as I have argued elsewhere (*"The Golden Bowl"* 68–82), James tried to improve on the art of his literary father instead of merely imitating it. Balzac's major limitation, according to James, was his inability to represent "superior virtue," especially in his female characters (*Literary Criticism: French Writers* 44). A figure such as Renee is supposedly virtuous, but, as James noted, she sometimes lapses from purity, and her sermonizing is less than persuasive. In creating Maggie Verver, James attempted a bold experiment: the fusion of dramatic power with thematic innocence, or, in broader terms, the amalgamation of Balzac's literary strengths with those of Hawthorne and Turgenev.

As readers know, however, the hybrid novel is also a problem novel. "Duplicity is more picturesque than honesty," James learned from Balzac (*Literary Criticism: French Writers* 49); so he played up Maggie's role as "a mistress of shades" (*Golden Bowl* 390). But this role is hard to reconcile with the images of purity that might better characterize Hawthorne's Hilda, Turgenev's Lisa, or James's own Milly Theale. Another radical stroke was to make Maggie's consciousness the sole center of the novel's second volume: " 'She'll carry the whole weight of us,' " Fanny Assingham explains (271). This move was designed to demonstrate Maggie's superiority to the Prince and Charlotte, as well as James's superior artistry in converting a small, uninteresting character into a great, dramatic one. Even so, as Brodhead has observed, readers are likely to question Maggie's status as the single artificer of the world in which she lives (196–200). Feminist critics, in particular, may challenge the novel's treatment of Charlotte. The more vividly Maggie pictures her rival's misery, the more we become aware of Charlotte's untold story—a story in which Adam, the Prince, and Maggie herself would be characterized much less sympathetically. Maggie's generous appraisal—" 'Charlotte's great' " (545)—presumably redeems the unhappy woman from the dismissive judgment of the Prince—" 'She's stupid' " (534). But again, the novel draws our attention to the themes it fails to develop.

Even more troublesome is Maggie's relationship with Adam, who epitomizes capitalist patriarchy (Kairschner 187–92; McCormack 88). "Nothing perhaps might affect us as queerer," the narrator observes, "had we time to look into it, than [Adam's] application of the same measure of value to such different pieces of property as old Persian carpets, say, and new human

acquisitions . . . " (138–39). James, in other words, might have
pursued this theme, as he had earlier exposed the sexism and
aestheticism of Gilbert Osmond. In this novel, however, the
focus is on Maggie and her redemptive perception: "[S]he was
lifted aloft by the consciousness that [Adam] was simply a great
and deep and high little man, and that to love him with tenderness was not to be distinguished, a whit, from loving him with
pride" (482). At this juncture *The Golden Bowl* invites comparison with *Le Père Goriot,* regarded by James as Balzac's greatest
work. Both novels present pictures of "distracted paternal love"
(*Literary Criticism: French Writers* 59), yet here the story of a
daughter's loyalty rivals, in its dramatic power, the Balzacian
narrative of treachery. Whether or not James intended this
comparison, he was closer to his nineteenth-century masters
than to twentieth-century feminists. Instead of challenging the
social order, he exploited it for the sake of his art. And he would
have questioned the presumption of critics seeking to undermine his creations. "We must grant the artist his subject, his
idea, his *donnee,*" he wrote in "The Art of Fiction." "[O]ur criticism is applied only to what he makes of it" *Literary Criticism:
Essays* 56).

Inevitably, we violate the master's prohibitions, even as we
offer our critiques of his novels and the culture that produced
them. Inevitably, too, we are tantalized and frustrated by James,
who gives us such compelling portraits of women without analyzing the system by which they are oppressed. " '[I]t's *always*
terrible for women,' " Maggie says to her husband near the end
of *The Golden Bowl.* But James allows the Prince to outflank her
with a comment diverting our attention from sexual politics:
" 'Everything's terrible, *cara*—in the heart of man.' " No wonder such vagueness dissatisfies us, especially when it is followed
by the bland assurance that Charlotte is " 'making her life' "
(535; New American Library edition).

Yet we return to James more often than to his competitors.
In many cases, the other novelists of the nineteenth century
had larger ambitions as philosophers and theorists, but their intentions exceeded their ability to realize them. Hawthorne
tried, not always successfully, to combine allegory with social
criticism; Eliot attempted, often ponderously, to formulate a
philosophy that might replace a discredited religious faith; Balzac aspired, with mixed results, to represent the whole of
French civilization. Even Alcott and Stoddard may be seen as
would-be philosophers hoping to reconcile their new under-

standing of sexuality with traditional Protestant theology. James was little of a theorist and not much of a feminist. But as a result of his single-minded—even narrow-minded—devotion to his own métier, he achieved a victory over his rivals: he was, on balance, a better novelist. Because his fiction may be enjoyed as well as studied, it will continue to provoke the discussion that, as he well knew, is the life of art.

Anerotic Excursions: Memory, Celibacy, and Desire in *The American Scene*

MARY ESTEVE

As MUCH AS JAMES'S *AUTOBIOGRAPHY, THE AMERICAN SCENE* IS AN EXploration of memory. As Gordon O. Taylor has written, *The American Scene*, "in a sense fusing its imaginative and documentary aspects, [is] a methodical rather than incidental work of autobiography, in which James repeatedly brings the remembered or reimagined past to bear on the present moment of his encounter with an altered America" (18). Indeed, from the first page of the preface, where James declares his willingness to "go to the stake" for his "gathered impressions," to the last page of the narrative, where we see him, the "lone observer," pondering the symbolic weight of the Pullman car (465), James assumes the role of a tenaciously reflective gatherer, a recollector. So much so that even the "present moment" of his visit is tinged with a sense of the past. Away from the United States for "nearly a quarter of a century," James represents himself as having the "advantage" of being both "inquiring stranger" and "initiated native": he is psychologically more removed than most Americans and therefore "vibrate[s] with more curiosity"; yet as a native he "should understand and should care better and more" than most foreign visitors (Preface). This unique position of observation enables James to cultivate a relation to his subject matter—American modernity—that is simultaneously detached and intimate. It contributes to what Taylor describes as *The American Scene*'s "alternative form [that] is often tentative, *con*fusing as well as fusing the documentary with the imaginative, the historical with the personal, and debating as well as assuming a kinship between such terms" (27).

This tentative, ambivalent form obviously depends not only on James's biographical circumstance (i.e., his lengthy absence) but also on his orientation toward the very activity of recollecting. In this essay I hope to demonstrate that James's mode of recollection in *The American Scene* aligns itself in remarkable ways with the contemporaneous and interrelated inquiries of William James and his French colleague Henri Bergson into memory and consciousness. Broadly stated, both William James and Bergson called into question prevailing assumptions within current psychophysiological and philosophical discourses, assumptions that engendered too facile equations between memory and/or consciousness and sense perception. Each was concerned to reveal the intimate yet radically detached—or immanent yet external—relations between these human capacities; each thereby called into question traditional notions of the harmonious, seamlessly self-conscious, and deeply interiorized human subject. In *The American Scene,* Henry James appears (however unconsciously) to put their new theories into practice. We shall see that in addition to fusing and confusing documentation and imagination of the past, as Taylor suggests, memory functions in James's work to point toward what can be called the impersonal limit of a subject's conscious experience. He *in*fuses, in other words, the interiorized subject's deliberate, conscious remembering of impressions with a *deinteriorizing* impulse. The more often James pronounces "I" and the more details he collects from his personal history, the more he reveals the cohabitation "within" of an impersonal subject.[1]

If James's enactment in *The American Scene* of an impersonally remembering consciousness reflects a conception of human subjectivity as constitutively disjoined, it also carries specific implications for his representation of desire and sexuality. On view in this narrative is what I call James's "*anerotics,*" which reconfigures the libidinal economy so that the productive role of celibacy is made visible. Within this economy, celibacy circulates as a kind of positive interruption: infused with anonymity, it functions as a de-interiorizing plenitude, an anerotic lure that draws subjective identity out of itself. James, in other words, instead of erecting a mutually exclusive opposition between erotic engagement and celibacy, suggests that the latter is in effect the limit-condition of the former. As is explained more fully below, James's introduction of impersonal memory into his economy of desire complicates the dynamics of his sexual orientation and libidinal passions. Stable sexual identification becomes difficult if not impossible to ascertain.

We may begin to see the ways in which James weaves this

thread of anerotic desire into his recollecting narrative by turning to one of those myriad figural flourishes in *The American
Scene* that simultaneously illuminate and obfuscate. In his
attempt to convey his marvel over New York's capacity to ac-
commodate indiscriminately all manner of architectural impor-
tation, such as the newly erected Tiffany building (done in the
Palladian style), James describes the surrounding "air" and
"the strong sea-light" (186). This "medium," he comments,
"has the abundance of some ample childless mother who consoles herself for her sterility by an unbridled course of adop-
tion" (186). This is surely one of James's more ungainly
analogies, whose nearly grotesque effect derives in part from
the sheer incongruity between an ample, childless, sterile, unbridled mother and the ethereal subject matter: light and air.
James's rhetorical figure appears as unbridled, as outlandish
and hyperbolic, as the human figure he invokes. But the image
itself is also startling because of what the woman embodies:
both a disconcerting, if not threatening, voluptuousness and a
pathetic barrenness.

Such clumsy misogyny as one may detect in this figure would
be more offensive if there were not so distinct a resemblance
between this childless mother and James himself. In a letter to
Edith Wharton, written during this same visit to the United
States, James describes himself as a "poor celibate exile" in the
midst of his brother William's "blooming" "Domestic circle"
(quoted in Edel 593). James's irony notwithstanding, the images both of himself and the childless woman register the dominant logic of nineteenth-century sociosexuality: one either
participates in a heterocentrist familial organization and
blooms or one is exiled to the impoverished state of sterility.
The central difference between the mother figure and James
would appear to be that the former consoles herself with others' biological children, and thereby fits her sterile, deprived
self—however pathetically or pathologically—into the model of
blooming fertility, while the latter, as our Romantic imagination of the solitary artist would have it, consoles himself with
an overabundance of rhetorical figures, of verbal progeny.
There is an alternate reading, however, one that I am advancing
in this essay, namely, that James does not console himself at all
but instead adopts a wholly different logic of expressivity in
which his celibacy itself instantiates asexual yet fertile fullness.
On this view, James's rhetorical figures—excessive, ample,
abundant as they may be—are not his surrogate children. They

are, rather, the result of what he at one point describes as his "excursions of memory—memory directed to the antecedent time—*reckless* almost to extravagance" (87, emphasis added). *To reck* means to number or to care; as James's figures escape the regime of being counted and cared for, they operate without exacting a consolatory return.

Precisely speaking, celibacy refers to marital status, but culturally it also suggests sexual inactivity—the lack or renunciation of carnal passion—which is why it does not seem redundant to call James, as critics often do, a celibate bachelor. As seen in James's comment to Wharton, celibacy contrasts with being biologically reproductive, thus bearing the further connotation of sterility. Recent critics have succeeded in minimizing the significance of James's self-declared celibacy by emphasizing his ostensibly livelier and largely concealed same-sex sexuality, whether in the form of homosocial bonding, homoeroticism, encoded homosexual practices and panics, or autoerotism. A compelling essay in this vein is Michael A. Cooper's "Discipl(in)ing the Master, Mastering the Discipl(in)e: Erotonomies of Discipleship in James' Tales of Literary Life."[2] Acknowledging the probability of James's sexual inactivity, Cooper goes on to speculate that "it was perhaps only when writing, when losing himself in the complex emotions and situations of his created characters, that he allowed guiltless ardor to wash freely over his psyche" (75). Cooper applies his analysis not simply to James's biography but also to certain characters in works of fiction. In either case, the translation of physical frigidity into textual lust fits well our general assumptions about Victorian culture's repressed sexuality and its strategies of sublimation; thus, it makes psychological sense. Indeed, the psychological apparatus that Cooper's argument deploys—a modified version of the return of the repressed, one that sees that return not as a debilitating neurosis but as a source of creativity—has become so naturalized as often to go unquestioned.

In *The American Scene,* however, James's anerotics cannot be squared with this deep psychological structure. That is, his celibacy is not the (fictional or biographical) locus of renunciation from which issue dialectically coherent (homo)sexual identifications and literary productions. Instead, celibacy provides the outside pressure of and on sexuality; as the limit-condition of sexuality, circulating through James's libidinal economy, it destabilizes sexual identity and erotic signification.[3] Moreover, James's keen attention to and analysis of urban modernity in this text reveal the inseparability of libidinal desire from capitalist desire. Indeed, James's libidinal affections coalesce and reach their height of intensity in his representation of the crowds of Wall Street, the cultural icon of urban modernity and finance capitalism. Having attained "the upper reaches" of one of New York's skyscrapers "looming through the weather with insolent cliff-like sublimity," James's affective distance renders him unable to "penetrate" the "magnitude and mystery" of the scene (80), yet he is simultaneously able to gain a seductive view of " 'the state of the streets' "—"the assault of the turbid air seemed all one with the look, the tramp, the whole quality and *allure*, the consummate monotonous commonness, of the pushing male crowd, moving in its dense mass . . . all the signs of the heaped industrial battlefield, all the sounds and silences too, of the universal will to move—to move, move, move, as an end in itself, an appetite at any price" (82–84). "Insolent" though these structures and their consequent human formations may be, they evidently have their "allure." Later, the fuller dimensions and implications of this highly homoeroticized yet also alter-eroticized scene will be the focus of my attention. But in order to understand the ways in which the "allure" and "quality" of urban modernity's monotonous appetites contribute to James's anerotics, it is necessary first to map out *The American Scene*'s narratological situation, to uncover its oddly splayed remembering consciousness. This requires returning to the thought of William James and Bergson.

In *The Principles of Psychology* (1890), William James disputes the traditional equation of memory and consciousness. Taking issue with Charles Richet's dictum, "Without memory no conscious sensation, without memory no consciousness," James responds with his own dictum, "Without memory no consciousness known outside of itself." Here he argues that consciousness is in fact greater than memory: "[A] momentary state of consciousness . . . though absolutely unremembered, might at its own moment determine the transition of our thinking in a vital way, and decide our action irrevocably" (1:644). For James, then, memory is bounded by its epistemological function; it "is the knowledge of a former state of mind after it has already once dropped from consciousness" (1:648). As such, memory cannot be equated with consciousness. It is a product of the nervous system, and the nervous system is fully contained by the individual subject. Consciousness, on the other hand, is conditioned by what James calls "a stream of *Scious-*

ness pure and simple" (1:304), which is immanent but also external to subjective self-consciousness. "Sciousness," James clarifies, does "not yet includ[e] or contemplat[e] its own subjective being" (1:304). As he writes elsewhere, "Consciousness connotes a kind of external relation" (*Radical* 14). In this sense, consciousness bears within itself its own nonconscious limit.[4]

William James's conception of (con)sciousness and Bergson's conception of memory have much in common. What Bergson calls the memory-image results from "the intelligent, or rather intellectual, recognition of perception already experienced" (*Matter* 81). It may seem that this act of recognition thus simply registers the phenomenological interplay between subjective persons endowed with consciousness and an objective world endowed with things, but in fact Bergson's theory scrambles such categorical concepts. According to Gilles Deleuze, this has to do with Bergson's "obsession with the *pure*," with his apprehension of a pure memory and a pure perception, which "goes back to [his] restoration of differences in kind" (as opposed to in degree) between memory and perception (*Bergsonism* 22). Hence, Bergson restores the "inhuman" or "superhuman" dimensions of the recollective event (28). In positing memory and perception as qualitatively distinct, Bergson makes a number of concomitant severances. First, he severs both pure memory and pure perception from psycho-physiological processes, that is, from cerebration, whether conscious or unconscious: "No perception can arise from [received excitations], and nowhere in the nervous system are there conscious centers"; rather, "perception arises from the same cause which has brought into being the chain of nervous events" (*Matter* 64). For Bergson, then, perception cannot be equated with physiological sensation: "[I]n its pure state," "external perception . . . [is] a part of things rather than of ourselves." Matter, he goes on to explain, "coincides, in essentials, with pure perception" (64–65, 73). While he grants that perception without sensation or a nervous system is a practical (though not a theoretical) impossibility, he insists that the nervous system "is a mere conductor, transmitting, sending back or inhibiting movement" (44–45). The subjective experience of an image, then, inherits this nonsubjective, "impersonal perception" (34).

Just as Bergson severs perception from the purely psychophysiological, so also, he separates memory from these more mechanical processes. Jettisoning psychologists' premise that the brain functions as a storehouse of memories, Bergson argues that in fact "pure memory . . . interests no part of my body. No doubt, it will beget sensations as it materializes, but at that very moment it will cease to be a memory and pass into the state of a present thing, something actually lived. I shall then only restore to it its character of memory by carrying myself back to the process by which I called it up, as it was virtual, from the depths of my past" (139). In contrast to sensations, which are extended and localized, a qualitatively different memory is "inextensive and powerless" (140). If, for the sake of semantic convenience, one wants to think of this memory as residing in an unconscious, this unconscious maintains "an *existence outside of consciousness*" (142); it is not repressed within subjective memory, as the Freudian model predicates.

In a journal entry from 1881, on the occasion of his Christmas visit to Cambridge, we see Henry James working out a strikingly similar notion of pure, external memory. Back in his old "sitting room," he is reminded of his earlier years spent there "scribbling, dreaming, planning, [and] gazing out upon the world," as well as of the "suffering tortures from [his] damnable state of health" (*Notebooks* 224). James goes on to comment on the effect of this remembered suffering and the process of remembering: "When the burden of pain has been lifted, as many memories and emotions start into being as the little insects that scramble about when, in the country, one displaces a flat stone" (225). It is crucial to understand the logic of memory that James presents here. Despite the fact that a "burden of pain" initially exerts pressure on James's remembering consciousness, this is clearly not a Freudian scenario wherein repressed memories re-emerge as either neurotic or creative thought and action. What interests him, indeed, is what happens once the "burden" has been "lifted": the way impassive memory (that which is rendered inert by the "flat stone" of the unconscious) transforms into active impressions (scrambling as "little insects"). By depicting memories and emotions as things that "*start into being*," James suggests that they are, prior to the "start," inhabiting a realm of nonbeing; which is to say that they are external to consciousness. Yet, like insects under a rock, they are also already in the realm of being. With this image, James captures the paradoxical condition advanced by Bergson of memory's external yet immanent relation to consciousness. Impassive, inactive, yet ceaselessly pressing itself into experience or "starting into being": this is what we may call a *deinteriorizing, impersonal* memory. This is memory as will, as self-differentiating impulse. And in *The American Scene*, it is precisely this kind of memory that enters, in the guise of celibacy, into James's libidinal economy.

Not long after Henry James had read some of his brother's philosophical works "with rapture," confiding to him that "[p]hilosophically, in short, I am 'with' you" (quoted in Perry 1:425), William James attempted to arrange a meeting between Bergson and his brother (when he himself was visiting England to deliver the Hibbert lectures at Oxford). Though the meeting seems not to have occurred, William James, having recently read *The American Scene* with some perplexity, perhaps could see that the "new, positive metaphysics" that he and Bergson liked to think they shared (quoted in Perry 2:612) pertained as well to his brother's sensibility. Similar to William James's defense of his conception of consciousness as *alogical* rather than *illogical*, as pointing toward a "reality [that] obeys a higher logic, or enjoys a higher rationality" (*Writings* 1034, 724–26), is Henry James's description of himself in Baltimore, where he realizes that while he is "mechanically so argu[ing]" with himself, his "impression" of the city "was fixing itself by a wild logic of its own" (*Scene* 308). As Ross Posnock has suggested, in James's wild logic of gathering and analyzing impressions, he "fashions a representational technique far more complex" than critics' usual tags of impressionism or aestheticism allow (148–49). In my view, it is a technique that points toward the outside limit— the "upper reaches" to borrow James's phrase—of representation.

The notebook James kept during his travels through the United States reveals that this complexity derives in part from his recollective practice. In an entry written in California, James comes back to his worry about being in "arrears" as far as the travelogue goes, having an "inward accumulation of material" but little written out. The worry, however, passes. He assures himself that he need "only invoke [his] *familiar demon of patience,* who always comes," thus allowing the recollective process to go on: "Everything sinks in: *nothing is lost;* everything abides and fertilizes and renews its golden promise" (*Notebooks* 237, emphasis added). James becomes so imbued with patience that he seems nearly to forget his present thoughts on what has passed and begins to imagine himself in the future, secluded in Lamb House with his "long, dusty adventure over":

I shall be able to [plunge] my hand, my arm, *in*, deep and far, and up to the shoulder—into the heavy bag of remembrance—of suggestion—of imagination—of art—. . . . These things are all packed away, now, thicker than I can penetrate, deeper than I can fathom, and there let them rest for the present, in their sacred cool darkness. (237)[5]

In imagining the recollective process as requiring a sort of mystically mediating "demon of patience" as well as "suggestion," which together retrieve impenetrably packed experience from its sacred darkness, James echoes not only Bergson's ideas on the gulf separating the impersonal past from the living present but also his own view recorded in a notebook entry in 1900. There he is mulling over his initial work on what will become the unfinished novel *The Sense of the Past*. But this entry also registers the way James seems to prepare for writing by working himself into a near state of hypnotic trance and thereby transporting himself to the impersonal limit of consciousness. Indeed, he writes as though he were muttering automatically. To capture this hypnotic tone and rhythm the passage must be quoted at length:

I turn about, I finger other things over, asking, praying, feel something that will do instead. I take up, in other words, this little blessed, this sacred small, "ciphering" pen that has stood me in such stead often already, and I call down on it the benediction of the old days, I invoke the aid of the old patience and passion and piety. They are always there—by which I mean *here*—if I give myself the chance to appeal to them. There are *tails* of things that one must, with one's quick expert hand, catch firm hold of. They seem to whisk about me—to ask only for a little taking of the time, a little of the old patient mystic pressure and "push." Adumbrations of "little" subjects flash before me, in short, and the thing is to make them condense. . . . Ah, things swim before me, *caro mio*, and I only need to sit tight, to keep my place and fix my eyes, to see them float past me in the current into which I can cast my little net and make my little haul. . . . Here truly *is* the tip of a tail to catch, a trail, a scent, a latent light to follow up. Let me, in the old way that I can't *think* of without tears, scribble things as they come to me, while little by little the wandering needle and the wild stitch makes the figure. (190)

Hereness and thereness destabilized, things swimming before him, Henry James waits for images to materialize out of an essentially unidentifiable or anonymous "mystic pressure and 'push.' " As this pressure bears down on his present perceptions and recollections, James's "patience and passion and piety" function to "aid" the translation into images and expressions. His "scribble," hypnotically fixing his eyes, takes "wandering" and "wild" shape. James thus reveals his orientation toward a recollective reality that "is just entering into experience, and yet to be named," to borrow William James's formulation regarding the formation of consciousness (*Pragmatism* 119). William James's former student, the psychopathologist Boris Sidis, will similarly describe this hypnotic state as one in which the subject is a "[n]obody, nothing," "a reality and still [the subject] has no being," for it is "both subpersonal and impersonal" (252).

If Henry James inscribes his recollecting consciousness within contemporaneous discourses of psychology and philosophy, as well as within that lowly esteemed branch of both—psychical research—his spin on them diverges from the sort proffered by his contemporary cultural conservatives. An instructive comparison is an article written by one Dr. John Duncan Quackenbos entitled "The Transliminal," which appeared in the *North American Review* in 1906, directly preceding one of the serialized portions of *The American Scene*. Citing William James's work on hypnotic suggestion, Quackenbos launches into a eulogy for "the transliminal sphere," championing it as the source of "moral uplift," as "that principle in us which dictates what is right and inclines to good," as a means of extirpating "any abnormal craving or passion"—in sum, as the source of our "ethical energy," according, of course, to Christianity's set of humanizing and self-justifying ethics (238–39, 241, 244). The transliminal is thus appropriated to buttress an ideology of moral introspection and individual responsibility. In Henry James's hands, by contrast, the transliminal—the neither here nor there, the neither something nor nothing, of external, impersonal, and inhumanizing consciousness—serves, by dint of its differentiating will, to heighten rather than to extirpate "abnormal craving or passion," and simultaneously to evacuate the autonomous subject. He thereby diverges dramatically from genteel cultural politics as usual.

In *The American Scene*, James's quarter-century-long absence from the place of his past makes him alert to the "strange law" by which he "had lived in the other time, with gaps . . . in [his] experience, in [his] consciousness, with so many muffled spots in [his] general vibration," leaving places and things "undiscov-

ered" even then, but "which were to live on, to the inner vision,
through the long years, *as mere blank faces, round, empty, metallic, senseless disks*" (52, emphasis added). This mode of consciousness, pocked as it is by disorienting, blank, senseless bits
of memory, correlates with James's self-description as a flâneur. He manifests an inclination to wander nomadically, to di-
gress, abruptly to shift attention, to endure shock and
disorientation.[6] The act of remembering, as fellow flâneur (and
reader of Bergson) Walter Benjamin remarks in his own auto-
biographical writing, "Berlin Chronicle," "is not an instrument
for exploring the past, but its theater. It is the medium of past
experience, as the ground is the medium in which dead cities
lie interred" (*Reflections* 25–26). Memory-images thus retrieved
do not reconstruct a smooth, continuous history or autobiography; rather, "severed from all earlier associations" they stand
like "fragments or torsos in a collector's gallery" (26). The
"strange form" of the memory-image at the moment of recollection—"it may be called fleeting or eternal—is in neither case
the stuff that life is made of" (28).

In a similar vein of fragmented, inhumanizing memory,
James's narrative mode in *The American Scene* takes on a "certain recklessness"; it becomes what he calls "a fusion of possible felicities and possible mistakes" (3, 68).[7] In part he achieves
this by transforming certain present scenarios into theaters of
the past, not so much to bring sense *to* the past as to stage the
disorienting, alogical sense *of* both the past and present. His
visit to Mount Auburn cemetery, where "ghosts swarmed all the
while too thick . . . to name" (68), is an exemplary case. Having
"felt the whole place bristle with merciless memories," James
nevertheless first displaces these memories with a digression
on what he presently saw there: "Just opposite, at a distance,
beyond the river and its meadows, the white face of the great
empty Stadium stared at [him], as blank as a rising moon—with
Soldier's Field squaring itself like some flat memorial slab that
waits to be inscribed" (68–69). James's analogy here, between a
playing field and a memorial slab, ensures that what is displaced—the activity of remembering—lingers on, not in a repressed but in a hovering manner.[8]

In his elaboration of this analogy, James both extends one of
his recurrent criticisms of the United States and knits precisely
what he criticizes to a recollection of his most cherished memory-images of intimate friends. The criticism has to do with certain crowd phenomena. Throughout his travelogue, James does

little to conceal his annoyance with the American "insistence on gregarious ways only," for which "the Elevator," reiterating as it does "the abject consciousness of being pushed and pressed in," stands as an "intolerable symbol" (186–87). In the cemetery scene he invokes the "inscribed" field—by which he means the phenomenon of the "great intercollegiate game of football," which he "had seen . . . a week or two before"—as yet another instance of "the capacity of the American public for momentary gregarious emphasis" (69). He lets these reflections for the most part go, being not "now relevant" to his present effort to attend to the memorializing slabs of intimates, "save so far as the many-mouthed uproar [the reflections] recalled was a voice in the more multitudinous modern hum through which one listened almost in vain for the sound of old names" (69). Thus occurs a transmutation of the modern hum of the gregarious stadium crowd into the private hum of "old Cambridge ghosts," whom James represents as all remaining unnamed but "two or three of them . . . [who could] push their way, of themselves, through any silence" (68). This further alternation of figures between an anonymous uproar, be it of football fans or ghosts, and an anonymous silence contributes to the larger effect of this scene. This effect scrambles the past's traditional continuity and linearity, as well as skewing without collapsing present distinctions between public and private realities, between recollection and presentation of experience.

James's disjunctive contact with his own consciousness marks not only his scenes of explicit recollection but also, as I have been suggesting, his scenes of perception that are less explicitly self-referential. The vacant materiality—"metallic, senseless disks"—of memory feeds his perception of the "undiscriminated, tangled actual" (15). This disjointedness is registered in what becomes his obsession with the "blankness" of American culture; he aims "to gouge an interest *out* of vacancy," to demonstrate how an "illustration might be, enormously, of something deficient, absent—in which case it [is] for the aching void to be (as an aching void) striking and interesting" (12, 56). Accordingly, James finds absences at every turn and in all shapes and sizes: in, for example, a strip of decadently luxurious villas, representing "the expensive as a power by itself" but a power "exerting itself . . . in a poor gentle, patient, rueful, but altogether helpless void" (9); in the "vast and vacant" room of a New England meeting house, in which the "Patron['s] . . . absence made such a hole" (24); in a fortuitously

unnamed stream—"a stream without an identity" (32); in the
"exquisite emptiness" and "constituted blankness" of Cape
Cod (35); in the "strangest air of active, operative death" of a
Shaker community (49).

The larger purpose to which James puts these perceptions of
blankness is often difficult to ascertain, as William James was
one of the first to declare. Balking at Henry's "perverse" and
"unheard-of method," William warns that in "this crowded and
hurried reading age" those rising to the book's task will be few
(*Letters* 2:278). Despite his zeal for experimentation within the
disciplines of psycho-physiology and even philosophy, William
clearly wants literature that "is solid." But for all his impa-
tience with *The American Scene,* he characterizes it with remarkable insight. As an "account of America" it is "largely one
of its omissions, silences, vacancies." It consequently produces
"the illusion of a solid object, made (like the 'ghost' at the Poly-
technic) wholly out of impalpable materials, air and the prismatic interferences of light, ingeniously focused by mirrors
upon empty space." The effect "is but perfume and simula-
crum" (2:277–78). What William James, in effect, describes
here is the verbal or syntactical embodiment of a swarm of
ghosts. The book's imagistic smoke and mirrors and its linguistic sleights of hand place it in an elusive realm between the real
and the fantastic. It thus also places its traveling narrator in
hovering suspension. No doubt, Henry James himself balks at
the "omissions, silences, vacancies" encountered throughout
the United States. But, for him, a balk does not mean a permanent arrest; his hesitation contributes, rather, to an endless and
circumlocutional series of arrests, some of which are intensely
erotic. James stages movements that carry on only because
they break down—"possible felicities and possible mistakes"
(68). His recollections and perceptions of blankness all feed
back into an unpredictable production of desiring effects, of
more recollections and perceptions, of prismatically altered
versions of the same recollections.

When, on the first page of the preface to *The American Scene,*
James describes "the contribution of the state of desire" to the
"freshness" of his "outward and inward" looking "eye," he indicates that his mode of desire, apprehending and absorbing
American culture's rampant blankness, functions in his recollecting and perceiving economy as the very source of "prismatic
interference." Two recent analyses of James's mode of desire
have been, in my view, particularly misguided, and, for the pur-

pose of clarifying my own argument, I want briefly to address them here. Donna Przybylowicz, drawing on Lacanian psychoanalysis, characterizes James as "frightened and suspicious," as trapped within "a realm of Imaginary specularity," and "want[ing] to expel certain repressed desires and fears by projecting them onto the external world" (22, 4, 202). She thus squeezes James into a psychoanalytic conception of desire, which, operating under the sign of a transcendental lack, renders the human subject always already incomplete and affectively impaired.[9]

Sharon Cameron takes nearly the opposite and, given the present discussion's focus on consciousness, more troubling tack. She accuses James of having de-psychologized, isolated, and consequently "divorced [consciousness] from the strictures of situation and character" to such an extent that it becomes a "pure subject," hence "empowered" to "translate what is there [in the world] into what is desired" (2, 7, 20). Thus, James's very success at achieving his desire incurs Cameron's critical suspicion; for it represents his "psychic, artistic, ultimately political" mastery to her (20). Leaving aside the dubious premise that widely divergent types of mastery are substantively analogous, it is important to note how Cameron triangulates consciousness, power, and "what is desired" in such a manner as to hypostatize all three. Instead of limit-conditions of experiential movement, she sees James as conceiving them as phenomenological, circumscribable entities: "Consciousness is held like a sum in reserve by James and then distributed as the source of power"; "power is dispensed by those who have consciousness"; or, as she most bluntly puts it, "In *The American Scene* others [i.e., human beings] are gotten out of the way" (171, 29). Cameron, like Przybylowicz, fails to recognize that what James desires is not a function of what he lacks or wants but of his constitutive plenitude. Taking no specific object or "other" for cathecting purposes, his desire plays itself out immanently *among* these others but detached from them, producing an involuting array of affective attractions and contractions, dispersals and disjunctions. Owing to what James calls his "excited sensibility" (*Scene* 7), this sixty-year-old's desire functions as the motor of his erotically and impersonally nomadic—rather than repressively or imperialistically monadic—investigations of personal and social topoi. A permutation of memory, of power as will and not as analogue to patriarchal domination, James's desire is, as it were, "de-sired."

There is perhaps no more intense illustration of James's desired desire than the scene invoked near the start of this essay, in which his "state of desire" comes into contact with the "state of the streets." Here, James takes his *flâneurie* to such an extreme that he transmutes into a self-interfering *badaud*. The latter, Benjamin observes, is "strange[ly]" different from the former in that—here he quotes Victor Fournel from his 1858 book on Paris—"under the influence of the spectacle [the badaud] becomes an impersonal being; he is no longer a human; he is [the] public; he is [the] crowd" (*Schriften* 5:540, my translation here and below). In the New York crowd scene, we witness James similarly becoming anonymously inhuman. Ever the "celibate exile," James notes that he "could begin neither to measure nor to penetrate" the world he encounters, "hovering about [it] only in magnanimous wonder," noting further that "[i]f it had been the final function of the Bay [described a few pages earlier] to make one feel one's age so assuredly, the mouth of Wall Street proclaimed it" (*Scene* 80–81). In the face of "youth on the run . . . and the new landmarks crushing the old quite as violent children stamp on snails and caterpillars" (81), James, through the process of sentimental association, marks himself, like the Trinity Church described three pages earlier, as one who "aches and throbs" because "so cruelly overtopped and so barely distinguishable," among the recently erected "tall buildings," and "the thousand glassy eyes of these giants of the mere market" (77–78).

Despite such deprecating, alienating gestures toward himself as one of the old and crushed, James weaves a highly eroticized and entangled web of desire in this scene. Its central images are "the pushing male crowd, moving in its dense mass"; the "emergent mountain masses" of New York skyscrapers, with their "constructed and compressed communities, throbbing, through [their] myriad arteries and pores with a single passion," "as if each were a swarming city in itself"; and his own ghostly persona—or, more precisely, personae (81–83). Staging himself, as we shall see in a moment, as a sort of swarm of celibate interferences, James reconfigures conventional oppositions between, and alters conventional assumptions about, asexuality and eroticism. His self-fashioning throughout *The American Scene* as a solitary traveler, as celibate and impersonal—as, in effect, promiscuously anerotic—contributes to the dispersive and entangling erotics of this New York crowd scene.

In many respects the New York crowd scene prismatically repeats its direct antecedent, namely, James's passage through the New York bay on a "train-bearing barge" (72). Although both the physical organization of the bay and his panoramic view of it guarantee the descriptive uniqueness of this scene, it shares a certain affective and rhetorical intensity with the one that follows it. Here James's susceptibility to "any large view of an intensity of life" stirs in him "vibrations," which "tend to become a matter difficult for even *him* to explain," thus leaving him "open to corruption" (74). This vulnerability leads to his mimetic engagement with the "dauntless power" and the "*applied passion*" of the goings-on in the bay (74–75). That is, James invests himself with "the motion and expression of every floating, hurrying, panting thing": "the throb of ferries and tugs . . . the plash of waves and the play of winds and the glint of lights and the shrill of whistles and the quality and authority of breeze-borne cries" (74). Besides this Whitmanesque, incantatory repetition of the conjunction "and," the passage is steeped in hyperbolic, sexualized metaphors. James describes the bay as a "monster [that] grows and grows, flinging abroad its loose limbs . . . as some unmannered young giant . . . [as] some steel-souled machine room of brandished arms and hammering fists and opening and closing jaws." Likewise, the "immeasurable bridges" spanning the bay become "horizontal sheaths of pistons working at high pressure, day and night, and subject . . . to certain, to fantastic, to merciless multiplication" (75).

What James calls the "fine exhilaration" of this encounter results in part from his "free wayfaring relation . . . to the waters of New York" and to the "great scale of space" (71). The scene thus serves as a sort of anticipatory, impressionistic foreplay to his more convulsive response to the Wall Street crowd encountered in the scene to follow. There his "relation" grows more thickly intimate, miming the crowded vertical assemblages of buildings, the "turbid air," and the constricted "dense mass" of the "pushing male crowd" (83). He is no longer drifting past on a barge, impressed by but nonetheless apart from the scene; now he stages himself as a part of the scene. He witnesses the "parts and pieces . . . of 'downtown' seen and felt from the inside" (80). A part, but here too, as shall soon become apparent, apart: he is positioned "inside" but also not inside the crowd. Like Benjamin, James experiences the crowd as "now landscape, now living room" (*Schriften* 5:54). Such is the crowd's internally differentiating, hence disorienting, power.

James intensifies this sense of disorientation by destabilizing through figures of speech the scene's discrete elements. The

street crowd is both a "dense mass" and a "muddy medium" of
both "sounds and silences" (83–84); the skyscrapers are both
"insolent, cliff-like" and themselves filled with "multitudinous
life, as if each were a swarming city in itself" (82–83). Perhaps
most disorienting is the way in which the entity "Henry James"
differentiates and multiplies into a number of incongruous narrating and observing selves. The reader marks James's view of
"one of [the white towers] from the inside" (81), within which,
as his involuted topology would have it, he encounters the
swarming city. Here James's observer-self is clearly remembered (he remarks on "the different half-hours, as memory
presents them" when he visited Wall Street [80]) and is also
clearly situated within the "new and crude and commercial and
over-windowed," phallic tower (81). Thus, as if desiring not to
lose track of his whereabouts, James triply interiorizes this observer-self: he is in the midst of the swarming city that is "inside" a tower that is "inside" downtown.

Ironically, however, the excitation experienced by this deep
penetration remains largely with the temporally distant observer-self. That is, similar to James's depiction in his notebook
passages of the instability of hereness and thereness, the *here*
where James, the past observer, physically encounters the
crowdedness of the crowd (the swarming city) is not the *there*
where James, the present narrator, works up and into his most
incantatory, hypnotic, and impersonal expressivity. This takes
place in relation to the street crowd, from which, however,
James the observer remains physically absent. We will return
to this narrating figure in a moment; it must first be noted that
in between these two personae, narrator and observer, James
the literary critic interferes, invoking one of French literature's
famed portraitists of crowds: "[M]y thought went straight to
poor great wonder-working Émile Zola and *his* love of the
human aggregation. . . . What if [his novels] could have but
come into being under the New York inspiration?" (82). Further, James the extravagant lover of figures of speech is compelled to confuse and complicate our vision of the buildings and
street crowds by describing his recollection of "the picture, as it
comes back to me . . . [as] *so crowded* with its features that I
rejoice, I confess, in not having more of them to handle." He
likens the force of his impressions to "*the mob* seeking entrance to an up-town or a down-town electric car fight[ing] for
life at one of the apertures" (80–81, emphasis added). Crowded-

ness, then, becomes not simply a physical condition to observe, but a state of mind in which to be immersed.

When James the narrator turns to the street crowd, he clearly does so from a distance, though, significantly, it is not exactly clear where. James has earlier noted that he "gazed across at the special sky-scraper that overhangs poor old Trinity" (83), and that is the last the reader hears of his whereabouts. It is possible that he is still up in the white tower, looking down, but there is nothing in the passage to turn the possibility into a certainty. Such ghostly hovering stylistically enables James to do with or in this crowd what he intimates he cannot do while roaming through the "swarming city" of the tower, namely, "to let himself go" (82). If, while observing the swarming crowd inside the tower, James keeps the "impression in question" from "spreading in a wide waste of speculation" (82), the "allure," as he calls it, of the pushing male street crowd proves too much to withstand. James's insulated, celibate voyeurism metamorphoses—while yet maintaining itself—into (occupation- or class-based) alter-erotic and (gender-based) homoerotic immersion. The "confusion carried to chaos for any intelligence, any perception" (83) refers not only to James's impressionistic representation of a crowd scene once observed from who knows where, but also to the intensely expressive presentation of James's *current* relation to his own narration. With a rush of rhythmic, climactic force, a "muddy medium" of words spills out into the space of writing like a crowd into the streets: a "welter of objects and sounds in which relief, detachment, dignity, meaning, perished utterly and lost all rights" (83). James, like the crowd, enacts the "universal will to move—to move, move, move, as an end in itself, an appetite at any price" (84). With this welter of contiguous nouns and reiterated verbs, his writing becomes the site for writerly convulsions and recollective expressions; such a dispersion of affectivity arises from the coincidence in him of celibate and erotic intensities.

Affectively immersed in "all the signs of the heaped industrial battlefield, all the sounds and silences, the grim, pushing, trudging silences too," yet physically removed from it, James not only disorganizes himself libidinally and narratologically, but he also forces a reconsideration of conventional assumptions regarding the logic of capital. Readers of such periodicals as *Harper's, North American Review,* and *Fortnightly Review,* where *The American Scene* was serialized, were treated to a regular diet of moderately toned articles envisioning a rational, more or less smoothly expanding circulation and exchange of producing and consuming entities. A perusal of one of the 1906 volumes of the *North American Review* reveals its concerns typically to revolve around issues such as Canada's tariffs, Mexico's finance minister, Puerto Rico's industrial progress, and the regulation of trust companies—issues that presuppose rational, deliberate economic principles and policies. Globally diverse, such articles reinscribe the nation's official aura of geopolitical maturity. In contrast to this stabilizing, confidence-inspiring rhetoric, James uncovers capital's essentially "wild" or "unbridled" logic. Essential, but only rarely operative: for capitalism, as Deleuze and Felix Guattari explain, "liberates the flows of desire, but under the social conditions that define its limit and the possibility of its own dissolution, so that it is constantly opposing with all its exasperated strength the movement that drives it towards this limit" (139–40). In James's representation, the crowd embodies this movement of desire toward its own limit. The "thrill of Wall Street[,] . . . the whole wide edge of the whirlpool" (80), operates with an "appetite at any price," with the "will to move—to move, move, move, as an end in itself" (84). This is pure, terrifying, utterly disorganized capitalist desire, desiring for its own sake. It is unmoored from coherent, exchangist visions of self and society, of monetary obligations and value, of history and future.

James both loses himself in this unfettered capitalism and severs himself from it by enacting a hovering, swarmlike relation to it. He embodies the potentiality of de-interiorized alterity that he suggests subsists and insists in urban modernity. As he will write in a later but thematically related passage, the apprehension of this logic of capitalism, this press toward its own disorganizing limit, affects him as "the last revelation of modernity" (*Scene* 183–84). Discerning that the American consciousness of prosperity is conditioned by a kind of potlatch contest—what Georges Bataille calls "a kind of deliriously formed ritual poker," an "unproductive expenditure" (122, 118)—James playfully imagines a New York neighborhood, which has been vacated for the summer season, as inhabited by an auction crowd: "It was as if, in their high gallery, the bidders, New Yorkers every one, were before one's eyes; pressing to the front, hanging over the balustrade, holding out clamorous importunate hands" and "offering any price, offering everything, wanting only to outbid and prevail, at the great auction of life" (184). If this scene serves as yet another example of Jamesian hyperbole, it also invites us to consider how James's travelogue, densely populated with such figures, itself operates according to a kind of literary potlatch. As he carries out his "excursions of memory . . . reckless almost to extravagance" (87), as he excessively and expressively de-sires the human subject, he reaches toward what Bergson would call the matter of memory, what William James would call the Sciousness of consciousness. He reaches, in other words, toward the point of no return.

Notes

Editor's note: Esteve's citations to The American Scene *are to the Indiana University Press edition.*

For their comments and suggestions on earlier versions of this essay, I am very grateful to Ross Posnock, Gregg Crane, and Kevin Gustafson.

1. James can thus be seen to reverse the means but achieve the effects that Maurice Blanchot shows to be central to Franz Kafka's writerly experience: "as if the more he distanced himself from himself, the more present he became" (87, my translation). In *The American Scene,* the more intimate James becomes with his own process of recollection, the more anonymous and impersonal his self-representation becomes.
2. Others who have examined James's same-sex sexuality include Leon Edel, Eve Kosofsky Sedgwick, Posnock, and Sheldon M. Novick.
3. My argument is based in part on Leo Bersani's recent theorization of the specificity of homosexual desire as "a sexual preference without sex," which "eliminates from 'sex' *the necessity of any relation whatsoever*" (118, 122). By reconceiving erotic desire as conditioned by a nonrelation, that is, as constitutively disjunctive, Bersani's theory renders subjective identity incoherent. In my analysis of *The American Scene,* I locate this nonrelation in the impersonal dimension of James's recollective process. In this narrative, memory turns out to animate what Bersani refers to as homosexuality's "narcissistic" yet "impersonal sameness [which is] ontologically incompatible with analyzable egos" and which thereby "block[s] the cultural discipline of identification" (124–25). In using Bersani to replace a deeply structured ego with subjective non-relationality, I am by no means attempting to reclaim a transcendental, universal mode of desire in *The American Scene.* Indeed, my effort is entirely in the reverse direction; I aim to uncover the deep specificity of James's mode of desire, so as to correct what I think are misreadings of his libidinal investments.
4. For a fuller discussion of William James's conception of the limit of consciousness, see my article "William James's Onto-Physiology of Limits," *Genre,* (forthcoming).
5. For a fanciful yet provocative reading of this passage as a testament to James's "greater acceptance and *specificity* of homosexual desire," see Sedgwick, 186.

6. For the most detailed and penetrating account of Henry James as flâneur, see Posnock.

7. James could be said to hybridize Benjamin's conceptions of flâneur and
collector. "Possession and having are associated with the tactical and stand to
an extent in contrast to the optical. Collectors are people with tactile instinct.
. . . [T]he *flâneur* [is] optical, the collector [is] tactile" (*Schriften* 5:274, my
translation). In collecting, "the object is detached from all original functions.
. . . This is the diametrical opposite to use [value]" (5: 271). The distinction he
makes between flâneur and collector notwithstanding, Benjamin also imagines the possibility of experiencing the Paris arcades "as though they were
possession in the hand of a collector." As it happens, Benjamin develops this
thought in conjunction with his reading of Bergson's *Matter and Memory*,
which prompts him to think of collected objects (as well as memories, knowledge, thoughts, images, etc.) as thrusting themselves into the experiential
realm of the collector, just as Bergson's perceptions do (5:272).

8. For a different reading of this scene, see Sharon Cameron. I take issue
with the premises of her approach to consciousness and James later in this
essay.

9. While dispelling metaphysical frames of unified, autonomous subjectivity, such a model serves only to reframe the now decentered subject in a predictably repressive and doomed libidinal economy, wherein the desired
production of transcendental signifiers always fails and the experienced consumption of mother's breast ersatz never satisfies. A fine model, perhaps, for
analyzing the normative patterns of modern popular consumption, but as we
shall see, it is hardly applicable to James's odd mix of prismatic lust and inter-
fering celibacy.

Contributors

SARAH B. DAUGHERTY, professor and graduate coordinator of English at Wichita State University, is the author of *The Literary Criticism of Henry James* and of numerous essays on James and Howells in journals such as the *Henry James Review, American Literary Realism*, and *Texas Studies in Language and Literature*. She is also a member of the editorial board of the *Henry James Review*.

MARY ESTEVE is a postdoctoral fellow at the Center for Research on Culture and Literature at Johns Hopkins University. She has published articles on nineteenth- and early-twentieth-century American literature and culture in such journals as *ELH, American Literary History*, and *Genre*. She is currently working on a book on the representation of crowds and anonymity in urban literature and culture of the United States.

BRUCE HENRICKSEN is a professor of English at Loyola University in New Orleans and is the author of essays on contemporary critical theory in various journals such as *PMLA, Diacritics, Novel*, and *Studies in the Novel*. He is the author of *Nomadic Voices: Conrad and the Subject of Narrative*. In addition, he has edited *Murray Krieger and Contemporary Critical Theory* and coedited with Thais Morgan *Reorientations: Critical Theories and Pedagogies*.

ERIC HARALSON is an assistant professor of English at the State University of New York at Stony Brook. He has published essays on Victorian masculinity and modern sexual politics in *American Literature* and *Nineteenth Century Literature* as well as in the collections *Queer Forster* and *Victorian Sexual Dissidence*, the *Cambridge Companion to Henry James*, and the *Oxford Historical Guide to Henry James*. His book in progress is entitled "Henry James and the Making of Modern Masculinities."

ANNY BROOKSBANK JONES is Senior Lecturer in Hispanic Studies at the University of Leeds, in Leeds, England. She is the author of *Women in Contemporary Spain* and is the coeditor with Catherine Davies of *Latin American Women's Writing: Feminist Readings in Theory and Crisis*. She has also published widely on Latin American and Spanish cultural studies as well as James in European, British, and American journals.

LELAND S. PERSON is professor and chair of the English Department at the University of Alabama at Birmingham. He has published *Aesthetic Headaches: Women and a Masculine Poetics in Poe, Melville, and Hawthorne* as well as many essays in such major journals as *PMLA, American Literature, American Quarterly, American Literary History*, the *Henry James Review, Studies in the Novel*, and *Nineteenth-Century Literature*.

JOHN CARLOS ROWE is professor of critical theory and American literature at the University of California at Irvine. His books include *Henry Adams and Henry James: The Emergence of a Modern Consciousness; Through the Custom House: Nineteenth-Century American Fiction and Modern Theory; The Theoretical Dimensions of Henry James; At Emerson's Tomb: The Politics of Classic American Literature;* and *The Other Henry James*. He is editor of *"Culture" and the Problem of the Disciplines* and *New Essays on "The Education of Henry Adams"* and coeditor with Rick Berg of *The Vietnam War and American Culture*. He has published numerous essays on James, American literature, and literary theory in major academic journals and collections of essays on American literary and cultural studies.

PRISCILLA L. WALTON is professor of English at Carleton University in Ottawa. She is the author of *The Disruption of the Feminine in Henry James* as well as *Patriarchal Desire and Victorian Discourse: A Lacanian Reading of Anthony Trollope's Palliser Novels* and is the coauthor with Manina Jones of *Detective Agency: Women Rewriting the Hard-Boiled Tradition*. She has published essays on a variety of American works in journals such as the *Henry James Review, Narrative, Victorian Review, Commonwealth Essays and Studies,* and *Ariel*.

MICHAEL L. J. WILSON is an assistant professor of historical studies at the University of Texas at Dallas. He has published essays on James in journals including the *Henry James Review,* the *American Journal of Semiotics,* and *Body Guards: The Cultural Politics of Gender Ambiguity.* Wilson's current research is a book entitled *Bohemian Montmartre: Art, Commerce, and Community in Fin-de-Siècle Paris.*

PEGGY MCCORMACK is an associate professor in the English Department at Loyola University in New Orleans, chair of Loyola's Film Studies Program, and a member of the Board of Editors of the *New Orleans Review.* She has published essays on James in journals, including *American Literature* and the *Henry James Review.* She is the author of *The Rule of Money: Gender, Class, and Exchange Economics in the Fiction of Henry James.*

Works Cited

Adams, James Eli. *Dandies and Desert Saints: Styles of Victorian Masculinity.* Ithaca: Cornell University Press, 1995.

Alcott, Louisa M. *Moods.* 2d Edition. Boston: Loring, 1865.

Allen, Elizabeth. *A Woman's Place in the Novels of Henry James.* New York: St. Martin's Press, 1984.

Anderson, Quentin. *The American Henry James.* New Brunswick, N.J.: Rutgers University Press, 1957.

Anesko, Michael. *"Friction with the Market": Henry James and the Profession of Authorship.* New York: Oxford University Press, 1986.

Ash, Beth Sharon. "Narcissism and the Gilded Image: A Psychoanalytic Reading of *The Golden Bowl.*" *Henry James Review* 15 (1994): 55–90.

Bakewell, Michael. *Lewis Carroll: A Biography.* London: Heinemann, 1996.

Balzac, Honoré de. *Cousin Bette.* In *Poor Relations: Cousin Bette. Cousin Pons.* vol. 11 *The Works of Honoré de Balzac.* University Edition. Philadelphia: Avil, 1901.

———. *The Two Young Brides.* Critical introduction by Henry James. London: Heinemann, 1902.

Bataille, Georges. *Visions of Excess: Selected Writings, 1927–1939.* Translated by Allan Stoekl. Minneapolis: University of Minnesota Press, 1985.

Bauer, Dale M. *Feminist Dialogics: A Theory of Failed Community.* Albany: State University of New York Press, 1988.

Bauer, Dale, and Andrew Lakritz. "Language, Class, and Sexuality in Henry James's *In the Cage.*" *New Orleans Review* 14, no. 3 (1987): 61–69.

Baym, Nina. *The Shape of Hawthorne's Career.* Ithaca and London: Cornell University Press, 1976.

———. *Woman's Fiction: A Guide to Novels by and about Women. 1820–1870.* Ithaca and London: Cornell University Press, 1978.

Beidler, Peter G. "The Governess and the Ghosts." *PMLA* 100, no. 1 (1985): 90–100.

Benjamin, Walter. *Gesammelte Schriften.* Edited by Rolf Tiedemann and Hermann Schweppenhuser. 7 vols. Frankfurt am Main: Suhrkamp, 1991.

———. *Reflections.* Translated by Edmund Jephcott. New York: Schocken, 1986.

Bergson, Henri. *Matter and Memory.* Translated by N. M. Paul and W. S. Palmer. New York: Zone, 1991.

Bersani, Leo. *Homos.* Cambridge and London: Harvard University Press, 1995.

Bewley, Marius. *The Complex Fate.* London: Chatto and Windus, 1952.

Bhabha, Homi K. "Introduction: Narrating the Nation." In *Nation and Narration*, edited by Homi K. Bhabha. London: Routledge, 1990.

Blanchot, Maurice. *De Kafka/ Kafka*. Paris: Gallimard, 1981.

Bloom, Harold. *The Anxiety of Influence: A Theory of Poetry*. New York: Oxford University Press, 1973.

Boone, Joseph Allen. *Tradition/Counter Tradition: Love and the Form of Fiction*. Chicago: University of Chicago Press, 1987.

Booth, Wayne. *A Rhetoric of Irony*. Chicago: University of Chicago Press, 1974.

Bordwell, David, Janet Staiger, and Kristin Thompson. *The Classical Hollywood Cinema: Film Style and Mode of Production to 1960*. London: Routledge, 1985.

The Bostonians. Directed by James Ivory. Merchant-Ivory, 1984.

Bradley, John R., ed. *Henry James and Homo-Erotic Desire*. New York: St. Martin's Press, 1998.

Brennan, Timothy. "The National Longing for Form." In *Nation and Narration*, edited by Homi K. Bhabha. London: Routledge, 1990.

Brodhead, Richard H. *The School of Hawthorne*. New York and Oxford: Oxford University Press, 1986.

Brooks, Van Wyck. *The Pilgrimage of Henry James*. New York: E. P. Dutton and Co., 1925.

Butler, Judith. "Gender Trouble, Feminist Theory, and Psychoanalytic Discourse." In *Feminism/ Postmodernism*, edited by Linda J. Nicholson. New York: Routledge, 1990.

Cameron, Sharon. *Thinking in Henry James*. Chicago and London: University of Chicago Press, 1989.

Cannon, Kelly. *Henry James and Masculinity: The Man at the Margins*. New York: St. Martin's Press, 1994.

Cargill, Oscar. *The Novels of Henry James*. New York: Macmillan, 1961.

Castle, Terry. *The Apparitional Lesbian: Female Homosexuality and Modern Culture*. New York: Columbia University Press, 1993.

Charteris, Evan, ed. *The Life and Letters of Sir Edmund Gosse*. London: Heinemann, 1931.

Chatman, Seymour. *Story and Discourse: Narrative Structure in Fiction and Film*. Ithaca: Cornell University Press, 1978.

Chauncey, George. *Gay New York: Gender, Urban Culture, and the Making of the Gay Male World, 1890–1940*. New York: Basicbooks, 1994.

Cohen, Ed. *Talk on the Wilde Side: Toward a Genealogy of a Discourse on Male Sexualities*. New York and London: Routledge, 1993.

Conrad, Joseph. *The Collected Letters of Joseph Conrad*. Vol. 2. Edited by Frederick R. Karl and Laurence Davies. Cambridge: Cambridge University Press, 1986.

Cooper, Michael A. "Discipl(in)ing the Master, Mastering the Discipl(in)e: Erotonomies of Discipleship in James' Tales of Literary Life." In *Engendering Men: The Question of Male Feminist Criticism*, edited by Joseph A. Boone and Michael Cadden. New York and London: Routledge, 1990.

Corse, Sandra. "Henry James on Eliot and Sand." *South Atlantic Review* 51 (1986): 57–68.

Culler, Jonathan. "Story and Discourse in the Analysis of Narrative." In *The Pursuit of Signs*. Ithaca: Cornell University Press, 1981.

Daugherty, Sarah B. "*The Golden Bowl*: Balzac, James, and the Rhetoric of Power." *Texas Studies in Literature and Language* 24, no. 1 (1982): 68–82.

———. "Henry James and George Eliot: The Price of Mastery." *Henry James Review* 10, no. 3 (1989): 153–66.

———. "Henry James, George Sand, and *The Bostonians*: Another Curious Chapter in the Literary History of Feminism." *Henry James Review* 10, no. 1 (1989): 42–49.

Davis, Robert Con, ed. *The Fictional Father: Lacanian Readings of the Text*. Amherst: University of Massachusetts Press, 1981.

Davis, Tracy C. *Actresses as Working Women: Their Social Identity in Victorian Culture*. New York: Routledge, 1991.

Dellamora, Richard. *Masculine Desire: The Sexual Politics of Victorian Aestheticism*. Chapel Hill: University of North Carolina Press, 1990.

Deleuze, Gilles. *Bergsonism*. Translated by Hugh Tomlinson and Barbara Habberjam. New York: Zone, 1988.

———. *Masochism: An Interpretation of Coldness and Cruelty*. Translated by Jean McNeil. New York: George Braziller, 1971.

Deleuze, Gilles, and Felix Guattari. *Anti-Oedipus: Capitalism and Schizophrenia*. Translated by Robert Hurley, Mark Seem, and Helen R. Lane. Minneapolis: University of Minnesota Press, 1983.

Doane, Mary Ann. *Femmes Fatales: Feminism, Film Theory, Psychoanalysis*. New York: Routledge, 1991.

Douglas, Ann. *The Feminization of American Culture*. New York: Knopf, 1977.

Doweling, Linda. *Hellenism and Homosexuality in Victorian Oxford*. Ithaca: Cornell University Press, 1994.

Edel, Leon. *Henry James: A Life*. New York: Harper and Row, 1985.

———. *Henry James: The Treacherous Years, 1895–1901*. New York: J. B. Lippincott Co., 1969.

———. "The James Family." *Henry James Review* 10, no. 2 (spring 1989): 90–94.

———. *The Untried Years, 1843–1870*. Philadelphia: Lippincott, 1953.

Edel, Leon and Sheldon M. Novick. "Oh Henry! What Henry James Didn't Do With Oliver Wendell Holmes (Or Anyone Else)." *Slate*. 11 December 1996: 8 Messages. Online. Internet. 24 September 1997. Available http://www.slate.com/Concept/96-12-11/Concept.asp

Eliot, George. *The Mill on the Floss*. Standard edition of *The Works of George Eliot*. New York: A. L. Burt, [1900].

The Europeans. Directed by James Ivory. Merchant-Ivory, 1979.

Felman, Shoshana. "Turning the Screw of Interpretation." In *Literature and Psychoanalysis: The Question of Reading: Otherwise*. Baltimore and London: Johns Hopkins University Press, 1982.

Forster, E. M. *Commonplace Book*. Edited by Philip Gardner. London: Scolar Press, 1985.

Foucault, Michel. *The History of Sexuality*, vol. 1. Translated by Robert Hurley. New York: Random House, 1978.

Freud, Sigmund. "The 'Uncanny.'" In *The Standard Edition of the Complete Psychological Works of Sigmund Freud.* Vol. 17, *An Infantile Neurosis and Other Works,* translated and edited by J. Strachey. London: Hogarth Press and the Institute of Psycho-Analysis, 1973.

Fussell, Edward Sill. *The French Side of Henry James.* New York: Columbia University Press, 1990.

Gabler-Hover, Janet. "The Ethics of Determinism in Henry James's *In the Cage.*" *Henry James Review* 13, no. 3 (1992): 253–75 .

Gard, Roger, ed. *Henry James: The Critical Heritage.* London: Routledge and Kegan Paul, 1968.

Gilmour, Robin. *The Idea of the Gentleman in the Victorian Novel.* London: Allen and Unwin, 1981.

Habegger, Alfred. *Henry James and the "Woman Business."* Cambridge and New York: Cambridge University Press, 1989.

Haralson, Eric. " 'Thinking about Homosex' in Forster and James." In *Queer Forster,* edited by Robert K. Martin and George Piggford. Chicago: University of Chicago Press, 1997.

Hawthorne, Nathaniel. *The Marble Faun.* New York and Toronto: New American Library, 1961.

———. *The Scarlet Letter.* New York and Scarborough, Ontario: New American Library, 1959.

Hayes, Kevin J., ed. *Henry James: The Contemporary Reviews.* Cambridge and New York: Cambridge University Press, 1996.

The Heiress. Directed by William Wyler. Warner Bros., 1949.

Hemenway, Robert. *Becoming a Poet: Elizabeth Bishop with Marianne Moore and Robert Lowell.* New York: Farrar, Straus and Giroux, 1989.

Henricksen, Bruce. " 'The Real Thing': Criticism and the Ethical Turn." *Papers on Language and Literature* 27, no. 4 (fall 1991): 473–95.

Hillis Miller, J. "The Figure in the Carpet." In *Modern Critical Interpretations: Henry James's "Daisy Miller," "The Turn of the Screw," and Other Tales,* edited by Harold Bloom. New York: Chelsea House Publishers, 1987.

Hollander, John, ed. *American Poetry: The Nineteenth Century.* Vol. 1. New York: Library of America, 1993.

Homans, Margaret. "The Name of the Mother in *Wuthering Heights.*" In *Wuthering Heights,* by Emily Bronte, edited by Linda H. Peterson. Boston: St. Martin's Press, Bedford Books, 1992.

Howells, William Dean. *Novels, 1886–1888.* Edited by Don L. Cook. New York: Library of America, 1989.

Irigaray, Luce. *Je, Tu, Nous.* Paris: Grasset, 1990.

———. *This Sex Which is Not One.* Translated by Catherine Porter with Carolyn Burke. Ithaca: Cornell University Press, 1985.

———. *Speculum of the Other Woman.* Translated by G. C. Gill. New York: Cornell University Press, 1985.

James, Henry. *The Ambassadors.* Edited by S. P. Rosenbaum. New York: W. W. Norton and Co., 1964.

———. *The American Scene.* Bloomington: Indiana University Press, 1968.

———. *The American Scene*. Edited by W. H. Auden. New York: Charles Scribner's Sons, 1946.

———. *The Bostonians*. New York: Modern Library, 1956.

———. *The Complete Tales of Henry James*. Vol. 5. Edited by Leon Edel. London: Rupert Hart Davis, 1965.

———. *The Complete Tales of Henry James*. Vol. 14. New York: Charles Scribner's Sons, 1936.

———. *The Golden Bowl*. Vols. 23–24. *The Novels and Tales of Henry James*. New York: Charles Scribner's Sons, 1909.

———. *The Golden Bowl*. Edited by John Halperin. New York: New American Library, 1972.

———. *In the Cage and Other Stories*. By Henry James; introduced and selected by S. Gorley Putt. Harmondsworth: Penguin, 1974.

———. *In the Cage and Other Tales*. Edited by Morton Dauwen Zabel. New York: W. W. Norton and Co., 1958.

———. *The Letters of Henry James*. Vol. 1. Edited by Leon Edel. Cambridge: Harvard University Press; Belknap Press, 1974.

———. *The Letters of Henry James*. Vol. 3. Edited by Leon Edel. Cambridge: Harvard University Press; Belknap Press, 1980.

———. *The Letters of Henry James*. Vol. 4. Edited by Leon Edel. Cambridge: Harvard University Press; Belknap Press, 1984.

———. *Hawthorne*. In *Henry James: Literary Criticism*. Vol. 1. Edited by Leon Edel and Mark Wilson. New York: Library of America, 1984.

———. *Literary Criticism: Essays on Literature, American Writers, English Writers*. Edited by Leon Edel. New York: Library of America, 1984.

———. *Literary Criticism: French Writers, Other European Writers, the Prefaces to the New York Edition*. Edited by Leon Edel. New York: Library of America, 1984.

———. HM—*The Tragic Muse* [1890] New York: Harper and Brothers, 1960.

———. SM—*The Tragic Muse* [1908] 2 vols. New York: Charles Scribner's Sons, 1936.

———. *The Complete Notebooks of Henry James*. Edited by Leon Edel and Lyall H. Powers. New York and Oxford: Oxford University Press, 1987.

———. *Notes on Novelists with Some Other Notes*. London: Dent, 1914.

———. *The Siege of London*. In *"In the Cage" and Other Stories*. Harmondsworth, England: Penguin Modern Classics, 1972.

———. *Stories of Artists and Writers*. Edited by F. O. Matthiessen. New York: New Directions, 1965.

———. *The Turn of the Screw and Other Short Novels*. New York: New American Library, 1962.

———. *The Wings of the Dove*. New York: New American Library, 1964.

James, William. *Essays in Radical Empiricism*. Cambridge: Harvard University Press, 1976.

———. *The Letters of William James*. 2 vols. Boston: Little, Brown, 1926.

———. *Pragmatism*. Cambridge and London: Harvard University Press, 1978.

———. *The Principles of Psychology*. 2 vols. New York: Henry Holt and Co., 1890.

————. *Writings, 1902–1910*. Edited by Bruce Kucklick. New York: Library of America, 1987.

Jameson, Fredric. *The Political Unconscious: Narrative as a Socially Symbolic Act*. Ithaca: Cornell University Press, 1981.

Kairschner, Mimi. "The Traces of Capitalist Patriarchy in the Silences of *The Golden Bowl*." *Henry James Review* 5 (1984): 187–92.

Kaplan, Fred. *Henry James: The Imagination of Genius*. New York: William Morrow and Co., 1992.

Kermode, Frank. *The Genesis of Secrecy: On the Interpretation of Narrative*. Cambridge: Harvard University Press, 1979.

Kincaid, James R. *Child-Loving: The Erotic Child and Victorian Culture*. New York, London: Routledge, 1992.

Kristeva, Julia. *Strangers to Ourselves*. Translated by L. Roudiez. Hemel Hempstead, England: Harvester Wheatsheaf, 1991.

Lemaire, Anika. *Jacques Lacan*. Translated by David Macey. London: Routledge and Kegan Paul, 1977.

Lockhart, John G. *Some Passages in the Life of Mr. Adam Blair. Minister of the Gospel at Cross-Meikle*. Edinburgh: Edinburgh University Press, 1963.

Macnaughton, William R. "The New York Edition of Henry James's *The Tragic Muse*." *Henry James Review* 13 (1992): 19–26.

McClintock, Anne. *Imperial Leather: Race, Gender, and Sexuality in the Colonial Contest*. New York: Routledge, 1995.

McCormack, Peggy. *The Rule of Money: Gender, Class, and Exchange Economics in the Fiction of Henry James*. Ann Arbor: UMI Research Press, 1990.

McFarlane, Brian. *Novel to Film: An Introduction to the Theory of Adaptation*. Oxford: Clarendon, 1996.

McWhirter, David. *Desire and Love in Henry James: A Study of the Late Novels*. New York: Cambridge University Press, 1989.

Miller, Elise. "The Feminization of American Realist Theory." *American Literary Realism* 23, no. 1 (1990): 20–41.

Mulvey, Laura. *Visual and Other Pleasures*. Bloomington: Indiana University Press, 1989.

Novick, Sheldon M. *Henry James: The Young Master*. New York: Random House, 1996.

O'Neill, John P. *Workable Design: Action and Situation in the Fiction of Henry James*. Port Washington, N.Y., and London: Kennikat Press, 1973.

Perry, Ralph Barton. *The Thought and Character of William James*. 2 vols. Boston: Little, Brown and Co., 1935.

Peterson, Dale E. *The Clement Vision: Poetic Realism in Turgenev and James*. Port Washington, N.Y., and London: Kennikat Press, 1975.

Pfitzer, Gregory M. "Sins of Omission: What Henry James Left Out of the Preface to *The Tragic Muse* and Why." *American Literary Realism* 25 (1992): 38–53.

The Portrait of a Lady. Directed by Jane Campion. Propaganda, 1996.

Posnock, Ross. *The Trial of Curiosity: Henry James, William James and the Challenge of Modernity*. Oxford: Oxford University Press, 1991.

Propp, Vladimir. *Morphology of the Folktale*. Translated by Laurence Scott. Austin: University of Texas Press, 1968.

Przybylowicz, Donna. *Desire and Repression: The Dialectic of Self and Other in the Late Works of Henry James*. Tuscaloosa: University of Alabama Press, 1986.

Quackenbos, John Duncan, M.D. "The Transliminal." *North American Review* 183 (1906): 237–49.

Radhakrishnan, R. "Nationalism, Gender, and the Narrative of Identity." In *Nationalisms and Sexualities*, edited by Andrew Parker, Mary Russo, Doris Sommer, and Patricia Yaeger. New York: Routledge, 1992.

Ralf, Norrman. "The Intercepted Telegraph Plot in Henry James' 'In the Cage.' " *Notes and Queries* 24 (1977): 425–27.

Rimmey, John. *Henry James and London: The City in His Fiction*. American University Studies, ser. 4, vol. 121. New York: Peter Lang, 1991.

Ross, Andrew. *No Respect: Intellectuals and Popular Culture*. New York: Routledge, 1989.

Rowe, John Carlos. " 'Swept Away:' Henry James, Margaret Fuller, and 'The Last of the Valerii.' " In *Readers in History: Nineteenth-Century American Literature and the Contexts of Response*, edited by James L. Nachor. Baltimore: Johns Hopkins University Press, 1993.

———. *The Theoretical Dimensions of Henry James*. Madison: University of Wisconsin Press, 1984.

———. "Who'se Henry James? Further Lessons of the Master." *Henry James Review* 2, no. 1 (1980): 2–11.

Russo, Mary. *The Female Grotesque: Risk, Excess and Modernity*. New York: Routledge, 1995.

Said, Edward W. *Culture and Imperialism*. New York: Vintage, 1993.

———. *Orientalism*. New York: Vintage, 1979.

Scheler, Max. *The Nature of Sympathy*. Translated by Peter Heath. Hamden: Archon, 1970.

Sedgwick, Eve Kosofsky. "The Beast in the Closet: James and the Writing of Homosexual Panic." In *Sex, Politics, and Science in the Nineteenth-Century Novel*, edited by Ruth Bernard Yeazell, 148–86. Baltimore and London: Johns Hopkins University Press, 1986.

———. *Between Men: English Literature and Male Homosocial Desire*. New York: Columbia University Press, 1985.

———. *Epistemology of the Closet*. Berkeley and Los Angeles: University of California Press, 1990.

———. *Tendencies*. Durham, N.C.: Duke University Press, 1993.

Seemueller, Anne Moncure Crane. *Emily Chester: A Novel*. 2d ed. Boston: Ticknor and Fields, 1864.

Seltzer, Mark. *Henry James and the Art of Power*. Ithaca: Cornell University Press, 1985.

Sheppard, E. A. *Henry James and "The Turn of the Screw."* Auckland: Auckland University Press, 1974.

Sicker, Philip. *Love and the Quest for Identity in the Fiction of Henry James*. Princeton: Princeton University Press, 1980.

Sidis, Boris. *The Psychology of Suggestion*. New York: Appleton, 1898.

Silverman, Kaja. *Male Subjectivity at the Margins*. New York: Routledge, 1992.

Stevens, Hugh. "Sexuality and the Aesthetic in *The Golden Bowl*." *Henry James Review* 14 (1993): 55–71.

Stevenson, Robert Louis. *The Strange Case of Dr. Jekyll and Mr. Hyde*. New York: Bantam, 1985.

Stoddard, Elizabeth. *Two Men: A Novel*. Philadelphia: Coates, 1901.

Symonds, John Addington. *The Memoirs of John Addington Symonds*. Edited by Phyllis Grosskurth. London: Hutchinson, 1984.

Taylor, Gordon O. *Chapters of Experience: Studies in Twentieth-Century American Autobiography*. New York: St. Martin's Press, 1983.

Torsney, Cheryl B. "Specula(riza)tion in *The Golden Bowl*." *Henry James Review* 12 (1991): 141–46.

Trilling, Lionel. "Reality in America." In *The Liberal Imagination*. New York: Anchor Books, 1953.

Trollope, Anthony. *Can You Forgive Her?* 2 vols. *The Oxford Trollope*. Crown ed. London: Oxford University Press, 1948.

Tseelon, Efrat. *The Masque of Femininity: The Presentation of Woman in Everyday Life*. Thousand Oaks, Calif.: Sage Publications, 1995.

Turgenev, Ivan. *A House of Gentlefolk: A Novel*. Translated by Constance Garnett. London: Heinemann, 1894. Reprint, New York: AMS Press, 1970.

———. *On the Eve*. Translated by Constance Garnett. London: Heinemann, 1895. Reprint, New York: AMS Press, 1970.

Veeder, William. "Toxic Mothers, Cultural Criticism: *In the Cage* and Elsewhere." *Henry James Review* 14, no. 3 (1992): 264–72.

Waldstein, Louis, M.D. *The Subconscious Self and Its Relation to Education and Health*. New York: Charles Scribner's Sons, 1897.

Walker, Pierre A. *Reading Henry James in French Cultural Contexts*. De Kalb, Ill: Northern Illinois University Press, 1995.

Walton, Priscilla L. *The Disruption of the Feminine in Henry James*. Toronto: University of Toronto Press, 1992.

———. "Jane and James Go to the Movies: PostColonial Portraits of a Lady." *Henry James Review* 18 (1997): 187–90.

Washington Square. Directed by Agnieszka Holland. Disney/Caravan, 1997.

White, James Boyd. *Justice as Translation: An Essay in Cultural and Legal Criticism*. Chicago: University of Chicago Press, 1990.

Whitford, Margaret. *Luce Irigaray: Philosophy in the Feminine*. London; New York: Routledge, 1991.

Wicke, Jennifer. "Henry James's Second Wave." *Henry James Review* 10, no. 2 (1989): 146–51.

Wilde, Oscar. *The Picture of Dorian Gray*. Harmondsworth, England: Penguin, 1985.

Wilson, Michael. "Lessons of the Master: The Artist and Sexual Identity in Henry James." *Henry James Review* 14 (1993): 257–63.

Wilson, R. B. J. *Henry James's Ultimate Narrative: "The Golden Bowl."* St. Lucia: University of Queensland Press, 1981.

The Wings of the Dove. Directed by Iain Softley. Renaissance Dove/Miramax, 1997.

Woolf, Virginia. "The Ghost Stories." In *Henry James: A Collection of Critical Essays,* edited by Leon Edel. Englewood Cliffs, N.J.: Prentice-Hall, 1962.

Zwinger, Linda. "The Sentimental Gilt of Heterosexuality: James's *The Golden Bowl." Raritan* 7 (1987): 70–92.

Index

Adams, James Eli, 118
Alcott, Bronson, 138
Alcott, Louisa May, 31, 180, 194
Allen, Elizabeth, 155
Ambassadors, The, 101, 137
American, The, 86; as film, 38
American Scene, The, 21, 32–34, 137, 196–216
Anderson, Hendrik, 100
Anderson, Quentin, 155
Anesko, Michael, 106
art, 17, 68, 72, 75–80, 86, 102 n. 2, 104–32, 187, 195
"Art of Fiction, The," 194
artist, the, 17, 23–26, 96, 106, 113, 116–18, 130–32, 198
Ash, Beth Sharon, 152, 163, 173 nn. 3–5
Aspern Papers, The, 81–82
Austen, Jane, 37–38, 190
"Author of Beltraffio, The," 19–20, 74, 75–80, 81, 82, 83–84
Awkward Age, The, 83

Bakhtin, Mikhail, 69
Balzac, Honoré de, 31, 80, 177, 178, 182, 185, 188, 190–94
Barber, Benjamin, 14, 49
Barthelme, Donald, 46
Barthes, Roland, 191
Bataille, Georges, 214
Bauer, Dale M., 88, 155, 157, 159, 160, 174 n. 11, 175 n. 12
Baym, Nina, 179, 185
Beast in the Jungle, The, 97
Benjamin, Walter, 206, 210, 211, 216 n. 7
Bergson, Henri, 32, 34, 197, 200, 201–02, 204, 206, 215, 216 n. 7
Bersani, Leo, 215 n. 3
Bhabha, Homi K., 12–13, 39, 47, 52
Blanchot, Maurice, 215 n. 1

Bloom, Harold, 176, 179, 185
Boone, Joseph Allen, 171, 173 n. 1, 175 n. 12
Booth, Wayne, 84 n. 2
Bostonians, The, 86, 89, 95, 136, 162, 176, 182, 186; as film, 13, 14, 45–46
Braidotti, Rosi, 56–57
Brennan, Timothy, 40
Brodhead, Richard, 176–77, 193
"Broken Wings," 71, 75
Brontes, the, 190
Brooks, Van Wyck, 40, 41–42
Butler, Judith, 22, 93, 95

Cameron, Sharon, 209
Campion, Jane, 14, 15, 38, 40–41, 47–49, 50, 52
Cannon, Kelly, 108
capitalism, 29–30, 32–34, 151–59, 170, 193, 200, 213–15
Cargill, Oscar, 155
Carroll, Lewis, 145
Carter, Helena Bonham, 49
Castle, Terry, 136
celibacy, 32–34, 197, 198–99, 203, 210, 213, 216 n. 9
Charcot, Jean-Martin, 60
Chauncey, George, 157, 170
Cherbuliez, Victor, 177
class, 15, 21, 22, 50, 92, 111, 114, 121, 124, 136, 170; and gender, 23, 86, 93, 94–95, 100, 101, 129, 137; and language, 21, 87, 88–89; and male entitlement, 139, 144, 146, 170
Cleveland Street brothel affair, 26, 27, 139
Clift, Montgomery, 43
Cohen, Ed, 139
Colby, F. M., 143
Conrad, Joseph, 134, 144
Cooper, Michael A., 199
Corse, Sandra, 183
Culler, Jonathan, 78, 79

229

Daisy Miller, 178
Daudet, Alphonse, 188
Daugherty, Sarah B., 12, 20, 30–32, 176–95
Davis, Tracy C., 122
"Death of the Lion, The," 70–71, 75, 80
Deleuze, Gilles, 29, 150, 154, 201, 214
Dellamora, Richard, 139
Derrida, Jacques, 56, 76
Dickens, Charles, 77
Doane, Mary Ann, 45
Dodgson, Charles, 145
Douglas, Lord Alfred, 26, 140
Droz, Gustave, 177

Edel, Leon, 11, 60–61, 83, 141, 146, 187
Eichhorn, Lisa, 44
Eliot, George, 31, 32, 177, 178, 183–85, 187, 190, 194
Eliot, T. S., 72
Elliot, Alison, 49
Esteve, Mary, 12, 32–34, 196–216
"Eugene Pickering, " 181
Europeans, The: as film, 13, 14, 44–45, 46
exile, the, 57–61; characters as, 29, 55–56, 58–61, 65, 72; James as, 198, 210

father, the, 22, 43–44, 69–70, 97–98, 154–55, 157, 164–65. *See also* Law of the Father
Felman, Shoshana, 138
female body, 15, 40, 44, 47, 52
feminine, the, 12, 56–57, 65, 78, 80, 86, 92, 124–30, 150, 155, 164, 168; and reading 79, 165–66; and writing, 20, 21, 77, 183, 188
feminist criticism, 56, 64, 128. *See also* James, and feminism
"Figure in the Carpet, The," 70, 80–81, 82, 84
film, 12–15, 37–52
Fish, Stanley, 79
Flaubert, Gustave, 177, 188
Forster, E. M., 27, 136, 141
Fournel, Victor, 210
Freedman, Jonathan, 106

Freud, Sigmund, 17, 60, 61–62, 65, 76, 97, 150, 202
Fuller, Margaret, 185
Fullerton, Morton, 100
Fussell, Edwin, 106

gender, 12, 34, 127, 145, 213; and the artist, 17–20, 23–26, 68–85, 104–32; and capital, 151–75; and nation, 15, 40–53; and work, 20–23, 86, 91–95, 100, 101, 102 n. 2. *See also* feminine, the; masculine, the
Gielgud, Sir John, 48
Goetz, Augustus, 42
Goetz, Ruth, 42
Golden Bowl, The, 28–30, 83, 149–75, 192–94
Goncourts, the, 188
Gone With the Wind, 13, 42–43
Gosse, Edmund, 140, 144
"Greville Fane," 18, 70
Guattari, Felix, 214

Habegger, Alfred, 176, 179, 181
Haralson, Eric, 12, 26–28, 133–48
Havilland, Olivia de, 13, 42–43
Hawthorne, 39, 185–87
Hawthorne, Nathaniel, 31, 160, 177, 178, 183, 185–87, 193, 194
Heiress, The, 13, 14, 42–44, 46
Henricksen, Bruce, 12, 17–20, 68–85
heterosexuality, 15, 51, 62, 100, 106, 108, 150, 155, 162–63, 167, 169, 170, 198
Holland, Agnieszka, 13–14, 38, 52 n. 2, 53 n. 6
Homans, Margaret, 18, 69, 83
homoeroticism, 15, 23, 29, 78, 80, 99–100, 156–57, 165, 169, 199, 200, 213
homosexuality, 12, 26, 51, 62, 100, 135–36, 139, 141, 145–47, 167, 168, 199
homosocial, the, 15, 29, 50, 156, 162–63, 168, 199
Hopkins, Gerard Manley, 144
Howells, William Dean, 144

imperialism, 12, 14, 47–49, 146
In the Cage, 20–23, 60, 86–102

Irigaray, Luce, 17, 50–51, 59, 61–62, 63–65
Iser, Wolfgang, 79
Ivory, James, 14, 38, 44–46

James, Alice, 177
James, Henry, 11–12, 83, 100–01, 105; as critic, 30–32, 176–95; critical reviews of, 11, 83, 133–38, 141, 143, 176, 194; as cross-national writer, 15, 16–17, 37, 39–40, 52, 104, 196, 205; and feminism, 66, 176–95; fiction by, 12, 16–30, 54–175; letters of, 140, 142, 176, 198, 199; film versions of works by, 12–15, 37–53; and memory, 32–34, 196–216; nonfiction by, 12, 30–34, 176–216; prefaces and self-commentary by, 55, 60, 62, 105–8, 115, 134–36, 143, 164–66, 176, 208; and theories of art, 68, 106, 115, 118–19, 130–31, 132; and women writers, 31–32, 122, 177, 179–85, 190. *See also titles of individual works*
James, William, 32, 34, 142, 143, 183, 197, 198, 200–201, 203, 205, 208, 215
Jameson, Fredric, 73
Jones, Anny Brooksbank, 12, 16–17, 54–67

Kafka, Franz, 82, 215 n. 1
Kairschner, Mimi, 157, 170, 174 n. 9
Kaplan, Fred, 11, 100–101
Kermode, Frank, 81
Kidman, Nicole, 48
Kincaid, James R., 137, 138
Kristeva, Julia, 57, 58, 59–60

Lacan, Jacques, 18, 20, 69–70, 75, 76, 78, 80, 209. *See also* Law of the Father
Lakritz, Andrew, 88
language, 12, 18, 65, 70, 76, 79–80, 87–88, 89
Law of the Father, 18, 20, 70, 71, 75, 76, 77, 80, 82, 83, 97, 154
Leavis, F.R., 37
"Lesson of Balzac, The," 190

"Lesson of the Master, The," 19, 74–75
Lévi-Strauss, Claude, 19, 74
Lockhart, John G., 185
Lodge, Oliver, 142

Macnaughton, William, 106
"Madonna of the Future, The," 19, 71–74, 83–84
marriage, 86, 111, 113, 119–20, 130, 132, 150–51, 153, 166–70, 178
masculine, the, 12, 23, 78, 79, 92, 97, 108–12, 114–18, 150; in *The Golden Bowl*, 28–30, 149–75; in *The Turn of the Screw*, 139, 144–47; and writing, 31, 164–66, 183, 190, 192
masochism, 29, 149–50, 153, 154, 162–63, 166, 167
McClintock, Anne, 12, 14, 40, 47
McCormack, Peggy, 11–34, 83, 105–6, 107, 150, 176
McFarlane, Brian, 12–13, 37, 38
McWhirter, David, 173 n. 2
Melville, Herman, 164
Merchant, Ismail, 14, 38, 44–46
"Middle Years, The," 84
Mildred Pierce, 42
Miller, Elise, 181
Miller, J. Hillis, 81
mother, the, 18, 22, 43–44, 63, 69, 70, 76, 77, 80–84, 96–98, 102 n. 10, 154, 198
Mulvey, Laura, 17
Myers, F. W. H., 142–43

nationality, 37–40, 54, 121; and gender, 40–53. *See also* James, as cross-national writer
Novick, Sheldon M., 11

O'Neill, John P., 189
Orientalism, 50, 51–52

Person, Leland S., 12, 28–30, 149–75
Peterson, Dale E., 188
Pfitzer, Gregory, 122
Portrait of a Lady, The, 86, 95, 161, 162, 180, 184, 188; as film, 13, 14, 15, 38, 41, 47–49, 52
Posnock, Ross, 203

Princess Casamassima, The, 89
Propp, Vladimir, 17, 69
Przybylowicz, Donna, 209

Quackenbos, John Duncan, 205

Radhakrishnan, R., 42
Raffalovich, Andre, 100
reader, the, 54, 79, 84, 105, 108, 212; and *The Golden Bowl*, 164, 165–66; and James's representation of women, 188–90, 192; and *The Turn of the Screw*, 133–39, 141, 143, 146
"Real Thing, The," 68, 71, 75
Redgrave, Vanessa, 46
Reeve, Christopher, 46
Reik, Theodor, 150
Remick, Lee, 45
representation, 12, 20, 21, 22, 38, 51, 86, 107, 116, 197, 203; of women, 19, 30–32, 68–83, 130, 176–95
repression, 12, 17, 23, 57, 60, 97, 100, 199, 202
Richet, Charles, 200
Ross, Andrew, 40
Rowe, John Carlos, 12, 20–23, 46, 86–103

sadism, 29, 150, 153, 162–63, 167
sadomasochism, 28–30, 149–75
Said, Edward, 50, 52
Sand, George, 31, 62, 177, 181–82, 183, 190
Scott, Sir Walter, 178
Sedgwick, Eve Kosofsky, 15, 27, 50, 97, 141, 156
Seemueller, Anne Moncure Crane, 179
Seltzer, Mark, 150, 162, 170, 174 n. 6, 174 n. 10, 174 n. 12
Sense of the Past, The, 204
sexuality, 17, 34, 78, 152, 195, 197; in films, 12–15, 45, 47, 48, 52; James's, 11–12; in *The Turn of the Screw*, 135, 138–39, 140, 142, 146; and Victorian culture, 135, 199. *See also* celibacy; heterosexuality; homosexuality
Sheppard, E. A., 141, 145, 146
Sidis, Boris, 205
Siege of London, The, 16–17, 54–67

Silverman, Kaja, 28, 149–50, 154, 164, 166, 174 n. 7
Slate, 11
Softley, Iain, 14–15, 38, 41, 47, 49–52
Spoils of Poynton, The, 89
Stevens, Hugh, 163
Stevenson, Robert Louis, 27, 113, 122, 143
Stoddard, Elizabeth, 31, 180–81, 194
Sturgis, Howard, 100, 101
Symonds, John Addington, 143, 145–46

Taine, Hippolyte, 191
Taylor, Gordon O., 196, 197
Thackeray, William, 192
Torsney, Cheryl, 156
Tragic Muse, The, 23–26, 31, 104–32
Trilling, Lionel, 40, 41–42
Trollope, Anthony, 31, 93, 94, 177, 178–79, 183
Turgenev, Ivan, 31, 177, 178, 184, 187–90, 193
Turn of the Screw, The, 20, 21, 26–28, 87, 88, 96, 133–48

uncanny, the, 17, 60–62, 65–66

Veeder, William, 102 n. 10
Virilio, Paul, 52

Waldstein, Louis, 142
Walker, Pierre, 106
Walton, Priscilla L., 12–15, 37–53, 164
Ward, Mary, 122
Washington Square: as film, 13–14, 38, 42–44, 52 n. 2, 53 n. 6
Wharton, Edith, 198, 199
White, James Boyd, 38–39
Whitman, Walt, 143
Wicke, Jennifer, 87–88, 95
Wilde, Oscar, 26, 27, 113, 134, 139, 140
Wilson, Michael L. J., 12, 23–26, 31, 104–32
Wilson, R. B. J., 155
Wings of the Dove, The, 94, 178, 187, 189–90, 193; as film, 13, 14–15, 38, 41, 47, 49–52
woman, 17, 41, 42
women, 54, 61–65; in James' art tales, 17–20, 68–84; as characters, 12,

177–79, 183–90, 191–94; and work, 86, 89–103, 119–32; as writers, 179–85, 190. *See also* female body; feminine, the; mother, the; woman
Woolf, Virginia, 27, 135–36, 141

Wyler, William, 42

Zola, Emile, 188, 212
Zwinger, Lynda, 155, 157